Mike McGrath & Michael Price

# Windows 10

in
easy steps

special edition

In easy steps is an imprint of In Easy Steps Limited
16 Hamilton Terrace · Holly Walk · Leamington Spa
Warwickshire · United Kingdom · CV32 4LY
www.ineasysteps.com

Notice of Liability
Every effort has been made to ensure that this book contains accurate
and current information. However, In Easy Steps Limited and the
author shall not be liable for any loss or damage suffered by readers
as a result of any information contained herein.

Trademarks
Microsoft® and Windows® are registered trademarks of Microsoft
Corporation. All other trademarks are acknowledged as belonging to
their respective companies.

In Easy Steps Limited supports The Forest Stewardship Council (FSC),
the leading international forest certification organization. All our titles
that are printed on Greenpeace approved FSC certified paper carry the
FSC logo.

MIX
Paper from
responsible sources
FSC    FSC® C020837
www.fsc.org

Printed and bound in the United Kingdom

ISBN  978-1-84078-646-0

# Contents

## 5   Windows 10 apps   71

## 6   Desktop and Taskbar   83

## 7   Built-in programs   105

# 21 Backup and recovery 353

# 22 Security and encryption 377

# 23 Command Prompt 393

# 24 Update and maintain 405

## 25 Windows performance 421

## 26 Windows Registry 441

## 27 Extending Windows 459

## Index 471

# 1 Introducing Windows 10

*This chapter introduces Microsoft's latest operating system, Windows 10. We see the new features, what editions are available, and take a look at some free Microsoft software.*

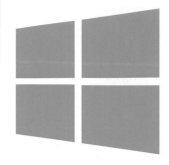

# Windows releases

There have been many versions of Microsoft Windows. The operating system was initially designed for IBM-compatible PCs, but was later extended to support larger computers such as servers and workstations. A derivative version, Windows CE, was also developed for smaller devices such as PDAs and cell phones.

The main versions of Windows that have been released include:

| Date | Client PC | Server | Mobile |
|------|-----------|--------|--------|
| 1985 | Win 1.0 | | |
| 1987 | Win 2.0 | | |
| 1990 | Win 3.0 | | |
| 1993 | | Win NT 3.1 | |
| 1995 | Win 95 | | |
| 1996 | | Win NT 4.0 | Win CE 1.0 |
| 1998 | Win 98 | | |
| 2000 | Win ME | Win 2000 | Win CE 3.0, Pocket PC 2000 |
| 2001 | Win XP | | Pocket PC 2002 |
| 2003 | | Win Server 2003 | Win Mobile 2003 |
| 2006 | Win Vista | | |
| 2007 | | Win Home Server | Win Mobile 6 |
| 2009 | Win 7 | Win Server 2008 | |
| 2010 | | | Win Phone 7 |
| 2012 | Win 8 | Win Server 2012 | Win Phone 8 |
| 2015 | Win 10 | | Win 10 Mobile |

**Hot tip**

The original IBM PC was supported by PC-DOS and MS-DOS operating systems, developed for IBM-compatible PCs.

**Hot tip**

Windows 10 for PCs and larger tablets comes in four editions:
· Windows 10 Home
· Windows 10 Pro
· Windows 10 Enterprise
· Windows 10 Education

The first three versions of Windows listed were designed for the 16-bit processor featured in the PCs of the day. Windows 95, 98 and ME added support for 32-bit processors. Windows NT was for 32-bit only while XP and 2000 added 64-bit support. Windows Vista, Windows 7, Windows 8, Windows 10, and the newer server editions, support both 32-bit or 64-bit processors. Each version of Windows builds on the functions and features included in the previous versions, so that the knowledge and experience you have gained will still be valuable, even though the appearance and the specifics of the operations may have changed.

# Windows 10 compatibility

With Windows 10, Microsoft has created an operating system designed to be compatible with a range of different devices. To make this possible, Windows 10 has a new feature called "Continuum" that helps the operating system work better with devices that support both a mouse and keyboard, and touch input. For example: Microsoft's Surface tablet or Lenovo's Yoga laptops. Continuum offers two operating modes for each type of device:

### Tablet Mode

When a device is in Tablet Mode the layout of the operating system is appropriate for touchscreen input. This means that the Start screen has tiles that you can tap to launch apps, the apps appear full-screen, and you can navigate using touch gestures. When you connect a mouse and keyboard, or flip your laptop around, you are prompted to change into Desktop Mode.

### Desktop Mode

When a device is in Desktop Mode the layout of the operating system is appropriate for mouse and keyboard input. This means that the Start menu has an A-Z list that you can click to launch apps, the apps appear in windows, and you can navigate using the mouse buttons or keyboard shortcuts. When you disconnect a mouse and keyboard, or flip your laptop around, you are prompted to change into Tablet Mode.

Tablet mode is less demanding of system resources and its introduction in Windows 10 clearly indicates that Microsoft considers mobile devices to be where the future lies.

Windows 10 shares its styling and kernel code with multiple platforms including smartphones, tablets, PCs and even the Xbox games console. This move towards cross-compatibility is one which is intended to establish Microsoft in the mobile market.

A key element in this is the OneDrive app, which we'll look at later. OneDrive enables users to store all their data and apps online and synchronize that data across all their devices. As a result, they will be able to log into OneDrive on any Windows 10 device and immediately access their data, preference settings, etc. Whatever or whoever's device they are using, it will be as though they are using their own.

The New icon pictured above indicates a new or enhanced feature introduced with the latest version of Windows. The Continuum feature is new in Windows 10.

OneDrive is the original SkyDrive facility. It was renamed for copyright reasons. Its features and functions remain unchanged.

# New features in Windows 10

Each new version of Windows adds new features and facilities. In Windows 10, these include:

### Familiar and improved

The customizable Start Menu is a new and welcome feature in Windows 10.

- **Customizable Start Menu** – a welcome return after the controversial removal of the Start menu in Windows 8.

- **Windows Defender & Windows Firewall** – integral anti-virus defense against malware and spyware.

- **Hiberboot and InstantGo** – fast startup and ready to instantly resume from Sleep mode.

- **Trusted Platform Module (TPM)** – secure device identification, authentication, and encryption.

- **Battery Saver** – limits background activity to make the most out of your battery.

- **Windows Update** – automatically helps keep your device safer and running smoothly.

InstantGo is a hardware-dependent feature and Trusted Platform Module support requires TPM1.2.

### Cortana Personal Digital Assistant

- **Talk or type naturally** – lets you ask for assistance by typing into a text box or by speaking into a microphone.

- **Personal proactive suggestions** – provides intelligent recommendations based upon your personal information.

- **Reminders** – prompts you according to the time of day, your location, or the person you are in contact with.

- **Search web, device, and Cloud** – find help, apps, files, settings, or anything, anywhere.

- **"Hey Cortana" hands-free activation** – passive voice activation recognizes your voice.

Cortana is a new feature in Windows 10 and requires you to have a Microsoft account. Performance may vary by region and device.

## Windows Hello

- **Native fingerprint recognition** – the ability to log in to the operating system using a fingerprint reader.

- **Native facial and iris recognition** – the ability to log in to the operating system using a camera.

- **Enterprise level security** – the ability to log in to the operating system using a 4-digit PIN code or picture.

## Multi-doing

- **Virtual desktops** – multiple desktops to separate related tasks into their own workspaces.

- **Snap assist** – easily position up to four apps on the screen.

- **Snap across** – easily position apps across different monitors.

## Continuum

- **Tablet Mode** – an interface appropriate for touch input and navigation using gestures.

- **Desktop Mode** – an interface appropriate for mouse and keyboard input, and navigation clicks and shortcuts.

## Microsoft Edge

- **Web browser** – streamlined for compliance with the latest HTML5 web standards.

- **Reading view** – instantly remove formatting distractions from web pages to make reading easier.

- **Built-in ink support** – add Web Notes to existing web pages then save or share the edited page.

- **Cortana integration** – search the device, web, and Cloud to quickly find what you need.

Windows Hello is new in Windows 10. Facial recognition requires a camera that has RGB, infrared, and 3D lenses.

Virtual desktops and Continuum are both new features in Windows 10.

Microsoft Edge is new in Windows 10. It lets you write Web Notes with your finger on touchscreen devices.

15

# Editions of Windows 10

There are four editions of Windows 10 for PCs and tablets of screen size over 8 inches – Home, Pro, Enterprise, and Education.

**Hot tip**

Windows 10 also brings Xbox gaming to the PC.

Windows 10 Home edition is the consumer-focused desktop version that includes a broad range of Universal Windows Apps, such as Photos, Maps, Mail, Calendar, and Groove Music. Windows 10 Pro edition is the desktop version for small businesses, whereas Windows 10 Enterprise edition is the desktop version for large organizations. Windows 10 Education edition builds on the Enterprise edition to meet the needs of schools.

The table below shows the features in Windows 10 and, as you can see, some of the features are specific to certain editions:

| Features | Home | Pro | Enterprise | Education |
|---|---|---|---|---|
| Customizable Start Menu | Y | Y | Y | Y |
| Windows Defender & Windows Firewall | Y | Y | Y | Y |
| Fast start with Hiberboot & InstantGo | Y | Y | Y | Y |
| TPM support | Y | Y | Y | Y |
| Battery Saver | Y | Y | Y | Y |
| Windows Update | Y | Y | Y | Y |
| Cortana Personal Digital Assistant | Y | Y | Y | Y |
| Windows Hello login | Y | Y | Y | Y |
| Virtual desktops | Y | Y | Y | Y |
| Snap Assist | Y | Y | Y | Y |
| Continuum Tablet & Desktop Modes | Y | Y | Y | Y |
| Microsoft Edge | Y | Y | Y | Y |
| Device Encryption | Y | Y | Y | Y |
| Domain Join | - | Y | Y | Y |
| Group Policy Management | - | Y | Y | Y |
| BitLocker | - | Y | Y | Y |
| Enterprise Mode Internet Explorer | - | Y | Y | Y |
| Assigned Access 8.1 | - | Y | Y | Y |
| Remote Desktop | - | Y | Y | Y |
| Client Hyper-V | - | Y | Y | Y |
| Direct Access | - | Y | Y | Y |
| Windows To Go Creator | - | - | Y | Y |

| Features | Home | Pro | Enterprise | Education |
|---|---|---|---|---|
| AppLocker | - | - | Y | Y |
| Branch Cache | - | - | Y | Y |
| Start Screen Control with Group Policy | - | - | Y | Y |
| Side-loading Line of Business Apps | Y | Y | Y | Y |
| Mobile Device Management | Y | Y | Y | Y |
| Join Azure Active Directory | - | Y | Y | Y |
| Business Store for Windows 10 | - | Y | Y | Y |
| Granular UX Control | - | - | Y | Y |
| Easy Upgrade Pro to Enterprise | - | Y | Y | - |
| Easy Upgrade Home to Education | Y | - | - | Y |
| Microsoft Passport | Y | Y | Y | Y |
| Enterprise Data Protection | - | Y | Y | Y |
| Credential Guard | - | - | Y | Y |
| Device Guard | - | - | Y | Y |
| Windows Update | Y | Y | Y | Y |
| Windows Update for Business | - | Y | Y | Y |
| Current Branch for Business | - | Y | Y | Y |
| Long Term Servicing Branch | - | - | Y | - |

There are two editions of Windows 10 for smartphones and tablets of screen size under 8 inches – Windows 10 Mobile, and Windows 10 Mobile Enterprise.

Windows 10 Mobile edition is designed to deliver the best user experience on smaller touch-centric devices. It provides the same universal Windows Apps that are included in the versions for PC and larger tablets. In addition, Windows 10 Mobile enables some new devices to take advantage of Continuum for Phone – so you can use your phone like a PC when connected to a larger screen. Windows 10 Mobile Enterprise edition is designed for businesses, so has extra security and mobile device management capabilities.

There are also special versions of Windows 10 Enterprise and Windows 10 Mobile Enterprise for industry devices, such as ATMs, retail point of sale, handheld terminals, and robotics, plus Windows 10 IoT Core for smaller devices, such as gateways.

Windows 10 is available in 111 languages!

# Microsoft OneDrive

A very important function built-in to Windows 10 is its ability to utilize what is commonly known as "The Cloud". Essentially, cloud computing is a technology that uses the internet and centralized remote servers to maintain data and applications. It allows consumers and businesses to use applications they don't own, and to access their personal files on any computer that has internet access. The technology enables much more efficient computing by centralizing data storage, processing and bandwidth.

So how do you get into the Cloud? There are actually several ways: One is to open an account with a dedicated service such as DropBox. You will be given a free amount of storage space, typically up to 18GB in which you can store virtually anything you choose to. If you need more, you will be charged a fee depending on the amount required.

A second way is to buy a product from a major software manufacturer. A typical example is True Image from Acronis – a data backup program. Buy this, and you are given 250GB of online storage that enables you to create Cloud-based backups.

A third way is courtesy of Microsoft OneDrive, which can be accessed online. OneDrive is basically a portal that allows you to access 15GB of online storage.

You need to have a Microsoft account to sign in to OneDrive.

Storage allowances discussed here are correct at the time of printing.

You can log in to access OneDrive with any web browser. Go online to **onedrive.live.com**

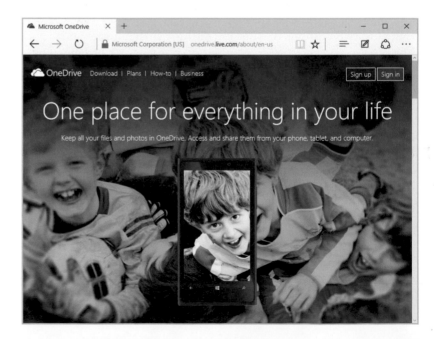

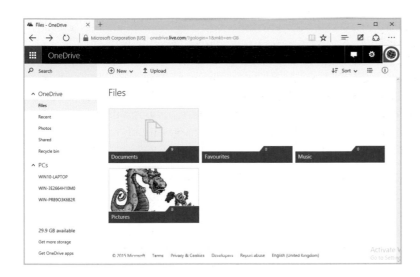

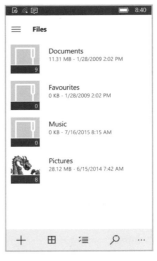

Once logged in, you will see that OneDrive has started you off with a number of pre-configured folders. Windows 10 is supplied configured to automatically synchronize these folders on OneDrive. You can delete these folders, rename them, create more folders, nest folders within folders, and upload/download files.

Once uploaded, your data can be accessed from any smartphone, tablet, or PC, from anywhere in the world and at any time. You can also access and upload data from within programs in Microsoft's Essentials suite of applications, and Microsoft Office.

One of the coolest features of OneDrive is that it enables online sharing and collaboration. For example, you can share your holiday snaps with friends and family regardless of where they are, while business applications provide access to documents while on the move or sharing documents between offices.

A key aspect of OneDrive is that it enables data to be synchronized across a range of devices. For example, emails on your PC can be automatically loaded onto your smartphone or tablet, and vice versa. You can also synchronize various settings, such as personalization, e.g. desktop background, theme, colors, passwords, app settings, and many more. This enables users to maintain the computing environment they are comfortable in across all their computing devices.

OneDrive on Windows 10 Home (above left) and on Windows 10 Mobile (above).

If you access OneDrive directly from a browser, you will have a "lite" version of Microsoft Office with which to create documents while online.

19

# Windows 10 connectivity

Windows 10 is terrific at connecting all your devices – whether it's a 3-year-old printer or projecting to your brand new TV with Miracast. Windows 10 is built on a common core and includes Universal Windows Apps so people using Windows 10 for both their PC and smartphone devices will get an optimal, seamless experience as they transition devices throughout the day.

Microsoft recognizes that many people also use iPhone, iPad or Android devices but want to ensure their Windows 10 content remains available to them across all the devices they own, regardless of the operating system. So Microsoft has produced a number of apps for Android, iPad and iPhone devices to make them work great with a Windows 10 PC.

So, whatever the operating system, this means that all your files and content can be magically available on your PC and phone:

Miracast is a wireless technology your PC can use to project the screen to a TV that also supports Miracast.

Cortana and the Groove Music app are new features in Windows 10.

- With the Cortana app on your phone you can have your Personal Digital Assistant always available.

- With the OneDrive app on your phone every photo you take shows up automatically on your phone and Windows 10 PC.

- With the Groove Music app you can access and play your music from OneDrive on your phone or Windows 10 PC.

- With the OneNote app on your phone any note you write on your Windows 10 PC will show up on your phone – and any note you write on your phone will show up on your PC.

- With the Skype app on your phone you can make video calls and messages – free over Wi-Fi.

You must use the same Microsoft account on your PC, phone, and tablet to automatically synchronize your content across these devices.

- With Word, Excel, and PowerPoint apps on your phone you can work on Office documents without moving files around.

- With the Outlook app on your phone you can get your email messages and calendar reminders everywhere.

To help people figure out how to make everything work together Windows 10 includes a Phone Companion app, which will help you connect your Windows 10 PC to your phone or tablet.

**1** The Phone Companion app begins by asking you to pick which type of device you have – here **Android** is chosen

**2** Next, the app asks to pick which app you would like to install on the selected device – here **OneNote** is chosen

**3** Now, you are asked to sign in with a Microsoft account, if not already signed in to the PC with a Microsoft account

**4** You are then given the opportunity to send an email containing a link to the chosen app

**5** After opening the email on the chosen device the link will allow you to install the chosen app – here from **Google Play**

**Hot tip**

With a Windows phone nothing else is needed – the apps are already installed on that device.

**NEW**

The Phone Companion app and support for other operating system connectivity is new in Windows 10.

**Don't forget**

You can, of course, search for the OneNote app on Google Play but the Phone Companion app makes life simple.

# Microsoft Office Online

Microsoft Office is a very important application for many people so here we will take a brief look at Microsoft Office Online and see how it fits in with Windows 10.

Office Online includes the core apps: Word, Excel, PowerPoint, Outlook and OneNote for both PC and touchscreen. Your completed documents, spreadsheets, and presentations can be saved online in your OneDrive for easy access or sharing. Alternatively, they can be downloaded to your computer and saved as a local file – just as you would with an installed app.

You will need a Microsoft account to sign in to Office Online apps.

**1** Open the Microsoft Edge web browser and navigate to **office.live.com/start/default.aspx**

**2** Click the **Sign in** button at the top-right of the page then type the email address for your Microsoft account

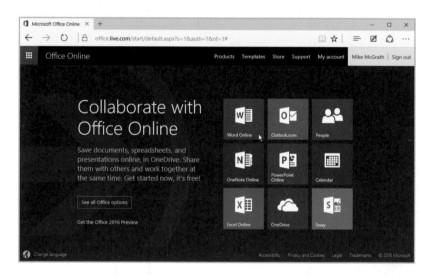

Other versions of Office can be compared at **products.office.com /en-us/compare-microsoft-office-products**

**3** Choose the online app you wish to use. For example, choose the **Word** app to create a cover letter

**4** When the Word app opens in the browser, you are presented with a number of ready-made templates. Choose the **Simple cover letter** template

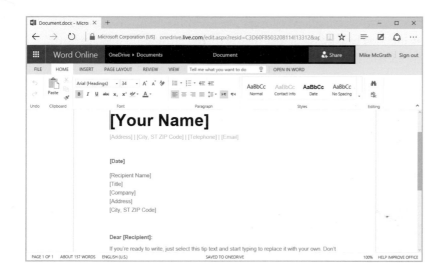

The Start menu in Windows 10 includes a **Get Office** item that makes it easy to start using Office apps.

**5** Edit the template to suit your requirements by inserting your name and address details, etc.

**6** When you are happy with the letter, click the **FILE** tab at the top-left of the window

**7** Now, choose where you would like to save the letter and in what document format

Use the **Rename** option before saving unless you are happy to use the automatically assigned default name.

# Windows Essentials

The mention of free Microsoft applications brings us to the Windows Essentials suite. This is a collection of free Microsoft applications that offer email, photo-sharing, blog publishing, security services, and more. Applications in the suite are designed to integrate with each other, with Microsoft Windows operating systems, and also with Microsoft web-based services such as OneDrive and Outlook.com, with the intention of providing a seamless computing experience.

Windows Essentials includes the following applications:

- Mail
- OneDrive
- Movie Maker
- Photo Gallery
- Writer

Windows Essentials is available for free download at **windows.microsoft.com/en-us/windows-live/essentials** Further free downloads are available to customize, protect, and enhance your computer. You can get desktop wallpapers and even language packs to see Windows in the language of your choice at **windows.microsoft.com/en-us/windows/downloads**

The latest version is Windows Essentials 2012 *(correct at the time of printing)*.

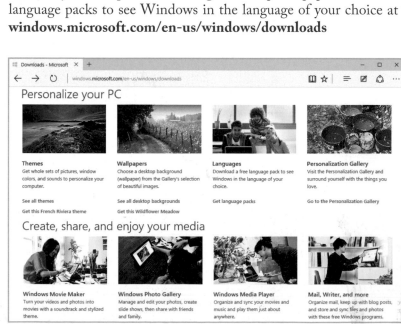

# 2 Choosing your computer

*In this chapter we examine the hardware requirements of both Windows 10 and the computers on which it can be run. For example: CPUs, memory, touchscreens, sensors, and much more.*

# Windows 10 Requirements

Traditionally, every edition of Windows has required more in the way of hardware resources than the editions that preceded it. This came to a stop with Windows 7, which ran quite satisfactorily on the same hardware that its predecessor, Windows Vista, did. This has continued with Windows 10, so users upgrading from either Windows 7 or Windows 8.1 do not have to also upgrade their computer hardware.

The official system requirements of Windows 10 are as follows:

● **Processor** – 1GHz or faster, or SoC (System on a Chip)

● **Memory (RAM)** – 1GB (32-bit) or 2GB (64-bit)

● **Disk space** – 16GB (32-bit) or 20GB (64-bit)

● **Graphics** – Microsoft DirectX 9 with WDDM driver

Please note that the above is the absolute minimum required. While Windows 10 will run on this hardware, it may not do so particularly well. To be more specific, it will probably be on the slow side, and if you run resource-intensive software such as 3D games, Photoshop, etc., it may struggle to cope. If you wish to avoid this, our recommendation is to install twice the recommended amount of memory, i.e. 2GB on a 32-bit system and 4GB on a 64-bit system.

In addition, the following will be required to use some features:

● **Touch gestures** – tablet/monitor that supports multi-touch

● **Snap app feature** – screen resolution of at least 1024 x 600 pixels

● **Internet access**

● **Microsoft account** – required for some features

● **Cortana support** – speech recognition requires a microphone

● **Windows Hello** – fingerprint reader or specialized camera

● **Continuum** – tablet or 2-in-1 PC, or manual mode selection

● **BitLocker To Go** – a USB drive

● **Hyper-V** – a 64-bit system with second level address translation (SLAT) plus an additional 2GB of memory

To get top performance from Windows 10 you need twice the recommended amount of memory.

Processor, disk space and video requirements on all modern computers are more than adequate in these respects.

Cortana Personal Digital Assistant, Windows Hello login, and Continuum mode features are all new in Windows 10.

# Processors

The Central Processing Unit (CPU), more than any other part, influences the speed at which the computer runs. It also determines how many things the PC can do concurrently before it starts to struggle, i.e. multi-task.

With regard to speed, a CPU is rated by its clock speed, for example 3.4GHz. We saw on the previous page that Windows 10 requires a 1GHz or faster CPU. As the slowest CPU currently on the market is 2GHz (twice as fast), the issue of CPU speed is not something the typical home user needs to be too concerned about. It's only important to users who require more power, such as hardcore gamers.

The CPU's, and hence the PC's, multi-tasking capabilities may well be a different story, though. Modern computers are frequently required to do a number of things at the same time. Each task requires a separate process or "thread" from the CPU, so anyone who is going to do a lot of multi-tasking will need a CPU that can handle numerous threads simultaneously.

This means buying a multi-core CPU. These devices are no faster than traditional single-core CPUs but because they have several cores, their multi-tasking capabilities are increased enormously. Currently, there are two-, four-, six- and even eight-core models on the market and, fairly obviously, the more your PC is going to have to do, the more cores you will need in your CPU.

There is also the issue of the CPU manufacturer. Currently, the majority of computing devices are laptops and desktop PCs. These both use CPUs from Intel and AMD exclusively. While Intel CPUs are considered to be better than AMD's offerings, there really isn't much in it. In other words, whichever of them you buy from, you won't go wrong.

For those of you looking to buy a smartphone or tablet, the issue of the CPU is more complicated. This is because the CPU in these devices is usually part of a combination chipset that also houses the system's graphics, memory, interface controllers, voltage regulators and more. This combination chip is referred to as a System on a Chip (SoC) and its main benefit is that it reduces the space needed for these components. This, in turn, lowers power requirements and increases battery life.

Don't get fixated with CPU clock speed. You should also consider things like the number of cores and the size of the cache.

For most users, anything over two cores is overkill. Don't waste your money on performance you will never use.

...cont'd

Things are further confused by the fact that most SoC manufacturers, including Apple, Samsung, Texas Instruments, and NVIDEA, use a CPU architecture called ARM that is produced and licensed by a company called ARM Holdings. Therefore, this part of an SoC will be identical regardless of the manufacturer – the rest of the SoC, however, will not be. This makes it very difficult to compare SoCs on a like-for-like basis.

Virtually all smartphones use SoCs, as do some tablets. There are some, though, (usually the more capable ones) that use a specially designed low-power CPU of the same type found in desktop PCs. Intel's Atom CPU is a good example.

However, whatever the type of CPU, be it a full-size AMD FX, an Intel Atom, or an SoC, the basic premise of clock speed determining the speed of the CPU and the number of cores determining its multi-tasking capability, or power, is the same.

# Hardware capabilities

If you are thinking about upgrading to Windows 10, there's a good chance you may also be considering upgrading your PC. If so, you need to give some thought to the hardware that will be in it. Alternatively, it may simply be time to give it a boost.

Whichever, to ensure your PC is capable of doing what you want it to, there are several components you need to consider. The CPU we've already looked at, but there is also the memory, video system and disk drive to consider.

### Random Access Memory (RAM)

As with the CPU, memory is a component that has a major impact on the performance of a computer. You can have the fastest CPU in the galaxy but without an adequate amount of memory, all that processing power will do you no good at all.

This is a more straightforward issue than CPUs. While there are many different types of memory, as far as desktop PCs and laptops are concerned there is only really one choice – DDR3. This is currently the memory of choice and is installed on all new PCs. DDR2 will be found on many older PCs and is still a perfectly good type of memory.

When you see the term ARM used in reference to a CPU, remember that the CPU is not manufactured by ARM but rather by a company licensed by ARM Holdings to use its CPU architecture.

If you wish to upgrade the memory on a PC that's more than two or three years old, it will almost certainly be using DDR2. You will not be able to replace it with the newer DDR3 – this requires a motherboard designed to use DDR3.

The only issues for owners of modern PCs are how much memory do they need, and how much can they install? With regard to the former, this is a difficult question to answer – it depends mainly on what type of programs are going to be run on the PC. Applications that shift large amounts of data, such as 3D games, video and sound editing, or high-end desktop publishing, will require a much larger amount of memory – typically 6GB or more. Less intensive applications, such as web browsing, word-processing and Freecell, will all run perfectly well on 2GB.

The amount of memory that can be installed is determined by the motherboard. This is not going to be an issue for the average user as current motherboards can handle anything up to 64GB. However, the computer architecture being used may well be. 32-bit computers running a Windows operating system can utilize a maximum of 4GB of memory regardless of how much is installed. 64-bit PCs, on the other hand, can use an almost limitless amount.

Memory modules are rated in terms of speed, which is another consideration. Currently, speeds range from 1GHz to 2.8GHz. The faster the memory, the more expensive it will be.

Smartphones and tablets require much less memory than desktop PCs. High-end devices of these types currently come with about 1GHz of RAM. They also make more efficient use of the available memory by "suspending" apps that are not being used, thus releasing memory for other apps.

When considering a smartphone or tablet, it is also necessary to see what it has to offer in the way of built-in memory for storage purposes, and if it can be expanded by adding larger capacity memory cards.

You might think that devices such as smartphones, which do not generally come with much in the way of internal storage, would almost certainly offer a memory card slot. However, this is not always the case, as owners of iPhones will testify.

## Video System

Video systems produce the pictures you see on the display. Two types are used in computers: integrated video that is built-in to the motherboard or CPU, and stand-alone video cards.

If you want to install more than 4GB of memory, you must be using a 64-bit PC.

Don't worry too much about memory speed. The real-world difference between the slowest and fastest modules is not significant. In any case, to get the best out of the high-speed modules, other parts, such as the CPU, also need to be top-end. Such a setup will be expensive.

**Hot tip**

If you have a need for speed, make sure your devices use SSDs.

### ...cont'd

Of the two, video cards produce by far the better quality video – for hardcore gamers they are essential.

The problem with video cards is that they are not only expensive; they are also bulky, noisy, and power-hungry. Desktop computers and high-end laptops are large enough and powerful enough to accommodate these demands, but for smaller devices, such as netbooks, tablets and smartphones, they are impractical.

Therefore, these all use an integrated video system. As we mentioned on page 28, in these devices the video will be just one part of a System on a Chip (SoC).

### Solid-State Drives (SSDs)

Disk drives, or hard drives as they are more commonly known, are the devices used to store a user's data. They are electromechanical devices that provide huge amounts of storage space at a low price.

A relatively recent development in the hard drive market has seen the introduction of solid-state drives (SSDs). These devices employ solid-state memory and contain no moving parts which, apart from anything else, makes them extremely reliable.

Other advantages include instant startup, extremely fast data access speeds, completely silent operation, a much smaller footprint, weight (they are much lighter than mechanical drives), and low power requirements.

These qualities all make SSDs ideal for use in low-power devices such as tablets and smartphones. Apple, for example, uses them in its highly successful iPads, iPhones and iPods.

However, their use in desktop computers is somewhat limited by two factors: The first is the high cost of SSDs compared with mechanical drives. The second is that they provide much smaller storage capacities than mechanical drives. This has lead to low-capacity SSDs, typically around 60GB, being used for the boot drive (where the operating system is installed), with a high-capacity mechanical drive to provide data storage.

The result is a PC that typically boots up twice as quickly, is snappy and responsive to the user's commands, and also has loads of storage space.

# Computer types

When it comes to buying a computer, buyers have quite a few different types to choose from, each having pros and cons that make them suitable for some purposes and less so for others.

### Desktop PCs

Traditionally, the desktop PC, comprising a system case that houses the hardware, plus a monitor, keyboard and mouse, has been the most popular type of computer.

Their main advantage is that the addition of peripherals, such as printers and scanners, turns them into workhorses that enable almost any type of computational work to be done.

Other advantages are that they are cheap to buy, easy to upgrade and repair, and easy to expand. Disadvantages are: size, noise, aesthetics, and lack of mobility.

### All-In-Ones

Increasingly popular due to their small footprint, all-in-one PCs are manufactured by a number of companies, including Apple, Lenovo and Samsung. Pictured below is the Lenovo IdeaCentre.

Other advantages include being lightweight, a minimal amount of messy wiring, many come with touchscreens, and a definite element of style – many of these devices look rather cool and not at all out of place in the living room.

The downside is that they are very difficult to repair/upgrade due to lack of accessibility. All-in-ones are also prone to heat issues due to the lack of air space in the case – this makes them unsuitable for high-end applications. Also, if one part goes wrong the whole unit has to go back – it's all or nothing.

Hot tip

A big advantage of desktop PCs is that they are easy to expand and to upgrade.

Hot tip

All-in-ones are produced by a limited number of manufacturers and tend to be expensive.

...cont'd

Hybrid PCs are ideal where mobility is an issue. Don't expect to do any serious work or gaming on them, though.

**32**

## Hybrid Computers

Continuing the all-in-one's theme of style and elegance, we have the hybrid computer. It is comprised of nothing more than a very small and usually stylish case that contains the hardware.

The user simply places it where it is to be used and connects a monitor, keyboard and mouse.

These devices have only one real advantage – they are extremely portable. They have the same disadvantages as all-in-one PCs and, as such, are only suitable for lightweight applications.

## Laptops

A laptop is basically a desktop PC condensed into a small, flat, portable case. It has the same components as a desktop, albeit on a smaller scale, and is capable of everything the desktop is.

Fairly obviously, their main advantage is portability – a laptop can be tucked under the arm and literally taken anywhere.

They also require little space and are easily secured, e.g. can be placed inside a safe.

If you buy a laptop with a view to portable computing, check out the battery capacity. Some models have low-capacity batteries that don't last long before needing to be recharged.

As ever though, there are downsides. Probably the main one is cost – laptops are considerably more expensive than desktops of equivalent capability.

These devices are also more difficult to use due to smaller screens and the need for touchpads. There is a high risk of physical damage as they can be dropped, they are easily misplaced or lost, and are prone to theft.

Variations of the laptop theme include Ultrabooks and Netbooks. The former are an Intel invention and manufacturers of these devices must conform to standards set by Intel.

These state that Ultrabooks must use low-power Intel Core CPUs, solid-state drives and unibody chassis. This is to ensure that Ultrabooks are slim, high-end devices able to compete at the top-end of the laptop market against the likes of Apple's MacBook Air.

A Netbook is simply a miniature laptop. They usually have 10-inch screens, scaled-down keyboards and touchpads to match, and are extremely small and lightweight. As a result, they are inexpensive and easily transportable. These have become less popular recently as their role is being taken over by Tablet PCs and Convertible Computers.

## Tablet Computers

Tablets are mobile computers that fit in between smartphones and Netbooks. The hardware is built in to a touchscreen and can be operated both by touch and by a keyboard (on screen or attached).

Unlike smartphones, the displays offered by tablets are large enough to enable serious work to be done. For example, with a suitable app you can easily write a properly punctuated letter, an email message, or even a novel.

You'll need to choose a Tablet PC that can run Windows 10 with an Intel processor or equivalent, or simply buy a Tablet PC with Windows 10 already pre-installed.

Tablet PCs then offer the best of all worlds. The convenience and ultra-portability of smartphones, a camera, plus the ability to carry out serious computer work. Some even have a phone as well!

Basically, Ultrabooks are aimed at the top-end of the laptop market, while Netbooks are aimed at the bottom-end.

Tablets are a good option if you need ultra-portability as well as computational functionality.

...cont'd

### Convertible Computers

A convertible computer is essentially a tablet computer that can be quickly transformed into a laptop by opening an integrated keyboard. Typically, this is achieved by means of a sliding or hinged mechanism. In all other respects they are just a tablet but are popular as they provide a degree of flexibility.

For example, by rotating the hinged keyboard, the Lenovo Yoga convertible computer, shown here, can be used in any one of its Tablet, Laptop, or Standing configurations.

### Smartphones

Windows 10 provides the opportunity to easily have all your files, music, photos, and videos available from anywhere. You can choose a cell phone running Windows 10 Mobile to carry your content in your pocket wherever you go.

Microsoft produces a range of Lumia smartphones for Enterprise and the individual, from budget to flagship.

Each device connected to the internet can share content via the magic of OneDrive. When you take a photo on your phone it gets added to the Camera Roll folder on your phone and can be automatically copied to any of your other Windows 10 devices. Similarly, any reminders you save in the OneNote app on your PC can be automatically copied to your phone. You can choose to share any content across devices.

Beware

Convertible computers offer a compromise in which you may consider the tablet too big, or the keyboard too small.

**NEW**

Windows 10 supports connectivity with Android, iPhone, and iPad devices.

Hot tip

Use a Windows 10 Mobile smartphone in conjunction with Windows 10 on your PC to really get the most from Windows 10.

# 32-bit versus 64-bit

All modern CPUs support 64-bit architecture. But what is it and how does it benefit the user?

The term "64-bit" when used in reference to a CPU means that in one integer register the CPU can store 64 bits of data. Older CPUs, which could only support 32-bit architecture, could store only 32 bits of data in a register, i.e. half the amount. Therefore, 64-bit architecture provides better overall system performance as it can handle twice as much data in one clock cycle.

However, the main advantage provided by 64-bit architecture is the huge amount of memory it can support. CPUs operating on a 32-bit Windows system can utilize a maximum of 4GB, whereas on a 64-bit system they can utilize up to 192GB.

The caveat is that a 64-bit system requires all the software to be 64-bit compatible, i.e. it must be 64-bit software. This includes the operating system and device drivers and is the reason why more recent versions of Windows, including Windows 10, are supplied in both 32-bit (x86) and 64-bit (x64) versions. Note that most 32-bit software will run on a 64-bit system but the advantages provided by 64-bit architecture won't be available.

So who will benefit from a 64-bit system and who won't? The simple answer is that every PC user will benefit as their system will be more efficient. Don't expect to see major speed gains over a 32-bit system when running day-to-day applications such as web browsers, word processing and 2D games, though – you probably won't notice any difference.

However, when running CPU-intensive applications that require large amounts of data to be handled, e.g. video editing, 3D games, or CAD software, 64-bit systems will be faster. Also, if you need more memory than the current small limit of 4GB possible with a 32-bit system, 64-bit architecture allows you to install as much as you want (up to the limitations of the motherboard).

Users running Windows 10 Pro, Enterprise, or Education editions have access to a virtualization utility called Hyper-V. One of the requirements for building virtual PCs with Hyper-V is that the computer must be running on 64-bit architecture.

To get a 64-bit system, simply buy a modern CPU and install a 64-bit version of Windows.

Modern CPUs automatically detect whether an application or operating system is 32-bit or 64-bit and operate accordingly.

If you opt for a 64-bit system, all your software, including device drivers, will have to be 64-bit compatible. Even though 64-bit systems are now common, there is still software on the market that runs only on 32-bit systems.

# Multi-touch

An important feature of Windows 10 is its support for touchscreen control. If you are considering buying a touchscreen monitor in order to take advantage of this feature, you should be aware of the following issues:

### Bezel Design
Some of the touch gestures required to control Windows 10 (opening menus, for example) are done by swiping a finger inwards from one edge of the screen towards the center.

However, it is a fact that many touchscreen monitors currently on the market have a raised bezel, which makes it more difficult than it need be to carry out this particular touch command. Our recommendation is that you choose a monitor in which the bezel is flush to the screen. Alternatively, look for a model that has at least a 20 mm border between the edge of the display and the start of the bezel.

### Multi-Touch
Multi-touch refers to a touchscreen's ability to recognize the presence of two or more points of contact with the surface. This plural-point awareness is necessary to implement functionality such as pinch to zoom-out or the activation of predefined programs.

All modern touchscreens have this capability. However, to get the best out of Windows 10's touch feature, you need a touchscreen that supports at least five touch points – this allows you to use five fingers simultaneously.

### Screen Technology
There are various types of touchscreen technology, but when it comes to computer monitors and mobile devices there are just two – resistive and capacitive. Resistive screens can be operated with any pointed object, such as a stylus or a finger. Capacitive screens rely on the electrical properties of the human body and thus only react to human touch (or a capacitive pen).

Of the two, the capacitive type is the one to go for – they are much more sensitive and accurate than resistive screens (these tend to be used more in business environments, e.g. shops and banks). Note that most current touchscreens are of the capacitive type, but do check it out just in case.

**Beware**

There are still touchscreens on the market that only support two touch points – don't buy one of these.

**Beware**

The downside of capacitive touchscreens is that they cannot be operated with a gloved finger (not so clever on a freezing cold day, perhaps!).

# Sensors

One of the main differences between static desktop PCs and mobile computing devices is the range of sensors employed by the latter. Some of these are important to the operation of these devices, while others add functionality. Sensors that you should look for include:

### Ambient Light Sensor (ALS)

This sensor enables screen brightness to be automatically adjusted in accordance with the ambient light level. If it gets darker then the screen brightness decreases; if it increases then the screen brightness increases. A useful side-effect of this is increased battery life.

### Proximity Sensor

The purpose of this device is to prevent accidental inputs – something that's easily done on a touchscreen. The most common scenario is the ear touching the screen during a call and triggering an event or action.

The proximity sensor is located next to the speaker and thus can detect when the ear (or another object) is close by. Any actions generated are assumed to be accidental and thus ignored.

### Accelerometer & Gyroscope

These two sensors are used to detect the orientation of a device so that the display can react accordingly. For example, if the device is moved from a vertical orientation to a horizontal one, the display will follow suit. Other uses include the camera – the sensors enable it to know if the picture is being taken in landscape or portrait mode.

### Global Positioning System (GPS)

An embedded GPS sensor used in conjunction with a mapping service enables any mobile device to get real-time position tracking, text- and voice-guided directions, and points of interest.

### Compass

Sensors that detect direction enable compass apps to be built. Sensors of this type do not sense magnetic fields as do traditional compasses but rather the frequency and orientation of radio waves. In doing this, smartphone compass sensors are assisted by gyroscopes.

Increasingly, data from the various sensors in a device is being combined to produce more elaborate applications.

New types of sensor are being developed for mobile devices. Examples are altimeters (will detect which floor of a building you are on, for example), temperature & humidity sensors and heart rate monitors.

# Other hardware features

Windows 10 includes several modern hardware features not seen in early Windows operating systems. We'll take a brief look at two of them here:

### Near Field Communication (NFC)

Near Field Communication (NFC) is a set of standards for mobile devices to establish radio communication with each other by touch or bringing them into close proximity – usually no more than a few centimeters. The technology is beginning to appear on mobile devices. Applications include:

NFC is similar in concept to Bluetooth but is somewhat slower in operation. It does, however, consume much less power.

**Purchase Payment** – used in conjunction with an electronic wallet, this effectively turns a smartphone into a credit card.

**Setting Up Connections** – connections such as Bluetooth can be quickly and easily established.

**Smart Tagging** – touching a smartphone to an NFC tag, e.g. tap-and-go at the gas pump.

**Peer-to-Peer** – sharing small snippets of information such as contacts, photos, and web pages is a typical use.

### Unified Extensible Firmware Interface (UEFI)

A computer needs an interface between its operating system and hardware to make sure they can work together. Traditionally, this role has been carried out by a chip called the BIOS (this produces the black boot screens you see when starting your PC).

If your PC has UEFI, it can be accessed from Windows 10's Recovery, Advanced Options menu.

UEFI is a replacement for the now archaic BIOS. Windows 10 takes advantage of a security feature in UEFI known as Pre-boot Authentication. This prevents any software that doesn't have a recognized and valid security certificate from running and, as a result, rootkits, viruses and malware are unable to load themselves into the system's memory during the boot procedure, i.e. before the operating system. (A virus that manages to do this could circumvent any antivirus measures on the PC.)

Another feature of UEFI is its graphical display that allows navigation with a mouse and keyboard. However, before you go looking for it, be aware that your computer's motherboard must provide UEFI support. Only computers built in the last year or two are likely to have UEFI.

# 3 Installing Windows 10

*Upgrading options for Windows 10 can be a confusing issue – this chapter explains exactly which editions of Windows can be upgraded to Windows 10. We compare installation options of upgrading and clean installing.*

# Upgrade paths

On this page we see the upgrade paths to Windows 10 from previous versions of Windows. It is not possible to upgrade from all earlier versions.

### Upgrade to Windows 10 Home

You can upgrade to Windows 10 Home and keep Windows settings, personal files, and applications from the following Windows operating system editions:

- Windows 7 Starter

- Windows 7 Home Basic

- Windows 7 Home Premium

- Windows 8.1

- Windows 8.1 with Bing

### Upgrade to Windows 10 Pro

You can upgrade to Windows 10 Pro and keep Windows settings, personal files, and applications from the following Windows operating system editions:

- Windows 7 Professional

- Windows 7 Ultimate

- Windows 8.1 Pro

### Upgrades unavailable

You <u>cannot</u> upgrade to Windows 10 from the following operating system editions:

- Windows 7 Enterprise

- Windows 8 (must be upgraded to at least 8.1)

- Windows 8.1 Enterprise

- Windows RT

- Windows RT 8.1

Windows 10 Home can be bought for $119.99/£84.99 and Windows 10 Pro costs $199.99/£119.99. *(Amounts correct at the time of printing.)* However, if you are already running an eligible version of Windows the upgrade to Windows 10 is free within one year of availability.

Windows Phone 8.1 users can also upgrade to Windows 10 Mobile.

40

# Upgrade options

Upgrading an operating system can be done in three ways:

- An inplace upgrade

- A clean installation

- A migration

We'll start with the most common method:

### Inplace Upgrade

With this method, the operating system is simply installed over the top of the old one. While this is the easiest way to do the job, it will produce the worst results. This is because any problems on the original setup (file corruption, malware, etc.) will be carried over to the new installation. Issues of this type can also cause an upgrade to fail.

The only advantages of upgrading in this way are that the procedure is straightforward and that the user's data, files and programs are not affected – they will still be there at the end of it.

### Clean Installation

With a clean installation, all potential problems are eliminated right at the start due to the format procedure, which wipes the drive clean of all data. Therefore, nothing is carried over to the new setup from the old one.

The drawback with this method is that the formatting procedure also removes all the user's data – settings, files and programs. So when the new operating system has been installed, it will then be necessary to redo all the settings, reinstall all the programs and restore the data. Another issue is the time it will take to do all this – the best part of a day in our experience.

### Migration

This is not a true upgrade option but we include it here as the procedure does transfer files and settings from one installation to another. It does not transfer programs, though.

To do a migration, you need a suitable application that copies the files and settings from the old setup to a medium, such as a USB flash drive, then transfers them to the new setup.

Hot tip

For best results, we suggest you back up your personal data and perform a clean installation.

# Walkthrough clean install

Unlike an upgrade, which can be initiated from within Windows, a clean install has to be done from an installation disk. If your copy of Windows 10 has been supplied on a DVD or USB then you're all set. If not, it will be in the form of an ISO image file. However, before you can use this it will have to be burned to a DVD, a procedure that will require a DVD burning program.

If you are upgrading from Windows 7, you have a DVD burner built in. Just pop an empty DVD in the DVD drive and follow the prompts from the AutoPlay window that will open shortly afterwards.

If you don't have a built-in burner, you can find a free one on the internet. One that we recommend is ImgBurn from **imgburn.com** Use it as described below:

Microsoft provides a free Windows 10 Media Creation Tool that allows you to easily download the Windows 10 ISO image file, which must then be burnt to a DVD. You can also use this tool to download for USB media. For details go to **microsoft.com/en-us/software-download/windows10**

42

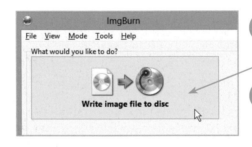

**1** At the opening screen, click **Write image file to disc**

**2** Under Source, click the browse link and select your ISO file

ImgBurn is just one of many free disk burners available on the internet.

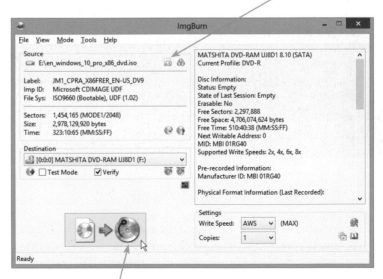

**3** Click Write and wait while the DVD is burned

## ...cont'd

### Set the boot drive

Having created your installation disk, you now need to configure your computer to boot from it. This is done as follows:

**1**    Start the PC and at the first boot screen, press the key required to open the BIOS. This is usually the Delete or F2 key (it is often specified at the bottom of the screen)

**2**    On the main BIOS page, scroll to **Advanced BIOS Features** and hit the Enter key

**3**    On the next page, scroll down to **First Boot Device**. Using the Page Up/Page Down keys, cycle through the options and select the CD/DVD drive

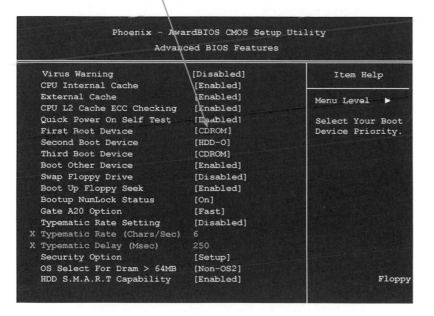

```
            Phoenix - AwardBIOS CMOS Setup Utility
                    Advanced BIOS Features

   Virus Warning                [Disabled]         Item Help
   CPU Internal Cache           [Enabled]
   External Cache               [Enabled]       Menu Level    ▶
   CPU L2 Cache ECC Checking    [Enabled]
   Quick Power On Self Test     [Disabled]      Select Your Boot
   First Boot Device            [CDROM]         Device Priority.
   Second Boot Device           [HDD-O]
   Third Boot Device            [CDROM]
   Boot Other Device            [Enabled]
   Swap Floppy Drive            [Disabled]
   Boot Up Floppy Seek          [Enabled]
   Bootup NumLock Status        [On]
   Gate A20 Option              [Fast]
   Typematic Rate Setting       [Disabled]
 X Typematic Rate (Chars/Sec)   6
 X Typematic Delay (Msec)       250
   Security Option              [Setup]
   OS Select For Dram > 64MB    [Non-OS2]
   HDD S.M.A.R.T Capability     [Enabled]                Floppy
```

**4**    Press the **Esc** key to return to the main page

Note that you must save the change before exiting the BIOS, otherwise it will revert to the original setting. The BIOS option for this is to **Save & Exit Setup**, typically with the F10 key.

**Hot tip**

If you can't find the key to open the BIOS, check the motherboard manual.

**Don't forget**

The BIOS screens in your PC may differ from the example on the left – it depends on the age of your PC and the BIOS manufacturer.

**Don't forget**

All the tools needed to do a clean install of Windows 10 are on its installation disk. So, you must set the CD/DVD drive as the first boot device.

# Windows setup

In the following pages, we are going to show you a step-by-step procedure for doing a clean installation of Windows 10.

**1** Place the Windows 10 installation disk in the CD/DVD drive and start the PC. When you see a **Press any key to boot from CD...** message, do so. Windows will now begin loading its installation files to the disk drive

**2** The first screen you will see is the language, time and currency format, and input method preferences. Make your selections and press the **Next** button

You have to configure the PC to boot from the CD/DVD drive.

**3** On the second screen click **Install now**

Before you start this procedure, make sure you have made a backup of any data that you want to keep.

# Enter product key

**4** Now, enter your product key, then click **Next**

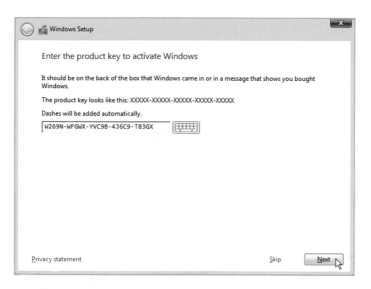

The product key will be found somewhere on the DVD packaging. If bought online, it will be in the email confirming the sale. If you are replacing Windows 7 or 8.1 the key may be on a sticker on the PC case or embedded in the BIOS. You can retrieve an embedded key using Windows OEM Key Tool. For details, see **neosmart.net/OemKey**

**5** Check the **I accept the license terms** box

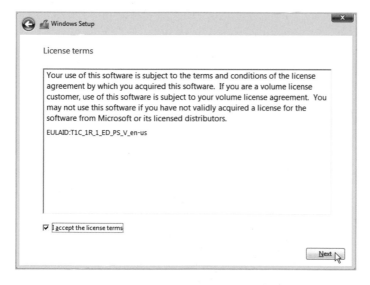

**6** Click the **Next** button to continue

# Type of installation

Drive options (advanced) enables the user to create and resize partitions.

If your current operating system is Windows 7, you will see a "Drive 0 Partition 1: System Reserved" entry. This is not relevant to Windows 10 so you can either ignore it or you can delete it in the advanced drive options.

**7** At the "Which type of installation do you want?" screen, select **Custom: Install Windows only (advanced)**

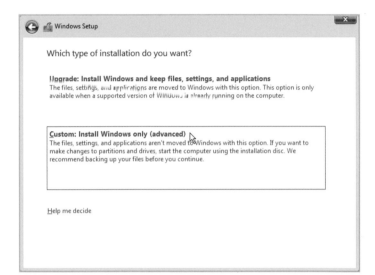

**8** In the "Where do you want to install Windows?" screen, select the required drive or partition

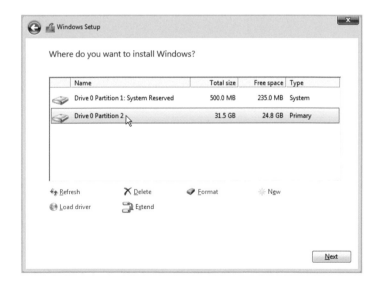

**9** Click the **Format** link then **OK** the warning dialog box. Note that this action will wipe your drive clean of all data

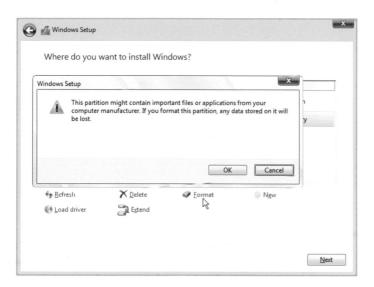

Your computer will reboot automatically during the installation procedure.

**10** The installation routine will now begin – just sit back until you see the first setup screen

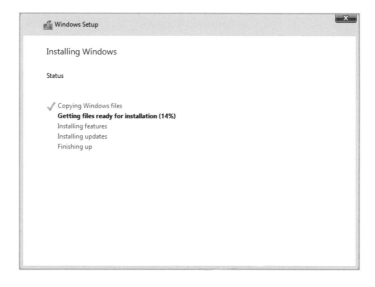

The end of the installation routine is signified by two screens – "Getting devices ready" and "Getting ready". The PC will then reboot into the new installation.

# First start

When Windows 10 starts for the first time, the first thing you will see is a "Get going fast" screen that describes the settings that will be used for your system:

The suggested default "Express settings" are recommended.

You can click the "Ease of access" icon to reveal the menu shown below, providing aids for those users with physical impairment difficulties.

**1** If you are happy to accept the suggested default settings simply click the **Use Express settings** button

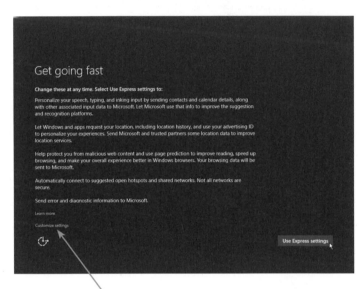

**2** Click the **Customize settings** link above the ⏱ "Ease of access" icon to change the settings

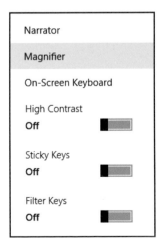

# Sign in to your PC

There now follows a screen that asks you to confirm whether the PC is owned by an organization, or by you. Selecting "I own it" enables you to sign in to the PC for the first time. This can be done via a Microsoft account or using a "local" account:

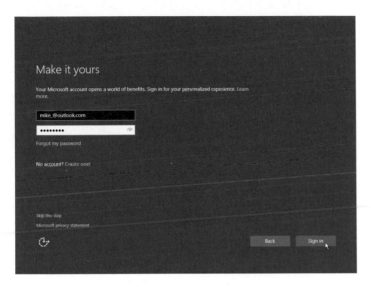

Ensure you have an internet connection or you will not be given the opportunity to sign in with your Microsoft account.

**1** Enter Microsoft account details, then click **Sign in**
OR
Click the **Skip this step** link, enter user details, then click the **Next** button to sign in with a local account

If you choose to sign in without a Microsoft account, certain Windows features will not be available to you (see page 52).

49

**…cont'd**

**2** Next, you are asked if you want to set up a PIN code that will allow you to log on to Windows using a 4-digit code

**3** The next screen allows you to automatically synchronize files between your PC and your OneDrive cloud folder. The PC will now reboot and you can finalize your settings

If you don't want to automatically sync your OneDrive folder with the Cloud, you can turn this off.

# Finalizing settings

The two final stages of the Windows 10 setting up procedure are:

**1** An introduction to the Cortana Personal Digital Assistant

If you are concerned with privacy you can change Cortana settings later to restrict access.

**2** Setting up and installing the apps

This won't take long

Setting up your apps

The final stage of setting up Windows is installing the apps. When this has been done, the PC is ready to go.

When these stages have been completed, your new Windows 10 installation is ready for use.

# Restoring your data

You now have a brand new operating system. However, apart from the apps bundled with Windows 10, that's all you have.

The first thing you have to do now is install essential system drivers. The most important of these are the chipset drivers and they will be found on the motherboard's installation disk. Pop this in the CD/DVD drive and wait for AutoPlay to open the disk's setup utility. Select the option that installs all the chipset drivers.

When the driver installation is complete, the PC will reboot. When back in Windows, the next step is to install the drivers for any hardware connected to the computer. Typically, these include video cards, sound cards, printers, scanners, routers, monitors, mice and keyboards.

Finally, install your programs and any data backed up from your previous installation.

### Local accounts

As a final note, on page 49 we mentioned that it is not essential to have a Microsoft account to use Windows 10 and, indeed, it isn't. However, if you choose this option, you will find that some features of Windows 10 are denied to you.

The first is that you won't be able to synchronize your settings, email, passwords, etc. across your various devices. This means that one of the big attractions of Windows 10 – the ability to create and maintain a consistent computing environment regardless of which device you are using – will not be available. While this probably won't be a big deal for many users, for some it most definitely will be.

Also, you won't be able to get apps from the Windows Store. It will still be possible to browse the Store but you won't be allowed to download any apps.

Furthermore, some Windows 10 apps won't work unless the user is signed into a Microsoft account. Examples include the Mail, Calendar, People, and OneDrive apps.

# 4 The Windows 10 interface

*In Chapter Four, we take an in-depth look at the Windows 10 interface. We also explain how to customize the Start menu.*

# Start Windows 10

When a Windows 10 PC is started, the first thing the user will see (once the boot screens have flashed past) is a black screen with the Windows logo, as shown below:

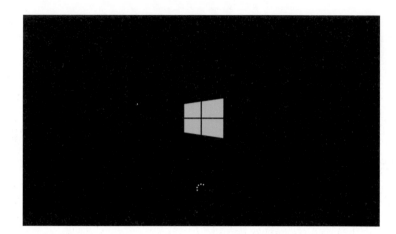

This is followed by the Lock screen. The basic purpose of this screen is to provide a protective barrier that prevents accidental inputs – this is necessary as Windows 10 is a touch-supportive operating system.

Microsoft has evolved this basic function by enabling users to customize the screen by changing its background, and by specifying various notifications to be displayed.

By default, the Lock screen shows the current date and time, and has power status indicator icons, as in the image above.

# Log on

Click or tap anywhere on the Lock screen and the log on screen will open. Above the log on box, you'll see the account picture. (This can be changed, as described on page 64.)

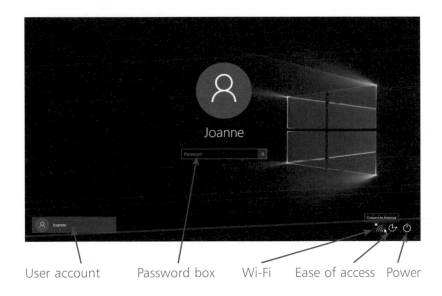

**Don't forget**

The log on screen will have a User account button for each account on the system – so you can choose which account to log on.

User account     Password box     Wi-Fi     Ease of access     Power

**User account** – a button that selects the user to be logged onto the system.

**Password box** – an input box where the user enters their password.

**Wi-Fi** – an icon button that allows you to connect to a network and indicates signal strength if already connected via Wi-Fi.

**Ease of Access** – an icon button that provides the pop-up menu shown on the right containing accessibility settings for users with impaired abilities. When this button is clicked, Windows reads and scans the menu as Narrator automatically provides audible guidance. Each item is explained and highlighted in turn. The user can select any item when it's highlighted by pressing the space bar.

**Beware**

The menus on the log on screen are easy to miss as they are very small and placed right at the bottom of the screen.

**Power** – an icon button that provides a pop-up menu containing Sleep, Shut down, and Restart options.

# Start screen

After logging on to a Windows 10 system you will see the Start screen in Desktop or Tablet Mode, appropriate for the device:

## Desktop Mode

The customizable Start menu and Taskbar Search box are new features in Windows 10.

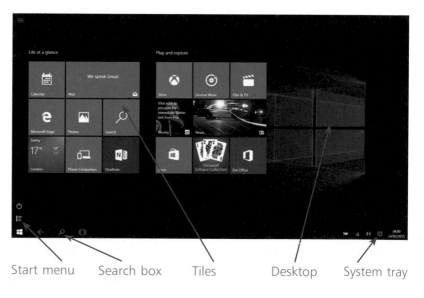

Start menu    Search box    Tiles    Taskbar    Desktop    System tray

Open the Start menu in Desktop Mode by clicking the ⊞ Start button, then click **All apps** to see the A-Z list of apps.

## Tablet Mode

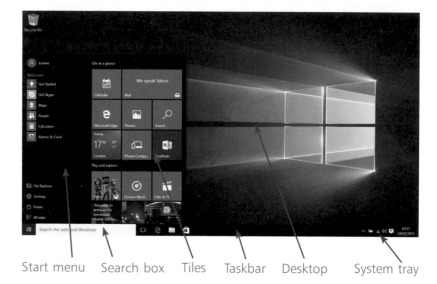

Tap the ▤ Start menu button in Tablet Mode to see the A-Z list of apps, then tap the 🔍 button to open the Search box.

Start menu    Search box    Tiles    Desktop    System tray

Each Start menu contains an A-Z list of all apps that launch within a window in Desktop Mode or full-screen in Tablet Mode.

## ...cont'd

Any app in the list can be added to the array of tiles by right-clicking on the listed app and choosing "Pin to Start" from a context menu. This allows you to populate the tiles with your favorite apps so you can quickly launch them by clicking, or tapping, on a tile. Apps can also be pinned to the Taskbar in Desktop Mode.

The Search box lets you easily locate anything you need on your system or on the web. The icons down the side of the open Search box give access to:

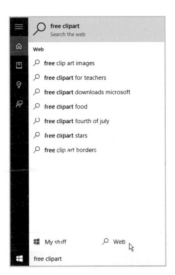

- Cortana Personal Digital Assistant (more on this later)

- Home, for news, etc.

- Notebook, for events, etc.

- Reminders, for appointments, etc.

- Feedback to Microsoft

The System tray contains icons that give access to:

- Show hidden icons, such as  "Safely Remove Hardware"

- Battery status and power settings

- Network status and settings

- Volume level control

- Action Center for notification messages and system settings

- Clock date and time settings

# Navigation

In its drive for Windows 10 to be all-encompassing, Microsoft has made it possible to navigate the interface in three different ways: by touch, the mouse, and the keyboard.

### Touch

Touch gestures include swiping, sliding, tapping, and pinching. The best way to get to grips with these is to experiment. The following, however, will get you off to a good start:

**Tap** – opens, selects, or activates whatever you tap (similar to clicking with a mouse).

**Tap and hold** – shows further info about the item or opens a context menu (similar to right-clicking with a mouse).

**Pinch or stretch** – visually zooms in or out, like with a website, map, or picture. Pinch to zoom out and stretch to zoom in.

**Rotate** – some items can be rotated by placing your fingers on them and turning your hand.

**Slide to scroll** – dragging your finger across the screen scrolls through items on the screen (similar to scrolling a mouse wheel).

**Slide to arrange** – dragging an item around the screen with your finger to position it (similar to dragging with a mouse).

**Swipe to select** – a short, quick movement will select an item and often bring up app commands.

**Swipe or slide from right edge** – opens the Action Center.

**Swipe or slide from left edge** – opens the Task View feature.

**Swipe or slide from top edge** – enables you to view the title bar in full-screen apps.

**Swipe or slide from bottom edge** – enables you to view the Taskbar in full-screen apps.

In many cases the touch commands available are dependent on the application in use. For example, various rotational commands can be used to manipulate objects in drawing and layout applications such as Microsoft PowerPoint.

## Mouse

Using the mouse to get around in Windows 10 is no different from any other operating system, although you can spin the mouse wheel while on the Lock screen to open the password box.

## Keyboard

Those of you who use the Windows 10 interface without the benefit of a touchscreen are well advised to get acquainted with the various keyboard commands relevant to it. In many cases, just as with keyboard commands and shortcuts in general, they are often quicker than using the mouse.

There is actually a whole bunch of these commands; the following being some of the more useful ones:

The key that will be used most is the Windows key (WinKey). Pressing this key opens and closes the Start menu. It can also be used in conjunction with other keys to perform other actions. For example, pressing **WinKey + X** opens the Power User Menu while **WinKey + C** opens the Cortana search feature.

The Home and End keys jump from one end of the "All apps" list on the Start menu to the other, while the arrow keys can be used to select a tile. The Enter key opens a selected app.

**WinKey + Tab** opens Task View, which allows the user to switch to a different app using the arrow keys to select an app. The Enter key can then be used to exit Task View and activate the app.

**Alt + Tab** opens a Switch list which allows the user to switch to a different app. Note that you must have at least two apps running for **WinKey + Tab** and **Alt + Tab** to work.

A rarely-used key known as the Context Menu key (usually located close to the space bar) brings up a menu of related options when pressed.

The Windows key is usually located at the bottom of the keyboard near to the space bar and often has an image of a flying window on it.

Two of the most useful keyboard shortcuts are **WinKey + C** to open Cortana search and **WinKey + X** to open the Power User Menu.

# Ask Cortana

One of the great innovations in Windows 10 is the Personal Digital Assistant named "Cortana". This is an enhancement to the Search box feature that allows the user to search, and much more, by verbal communication once it has been enabled:

**1** Click in the Taskbar Search box then, when asked, enter your name and agree to give access to your location

**2** Ensure your microphone is correctly configured then click the microphone icon at the right of the Search box

**3** Repeat the phrase that Cortana gives you, being sure to speak clearly without any background room noise, then click **Next** to close

**4** Click the Search box then click the Notebook icon and choose the **Settings** option

**5** Slide both the **Cortana** and **Hey Cortana** toggle buttons into the **On** position

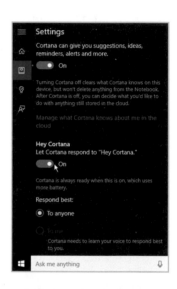

**6** Upon completion of setup just say "Hey Cortana" to make Cortana listen

**7** Now, ask Cortana anything you like. For example, try asking about the weather

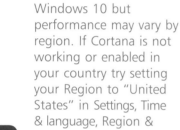

Cortana is new in Windows 10 but performance may vary by region. If Cortana is not working or enabled in your country try setting your Region to "United States" in Settings, Time & language, Region & language.

You can also click the microphone icon in the Search box to make Cortana begin listening.

60

The best way to learn Cortana commands is to simply try out different ways to phrase your question. Here are some Cortana commands that worked successfully when we tried them and demonstrate some of the many things you can have Cortana do:

- **Cortana Search** – "Pink discography"

- **Cortana Calendar** – "Create a meeting with David"

- **Cortana Reminder** – "Remind me at 4pm"

- **Cortana Alarm** – "Wake me up in 2 hours"

- **Cortana Maps** – "Show me a map of Washington DC"

- **Cortana Weather** – "What's the forecast this weekend?"

- **Cortana Music** – "Play music", "Pause music", "Resume music"

- **Cortana Pictures** – "Show me a picture of Cortana"

- **Cortana App Launch** – "Open Command Prompt"

- **Cortana News** "Show me today's news"

- **Cortana Finance** – "How is Microsoft Stock doing today?"

- **Cortana Sports** – "New York Jets' next game?"

- **Cortana Fun** – "Sing me a song"

Cortana requires an internet connection so will be unable to answer if you should lose your Wi-Fi connection. More features, such as the ability to take notes, will be added to Cortana in the future.

Cortana collects users' personal data to further personalize results and as such is subject to child-protection laws. Therefore the user must be at least 13 years of age (checked against age data in user profiles) or Cortana will refuse to answer questions.

# Personalization

You can easily customize your Desktop by replacing the default Windows 10 background with a picture of your choice or with a solid color by choosing from a swatch selection:

You can click Browse to choose an image from your Pictures folder. Search the web for background wallpapers to suit the resolution of your PC screen.

**1** Click the Start button then choose the **Settings** option

**2** On the Settings screen click the **Personalization** icon

**3** Click the **Background** dropdown menu and select **Picture** then choose an image, or select **Solid Color** then choose a color from the swatch that appears

There is also a dropdown option to create a Slideshow that changes the background image at a frequency of your choice, and you can choose how to fit images on your screen.

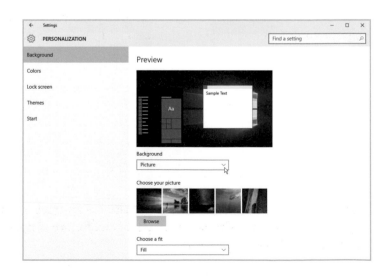

**...cont'd**

The Lock screen, that appears when you boot your PC, or when it's sleeping, can be customized in two ways:

## Appearance

**1** Go to Settings, Personalization then click the **Lock screen** option on the left pane

**2** Click the **Background** dropdown and select a picture

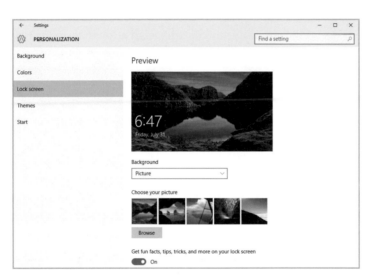

If you are leaving your PC and want to turn on the Windows 10 Lock screen, simply press **WinKey + L**.

63

## Notifications
If you look below the default Background images you will see options to change the notifications displayed on the Lock screen.

You can use the Lock screen to display useful information. For example, unread emails.

The only app showing a notification on the Lock screen in the picture above is the Calendar app. You can add more simply by clicking one of the **+** add icons.

# User settings

The Windows 10 interface provides a range of settings with regard to users. Amongst other things, these include switching accounts and changing account passwords.

### Switch accounts

Windows 10 allows two types of account – a Microsoft account, which enables all of Windows 10's features to be used, and a local account, which has restrictions. To switch from one to the other:

**1** On the Start menu, click **Settings** then choose **Accounts**

**2** Click the link to **Sign in with a local account instead**

**3** In the screen that opens, enter your current password

**4** In the next screen, enter a username, password and password hint for the account

**5** Click **Sign out and finish** to be taken to the Lock screen where you must log in with the new account's credentials

**Hot tip**

Two types of account can be used with the Windows 10 interface – a Microsoft account and a local account.

**Hot tip**

The "Switch to a local account" option effectively creates a new user account.

## Change account password

Should you ever wish to change your account's password, do it as described below:

**1** On the Start menu, click **Settings** then choose **Accounts**

**2** On the left pane, click the **Sign-in options** item and you will see a **Change** button for your password

It is recommended that account passwords should have at least eight characters and include digits plus mixed-case letters.

**3** Click the button to open the "Change your Microsoft account password" window

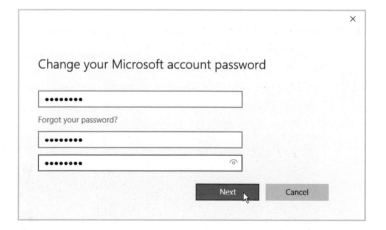

**4** Enter your old password, then enter your new password twice and click **Next**

# Account picture

Should you wish to change your account picture you can choose any image to associate with your identity:

**1** Go to Settings, Accounts then click the **Your account** option on the left pane

**2** Click the **Browse** button and select a picture

You can also click the Camera icon to have your webcam create a photo to use as your account picture if you like.

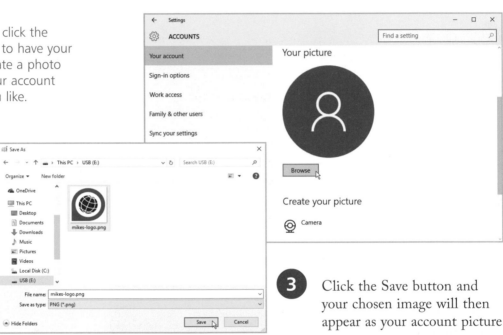

**3** Click the Save button and your chosen image will then appear as your account picture

# Picture password

Windows 10 allows users to present their login credentials in the form of a picture password rather than a text password. Set this up as follows:

**1** On the Start menu, click **Settings** then choose **Accounts**

**2** On the left pane, click the **Sign-in options** item and you will see an **Add** button for your picture password

**3** Click the button then verify you are the account holder by entering the existing text password

**4** At the next screen, click the **Choose picture** button to open File Explorer in your Pictures folder

**5** Choose a suitable image and click the **Open** button

**6** Now, click the **Use this picture** button to enter a "Set up your gestures" screen

Because there are so many possible combinations of pictures and gestures, picture passwords can be more secure than text passwords.

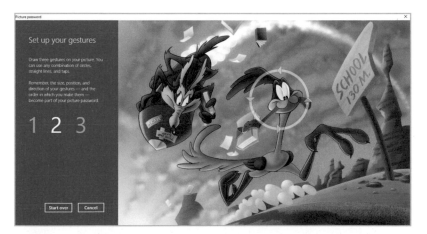

**7** Create three separate marks or gestures on the picture. Each gesture can be a straight line or a circle or a tap

If you make an error when confirming the gestures, hit **Start over**. Windows draws the gestures on the screen as guidelines.

The next time you log in to the PC, you will have the choice of using your text password or the picture password.

# PIN code

PIN (Personal Identification Number) codes are another security feature in Windows 10, and enable users to secure their computer with a four-digit code. You may question the need for this as there are already plenty of security options provided, not to mention the fact that a four-digit code isn't particularly secure anyway.

However, the feature is intended for use in tablets and smartphones, where the small keyboards provided make it difficult to enter a complex alpha-numeric password.

The PIN code feature is intended for use on small touchscreen devices.

**1** On the Start menu, click **Settings** then choose "Accounts"

**2** On the left pane, click the **Sign-in options** item and you will see an **Add** button for your PIN

**3** Click the button and enter a four-digit PIN – the PIN code option will now be available at the login screen

# Add a user

An important feature in Windows 10 is the provision for setting up more than one user account. This allows a single PC to be shared by a number of people, each with their own computing environment. The procedure for adding a user is as follows:

**1**    On the Start menu, click **Settings** then choose **Accounts**

**2**    On the left pane, click the **Family & other users** item and you will see an **Add someone else to this PC** button for "Other users"

When a user is added to a Windows 10 PC, the account type can be either a Local account or a Microsoft account.

**3**    Click the button then enter user details of a Microsoft account, or click the link to enter user details without a Microsoft account then enter the user details

**4**    The user will be added to the "Other users" list and will be able to log in the next time the PC is started

69

# Close Windows 10

Windows 10 offers several ways of closing the system down:

### Desktop Mode
Click the ■ **Start** button icon and choose to "Sleep", "Shut down", or "Restart" from the pop-up menu options.

You can also **Shut down** or **Sign out** from the Power User Menu (see page 98).

### Tablet Mode
Click or tap the ⏻ power button icon and choose to "Sleep", "Shut down", or "Restart" from the pop-up menu options.

### Keyboard
A keyboard command that has been around for a long time is still available in Windows 10. This is **Ctrl + Alt + Del**. Pressing these keys opens the options screen shown on the right – from where you can access the pop-up menu power options.

### Shutdown/Restart Shortcuts
This procedure lets you create your own power option shortcuts.

You can also create a "Sign out" tile using the value **shutdown /l**

**1** Create a shortcut named "Shutdown" on the Desktop with value **shutdown /s /t 0**

**2** Right-click the shortcut and select **Pin to start**

**3** Repeat to create and pin a shortcut called "Restart" with value **shutdown /r /t 0**

You will now see Shutdown and Restart tiles on the Start menu.

# 5 Windows 10 apps

*Apps are an integral part of*

*the Windows 10 interface.*

*We explain how they work,*

*how to access their options,*

*plus show some useful tips.*

*We also review all the apps*

*bundled with Windows 10.*

# Supplied with Windows 10

Windows 10 comes with lots of pre-installed applications ("apps"). There are familiar traditional programs, such as Notepad, but the A-Z list of "All apps" on the Start menu contains many new "Universal Windows App" programs designed to run on PCs, tablets, and smartphones. The A-Z list of "All apps" looks like this:

**Don't forget**

Several of the bundled apps require the user to be logged in with a Microsoft account.

Universal Windows Apps are new in Windows 10 and are intended to provide a common experience across many devices.

**Hot tip**

If you need apps not supplied with Windows 10, you can find many more apps at the Windows Store.

- **3D Builder**
- **Alarms & Clock**
- **Calculator**
- **Calendar**
- **Camera**
- **Candy Crush Saga**
- **Contact Support**
- **Cortana**
- **Get Office**
- **Get Skype**
- **Get Started**
- **Groove Music**
- **Mail**
- **Maps**
- **Microsoft Edge**
- **Microsoft Solitaire Collection**
- **Money**
- **Movies & TV**
- **News**

- **OneDrive**
- **OneNote**
- **People**
- **Phone Companion**
- **Photos**
- **Settings**
- **Sports**
- **Store**
- **Twitter**
- **Voice Recorder**
- **Weather**
- **Windows Accessories** *
- **Windows Administrative Tools** *
- **Windows Ease of Access** *
- **Windows Feedback**
- **Windows PowerShell** *
- **Windows System** *
- **Xbox**

Items marked with an * are folders containing more apps. For example, **Windows Accessories** contains Notepad, Paint, Sticky Notes, WordPad, Internet Explorer, and many more.

# Start apps

We will take a brief look at some of the pre-installed apps – the ones not covered here will be reviewed in later chapters.

## People

Windows operating systems have always provided a contact manager, which provided a useful means of keeping phone numbers, addresses, etc. in one place. However, the advent of social media websites, such as Twitter, Facebook and LinkedIn, has seen this type of information stored and used in new ways.

The **People** app is Microsoft's attempt to update its old Contacts manager to make it relevant to today's needs. It stores the data from your contacts in a cloud-based location, which means they can be accessed from anywhere in the world, and via any of your Windows 10 devices.

Furthermore, the app amalgamates data from all supported networks. Thus, people who use more than one social network will be recognized by the app as being the same person and all their data, whatever the source, is presented as a single contact link.

## Skype

This app replaces the Messaging app provided with Windows 8. It allows you to make audio and video calls to other Skype users on almost any device, pretty much anywhere in the world, for free.

It is also possible to share files, photos, and links with people you're chatting with. When you sign in to the app, all your contacts from the old Messaging app are automatically added to your existing list of contacts. The **Get Skype** item on the "All apps" list lets you easily download and install the Skype app.

## Calendar

An updated version of a traditional Microsoft application, the **Calendar** app doesn't really offer anything new. It has been designed to be easy to read, and free of unnecessary distractions.

To this end, by default, the content displayed is kept to a minimum. Ease of navigation has been improved, there is a simple interface for adding events, many notification options, and some good advanced scheduling options.

The People app also integrates with other Universal Windows Apps. So from the People app, you can send emails via the Mail app, map addresses with the Maps app, and more.

Calendar syncs with Hotmail, Outlook, and Google accounts to bring all your events together for easy viewing.

...cont'd

### Money

The **Money** app provides a wealth of finance-related information, with various menu options providing different types of data. You can drill down into items of interest to get detailed information.

The Markets option and World Markets option provide up-to-date stock, commodities, and bond market data. A Watchlist option provides a customizable list of companies you may want to follow closely. Information that can be monitored includes stock market performance (current and historic), revenue, profit, company profile, and more.

The Currencies option provides a handy Currency Converter and up-to-date exchange rates of world currencies. There is also a Mortgage Calculator option to calculate monthly payments.

### Weather

The **Weather** app provides several menu options. The Home screen displays weather conditions for the current location. This includes an overview, an hourly breakdown, and a range of weather-related details.

The Maps option shows a temperature map of your location and a Historical Weather option displays a graph of past monthly temperature and rainfall at your location.

The Places option allows more locations to be selected to create a Favorite Places list so that multiple locations can be monitored in addition to those displayed on the Home screen.

A News option displays weather-related news items from around the world, describing typhoons, earthquakes, etc.

### Sports

As with the Money and Weather apps, the Sports app is dynamic and provides updated content in real-time. It provides an edition related to your location. For example, the US edition is devoted to popular American sports such as Football, Basketball, Baseball, Ice Hockey, Golf, and Soccer.

The My Favorites option allows you to choose your Favorite Teams and Favorite Sports to follow more closely. Drilling down enables you to access detailed information such as the latest team news, results, fixture lists, leading players, etc.

Right-click or select the App Commands menu item to drop down the Features list, then choose a feature and scroll or swipe through its tabs.

The new Universal Windows Apps of Money, Weather, Sports, and News provide the latest information on any device, wherever you are.

**...cont'd**

## News

Most people like to keep abreast of what's happening both in their locality and on the world stage. The **News** app provides the conduit and, like the Sports app, provides an edition related to your location. For example, the US edition is devoted to American news items.

The Home screen displays My News items with tabs for categories of news you can customize using the Interests menu option.

The Local option allows you to receive items of local news from a location of your choice, and the Videos option shows a selection of recent news videos from the internet.

## Contact Support

A new app in Windows 10, **Contact Support** is useful for those wanting assistance with Microsoft's latest operating system. It is split into two sections – **Accounts & billing**, **Services & apps**.

The **Accounts & billing** section provides links to manage your Microsoft account, and seek information for Xbox, Skype, or Windows Phone billing queries. It also lets you get help via Online Chat or Scheduled Call to a Microsoft Answer Tech.

The **Services & apps** section provides links to seek help on Windows installation, settings, activation, errors, performance, and security issues. It provides links to get answers from the Microsoft Community forum, and also lets you get help via Online Chat or Scheduled Call to Microsoft Answer Tech.

## Maps

Windows 10's **Maps** app is a particularly useful app. You can enter any address using its Search option and the app will attempt to produce a map showing that location and a street view photo if available. If the address is found by the app, you can get directions from a starting point of your choice to that address, and discover nearby hotels, coffee shops, restaurants, stores, and museums.

The Directions option lets you seek directions between any two points of your choice, and you can store your maps using the Favorites option.

There is also a 3D Cities option that provides aerial photographic views that you can zoom, tilt, and rotate.

When a news story is clicked, it opens in the website that provides it.

The Contact Support app is new in Windows 10 and makes it easy to get help directly from a Microsoft Answer Tech.

# App options

In addition to options provided on an app's toolbar, Windows 10 apps offer a range of options on a dropdown menu from a "hamburger button".  Let's start by adding a favorite app to a custom Start group.

A good way to open the Start menu is to simply press the WinKey.

**1** To add any app to a Start group first click on the Start button then find the app in the alphabetical **All Apps** list

**2** Next, right-click on the app item to open a context menu, and choose the **Pin to Start** option

Use the  icon at the right of a Start group title bar to drag that group, to arrange your Start menu groups.

**3** Click the group title bar above the app icon that has been added to the Start group and enter a custom group name

You can open a context menu of options by right-clicking on any app icon in a Start group. With an open app, clicking the app window's ☰ "hamburger button" reveals a list of options for that app. The app's ⚙ Settings button can reveal settings options.

**4** Launch an app (say, Weather) from the Start menu then click the app's hamburger button to see the app's options

**Hot tip**

Windows can display apps in full-screen or the window can be resized to display the app in a small floating window.

**5** Click the Settings button to reveal the settings options

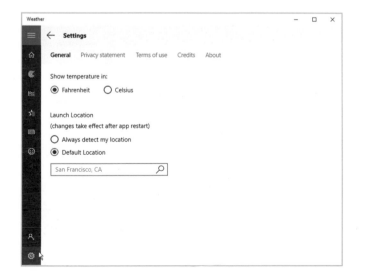

**Don't forget**

App options offered are related to each particular app in use.

77

# App switcher & Task list

The Windows 10 App switcher can be used to quickly switch between running apps. It displays all running apps on the Desktop so you can easily select the one you want to work with. The App switcher is launched using a keyboard shortcut of **WinKey + Tab**.

**1** Open the App switcher by pressing **WinKey + Tab**

"WinKey" refers to the Windows key. This is usually located close to the space bar (see page 59).

**2** Tap or click to select the app you want to work with, or press **WinKey + Tab** again to close the App switcher

Alternatively, you can quickly select a running app to work with from a Task list. This too displays all running apps on the Desktop so you can easily select the one you want to work with. The Task list is launched using a keyboard shortcut with **Alt** and **Tab** keys.

**3** Open the **Task list** by holding down the **Alt** key and by pressing the **Tab** key once

When using the Task list, you can also select programs with the arrow keys.

**4** Keep the **Alt** key depressed and tap the **Tab** key to move through the list. When the focus is on the app you want to work with, release the **Alt** key to select that app

# Snap apps

Windows 10 apps can run full-screen. With the large wide-screen monitors available today, many users will find it irritating to have their entire desktop real-estate taken up by just one program.

To address this issue, Windows 10 offers a feature called Snap, which enables users to run up to four apps side-by-side. The actual number depends on the monitor's resolution. Resolutions of 2,560 x 1,440 pixels can snap four apps. Resolutions less than this will only be able to snap two or three apps.

For the Windows Snap feature to work, the device must have a screen width of at least 1,366 pixels. If you are having problems, check this out by going to Control Panel, Display, Adjust Resolution.

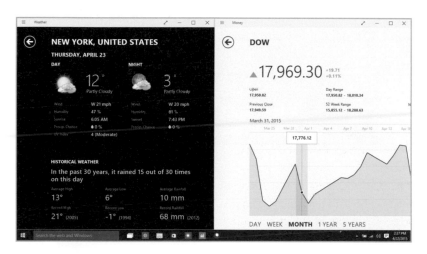

Here two apps are snapped – the Weather app and the Money app

**1** Open an app full-screen and click its ☐ down-size button to put the app in a floating window, then repeat this process for a second app

**2** Click on the title bar of the first app and drag it out to the left edge of the screen – then release it to see the window snap to fill the left half of the screen

**3** Click on the title bar of the second app and drag it out to the right edge of the screen – then release it to see the window snap to fill the right half of the screen

In addition to snapping apps to left and right, Windows 10 lets you snap in a third and fourth app if the screen resolution allows it.

# Close apps

Closing an app is very simple to do but it must be pointed out that usually it is not actually necessary to close apps. This is because when a new app is opened, other running apps are switched to a state of suspension in which they use very little in the way of system resources.

However, there may be situations in which it is desirable or even necessary to close down an app. Here are five ways to do this:

Most of the time, it is not necessary to shut an app down. Due to the way that Windows 10 minimizes the system resources required by apps that aren't being used, you can, in fact, have a whole bunch of apps running at the same time without any noticeable degradation of system performance.

80

- Simply press **Alt + F4** – this kills the app instantly

- Click the Close button on the window bar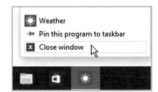

- Right-click the app in **App Switcher** and select **Close**

- Hover over the app icon on the Taskbar and select **Close window** in the pop-up context menu that appears

- Press **Ctrl + Shift + Esc** to open the Task Manager, then select the app on the Processes tab and click the **End Task** button

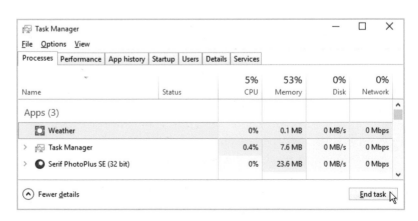

# Reader

Reader is an app provided by Microsoft that can open PDF files. By default, this app is not bundled with Windows 10 so you have to download it from the Microsoft Store. Using the Search box for "reader" takes you to the Reader download in the Store.

Once installed, click the Start button and choose **All apps** to see the A-Z list of programs on the PC. Under the letter R you will see the Reader app has been added. Click to open it. Reader launches by default in full-screen mode and is straightforward in concept. Open a PDF file and that's all you will see – the PDF file. No toolbars or options.

**Hot tip**

You can zoom in and out of a PDF document with the **Ctrl +** (zoom in) and **Ctrl –** (zoom out) keyboard shortcuts.

Right-click on the screen, however, and the feature set is revealed.

Reader provides three reading modes: One Page, Two Pages, and Continuous. In One Page view, only one whole page will be seen at a time. In Two Pages view, Reader will display two pages side-by-side. Pages can be navigated both vertically and horizontally, depending on the page view being used. It is possible to zoom in and out, and also find specific words with the Find feature.

You can print from the app by pressing **WinKey + P** to open the Printer list. It is also possible to highlight text, add notes and fill out forms.

**Hot tip**

Reader may be simple but it performs very well. It actually opens PDF files much faster than the native PDF application, Adobe Reader.

# OneDrive

OneDrive is a Microsoft facility that allows users to store data in the Cloud via a Microsoft account. To get started, click the OneDrive item on the **All apps** menu and log in with your Microsoft account (if you don't have an account you will need to create one). You will then be asked to choose which folders on your PC you wish to synchronize on OneDrive. Your selection now appears under the OneDrive category on your PC marked with green check mark icons when they have been synchronized.

A OneDrive account can be accessed in two ways – directly from a web browser and via a OneDrive app. More options are available when it is accessed via a browser.

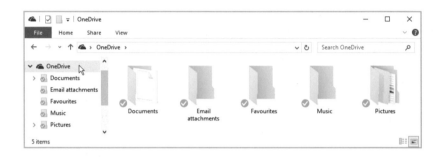

Copies of content added to these local folders are automatically uploaded to your online OneDrive folder to synchronize photos, video, email, documents, etc. across a number of separate devices, such as PCs, smartphones, and tablets. Your content can be accessed from anywhere using a OneDrive app on a device or by browsing to **onedrive.live.com**

You can create **New** online folders and add files, or **Upload** folders and files to the online OneDrive folder from your device.

OneDrive is more important than ever in Windows 10 as it seeks convergence for all devices to make your data available to you wherever you may be.

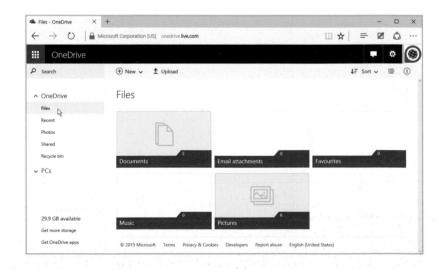

# 6 Desktop and Taskbar

*You can control how Windows sets up the screen so that it displays text and graphics at the right size. You can also take advantage of multiple monitors and you can choose a desktop theme with the style, appearance and features that most appeal to you.*

# Switching desktops

Windows 10 has a virtual desktop feature called "Task View". This allows you to have multiple desktops so you can spread out various projects, so that each project is on a separate desktop. When you need to jump from one project to another you can just switch desktops and everything is right there waiting for you – no need to minimize and maximize windows to get back to work:

**1** Click the 🔳 button on the Taskbar to access the Task View feature – thumbnail icons of all running apps and a **+ New Desktop** button appear on the screen

**2** Next, click the **+ New Desktop** button – thumbnails of the original desktop and one more desktop appear in a bar across the bottom of the screen

**3** Each desktop thumbnail has a pop-up **X** button you can use to close that desktop

**4** Select any desktop thumbnail to switch to that desktop, where you can open apps, or move open apps from one desktop to another

You can also access Task View by pressing **WinKey + Tab**.

Virtual desktops have been available in other operating systems for quite some time but are new in Windows 10.

In Task View you can move between desktops by holding down **Ctrl + WinKey** then pressing the left- or right-arrow keys.

**5** In Task View, right-click on the thumbnail icon of an open app you want to move then select **Move to** and choose a desktop from the context menu

**Hot tip**

When you close a desktop, all open apps on that desktop automatically move to another existing desktop.

**Don't forget**

You can click an app thumbnail to switch to the desktop in which it is open and activate the app, or click the Task View button once more to exit the feature.

# Launching apps

There are various ways of launching an application:

### Start menu/desktop icons
Start menu items and desktop icons are actually shortcuts that link to a program's executable file. So, to launch an app, just click on the menu item or desktop icon – this activates the app, which then opens on the screen.

### Taskbar icons
Icons on the Taskbar are application shortcuts as well. Click one, and the associated application will open on the Desktop.

### Search box
Applications that are located on the Start menu, Desktop, or Taskbar are easy to locate – they are literally right in front of your eyes. How about programs you can't see, though?

Windows 10's Search box is the answer:

**1** Enter the name of the app in the Search box

**2** Choose the appropriate app from the search results

You can launch any program on the PC from the Search box.

The Taskbar Search box is new in Windows 10.

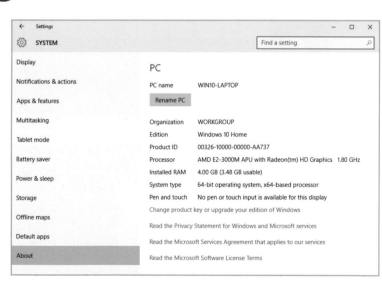

# Personalize

You can give your computer a personal touch by changing the computer's window color, sounds, desktop background, screen saver, and other aspects. You can change the attributes individually, or select a pre-configured theme.

There are two ways to view and change the current theme:

**1** Right-click the Desktop and select **Personalize**

**2** On the Personalization screen that opens, choose **Themes** on the left pane, then select **Theme Settings** on the right

OR

**1** Go to the Control Panel and under the "Appearance and Personalization" category, click **Change the theme**

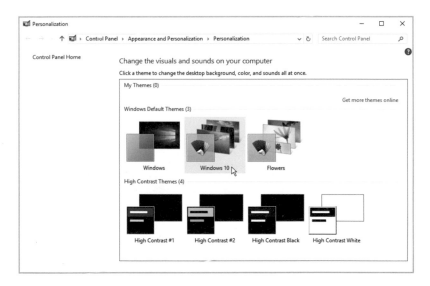

**2** You'll see the current theme with its desktop background

**3** Select any of the suggested themes, and it is immediately applied, and its components are displayed

**Hot tip**

You can click the **Get more themes online** link on the Personalization, Themes screen to add more great themes to your PC.

**Don't forget**

There's no screen saver included in most themes since they already include a varying background. However, you can add a screen saver to any theme.

**...cont'd**

In the example below, a standard Windows 10 theme has been selected.

There will be a theme for the location appropriate to your installed version, for example, USA or UK.

If you don't like the background image of a particular theme, right-click the Desktop then select **Personalize** and click **Background** to choose another.

To retain the previous accent for icons and tiles select **Colors** then turn off the option to "Automatically pick an accent color from my background". Below, we see the Windows 10 theme as above but now with a different background.

By default, the images advance every 30 minutes, but you can adjust the timing and select a random order.

# Create a theme

**1** Right-click the Desktop and select **Background** on the Personalization screen

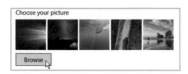

**2** Next, click **Browse** and select the background image required, then click the **Choose picture** button

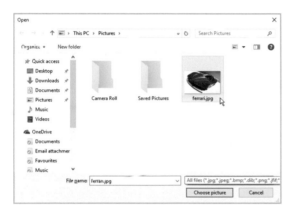

**3** The selected image now appears in the Preview area

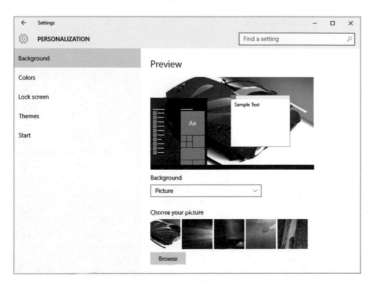

To create your own theme, start with an existing theme, the Windows 10 theme for example, and revise its components.

Select all the pictures or just a selection, set the timing, then click Save changes to add them to the theme you are creating.

**...cont'd**

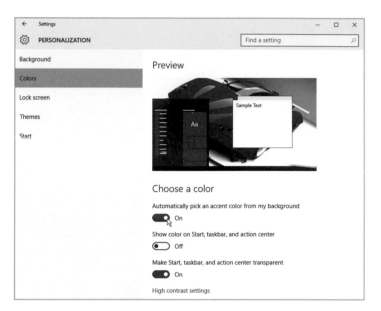

**Hot tip**

The modified theme is added to the My Themes section, as an unsaved theme.

**4** Select **Colors** and turn **On** the option to "Automatically pick an accent color from my background" for color tiles

**5** Adjust the other toggle buttons for color and transparency on the Start menu, Taskbar, and Action Center. Your changes appear in the Preview area and on your Desktop

**Don't forget**

You can click the **High contrast settings** link to customize colors for high contrast themes.

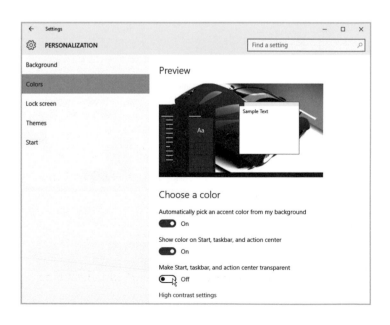

## ...cont'd

### Sound scheme

Next, choose a sound scheme:

**1** Right-click the Desktop and select **Themes** on the Personalization screen, then choose the **Advanced sound settings** link

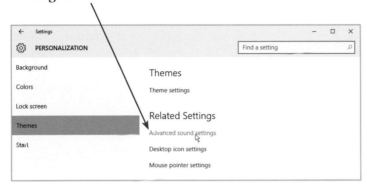

Most of the Windows themes provide their own sound scheme, so you can try these out to see which you prefer.

The default Windows 10 sound scheme has more mellow sounds than earlier versions.

**2** Select the **Sound Scheme** box and choose from the predefined sound schemes to find which you prefer

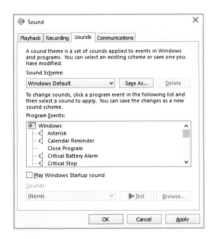

**3** Select a program event such as "Windows Logon" and click **Test** to listen to the sound

**4** Click **Browse** to choose a different sound file

**5** Click **Save As** to save the revised sound scheme

Check the box **Play Windows Startup Sound** to hear sound when Windows starts up, or uncheck it to avoid the sound.

...cont'd

## Desktop icons & Mouse pointer settings

Choose which icons to display on the Desktop:

**1** Right-click the Desktop and select **Themes** on the Personalization screen, then choose the **Desktop icon settings** link

**2** Check the box of any icon you want on the Desktop, then click the **OK** button to save your selection

**Don't forget**

Check the box to "Allow themes to change desktop icons" if you want to use themes with their own custom icons.

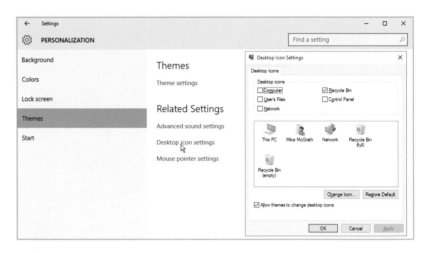

**3** Now, choose the **Mouse pointer settings** link on the Personalization screen, then choose the **Desktop icon settings** link

**4** Customize the performance of the mouse and the appearance of pointers using the tab options

**5** Click the **OK** button to save the settings

**Hot tip**

The Mouse Properties' Pointers tab lets you select from a variety of Windows pointer schemes.

## Save the theme

To save your theme:

**1** Right-click the Desktop and select **Themes** on the Personalization screen, then choose **Theme settings**

**2** Select the Unsaved Theme and click the **Save theme** link

**3** Provide a name for your new theme and click **Save**

**4** The theme remains in "My Themes", under its new name

The theme file is stored in the user's applications data area, e.g. **C:\Users\Michael\AppData\Local\Microsoft\Windows\Themes**, along with any Windows themes that have been downloaded.

Your theme is stored as an Unsaved Theme until you choose to Save the theme.

If you cannot see the AppData folder in your User folder, you may need to check "Hidden items" on File Explorer's View menu.

**...cont'd**

To make the theme available to other users:

**1** Right-click the theme and select **Save theme for sharing**

**2** Specify the name and folder for the theme and click **Save**

**3** The background images, colors, sounds and other settings for your theme are saved in a file of type **.deskthemepack**

Ferrari Theme.deskthemepack

Downloading this file or selecting it on a shared network drive will make the theme available to the other users. You can remove themes from My Themes when they are no longer needed.

**1** Make sure that the theme is not currently selected

**2** Right-click and select **Delete theme**

# Screen resolution

To adjust the screen resolution:

**1** Right-click the Desktop and select **Display settings** from the menu

**2** Next, click the **Advanced display settings** link

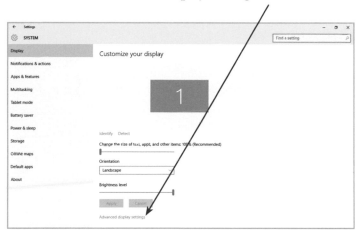

**3** Now, click the **Resolution** box and choose a setting from the dropdown menu

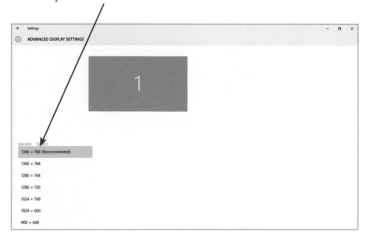

**4** Click **Apply** to see the resolution change for 15 seconds

**5** Click **Keep changes** during the change period to retain the new resolution you have selected

Hot tip

The screen resolution controls the size of the screen contents. Lower resolutions (e.g. 800 x 600) have larger items so fewer can be displayed. Higher resolutions (e.g. 1920 x 1200) have smaller and sharper items, and more can be viewed on the screen.

Don't forget

You can also change the orientation from Landscape to Portrait – useful for tablet PCs and for a monitor that can be rotated.

# Taskbar

The purpose of the Taskbar is to launch and monitor running applications. The version provided in Windows 10 has two specific regions – a small section at the right called the system tray Notification area, and the main body of the Taskbar on which program icons and the Start button are displayed.

To explore the Taskbar properly and see what it can do, it is necessary to go into its properties (right-click on the Taskbar and select Properties).

**Don't forget**

Before you can move or resize the Taskbar, it must be unlocked.

The Taskbar tab provides various options. These include:

- Locking and unlocking the Taskbar. When unlocked it can be moved to any edge of the screen and also its depth can be increased.

- Those of you with keen eyesight can reduce the size of the Taskbar icons. This enables the bar to hold more of them.

You can alter the way Taskbar icons are presented. Options include:

- **Always combine, hide labels** – each app appears as a single, unlabeled icon, even if several windows for that app are open.

- **Combine when Taskbar is full** – each window is shown as an individual icon. When the Taskbar becomes crowded, apps with multiple open windows collapse into a single icon.

- **Never combine** – each window is shown as an individual, labeled icon and are never combined, regardless of how many are open. As more apps and windows open, icons get smaller, and will eventually scroll.

From the Taskbar tab, you can also customize the Notification area, e.g. which icons and notifications to display.

**Hot tip**

When the "Use Peek to preview the desktop..." option is enabled, hovering your mouse at the far-right of the Taskbar will return you to the Desktop view, i.e. all open windows will be minimized. To get them back again, just left-click.

**...cont'd**

You will also find options for configuring the Taskbar on multiple displays, as shown below. For example, you can choose to have the Taskbar showing on all your displays, and also how program icons are displayed:

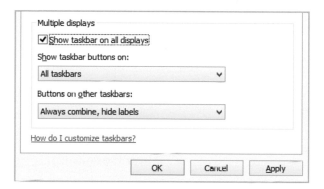

Start screen apps can be pinned to the Taskbar by right-clicking and selecting **Pin to Taskbar**.

The Navigation tab provides options relevant to the Start screen and the Toolbars tab shows a list of pre-configured toolbars that can be added to the Taskbar. For example, select **Address** then click **Apply** to add an address toolbar to the Taskbar:

By right-clicking on the Taskbar and selecting Toolbars, New toolbar..., you can create your own Taskbar toolbars.

Folders and files cannot be added to the Taskbar. However, they can be dragged to the File Explorer icon on the Taskbar and accessed from its jump list. You can Pin a folder to the Start menu tiles, then Pin that tile to the Taskbar.

Any program can be "pinned" to the Taskbar – simply right-click and select **Pin to Taskbar**, or just drag-and-drop onto the Taskbar.

# Power User Menu

One of the major changes in Windows 8 was the omission of the Start button, which provided access to many different sections of the operating system in previous versions of Windows.

In Windows 10, however, the Start button is back. Instead of left-clicking on it to go to the Start menu, right-click. This will open the Power User Menu shown below:

**Hot tip**

Another method of opening the Power User Menu is to use the **WinKey + X** keyboard shortcut.

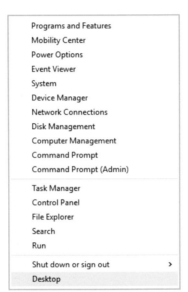

The more useful options include:

- **Programs and Features** – manage the programs installed on the PC, e.g. uninstall, repair.

- **Power Options** – this lets you configure a suitable power plan for the PC. Particularly useful for laptop and tablet users.

- **System** – provides details about your system, plus related links.

- **Device Manager** – enables all the PC's hardware to be viewed and configured.

- **Disk Management** – provides drive management tools, e.g. formatting and partitioning.

- **Computer Management** – tools for advanced system management. These are useful for system administrators.

- **Task Manager** – a program management tool that provides a range of options regarding the software running on the PC.

- **Control Panel** – an important section of the operating system that allows users to view and configure system settings.

- **File Explorer** – a combined file manager application and navigation tool. Replaces Windows Explorer.

- **Search** – opens the Start screen's Search app. Enables users to locate data, programs, emails, etc.

# Multiple displays

The graphics adapter on your computer is probably capable of handling more than one monitor, having for example both VGA (analogue) and DVI (digital) connectors. You can also attach a second monitor to a laptop. To see how Windows handles this:

**1** Right-click the Desktop and select **Display settings** from the menu

**2** Now, attach a second monitor and see the monitors are duplicated

Your monitor may have both VGA and DVI cables, but you should never attach the monitor to two connections on the same computer.

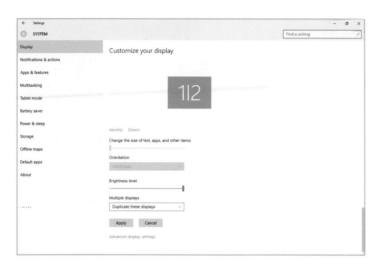

Windows resets both monitors to a resolution that both will be able to handle. If you want to continue duplicating the display, you can choose another more suitable resolution that both monitors can support.

To use the monitors for different information:

**1** Select the **Multiple displays** box and choose **Extend these displays**

**2** Click **Apply** to see the arrangement change for 15 seconds

**3** Click **Keep changes** during the change period to retain the new arrangement you have selected

If you pick a resolution that is not supported by one of the monitors, you will get a warning message and the change will not be applied.

...cont'd

 **4** By default, the first monitor is the main display. To make the second monitor the main display select the number two block then check the **Make this my main display** box

**5** Click **Identify** to briefly display the numerals 1 and 2 on the monitor screens for identification

**Hot tip**

When you press **PrtScn** with dual monitors, you will capture an image of both monitors, in the positions as arranged.

**6** By default, the monitors are arranged horizontally, so the mouse moves between them at the screen left and right. To arrange the monitors vertically, so the mouse moves between them at the screen top and bottom, drag one of the monitor blocks above the other, then click **Apply**

**Don't forget**

You can drag an application window from one monitor to the other, or across both monitors.

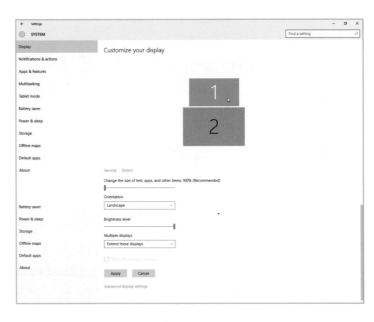

# Application windows

A very useful function in Windows is the ability to move and resize application windows. Apps in the Windows 10 interface can run in full-screen mode and can be resized.

**1** To move a window, click the title bar area, hold down the mouse button and drag the window

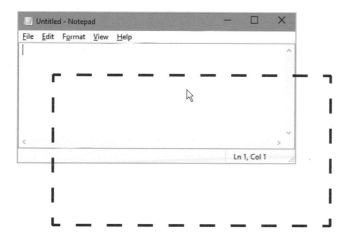

**Hot tip**

When you drag a corner of the window, you can adjust the two adjacent borders simultaneously.

**2** To resize a window, move the mouse pointer over any border or any corner until it becomes double-headed. Then click and drag until the window is the desired size

**Hot tip**

Double-clicking the title bar is an alternative to selecting the Maximize and Restore buttons.

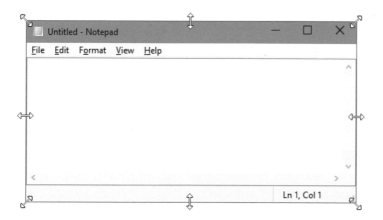

**Don't forget**

By default, the window contents show as you drag. To display just the frame, select System Properties, Advanced system settings, and then Performance Settings.

**3** To make the window full-screen, click the Maximize button. The button will now change into the Restore button – click it again to return to the original size

**Hot tip**

You can also use Snap to maximize a window to full-screen by dragging it to the top or bottom edges of the screen.

# Snap and Shake

Windows 10 includes two neat window manipulation features carried over from Windows 7. These are Snap and Shake.

## Snap

Snap is a window docking feature that resizes two windows, each to half the size of the screen, and places them side-by-side. It is almost instant, requiring just two clicks to achieve what previously would need much dragging and resizing. Do it as follows:

**1** Drag the title bar of a window to the left or right side of the screen until an outline of the expanded window appears

**2** Release the window, which then expands to fill one half of the screen

**3** Repeat with another window on the other side of the screen. You will now have two windows of equal size side-by-side and filling the screen, as shown below

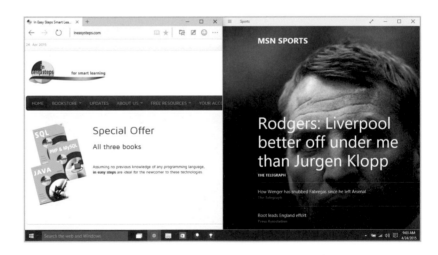

**NEW**

Snap is improved in Windows 10 with the new Snap Assist feature. This provides a thumbnail list of other open apps when you snap one app to a screen edge. Click any thumbnail to snap it to the other edge.

## Shake

Ever need to cut through a cluttered desktop and quickly focus on a single window? Just click the top of a pane and give your mouse a shake. Voilà! Every open window except that one instantly disappears. Shake it again – your windows are restored.

# ClearType

ClearType font technology makes the text on your screen appear as sharp and clear as text that's printed on paper. It's on by default in Windows 10, but you can fine-tune the settings.

**1** Go to Control Panel, Appearance and Personalization, then under Fonts, click **Adjust ClearType text**

**2** Check the **Turn on ClearType** text box (if unchecked)

For the full benefit of ClearType, you need a high-quality, flat-panel monitor, such as LCD or plasma.

**3** Click **Next** and Windows checks that you are using the native resolution for your monitor

If the monitor is not set to the recommended resolution, you are given the opportunity to change it.

**4** Click **Next** to run the "ClearType Text Tuner"

## ...cont'd

**5** Click the text box that looks best to you, then click **Next**

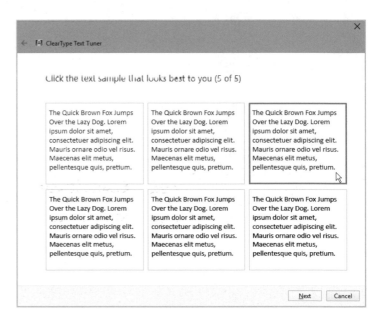

**6** Click **Finish** to close the "ClearType Text Tuner"

# 7 Built-in programs

There are programs built into Windows to help you in many areas, including text processing, scanning, faxing, image management, and calculations. There are tools to record and process sound and images. There are also special tools available, such as Command Prompt and Windows PowerShell.

# All apps

Windows 10 comes with a number of applications, services and functions, the presence of which many users will be completely unaware. Usually, these will be features and programs that they will never need to use. There will be times, though, when they miss out on something that would have been useful if only they had known it was there.

To make sure this doesn't happen to you, check to see exactly what is available in Windows 10:

In Windows 10 most items in the **All apps** A-Z list are new Universal Windows Apps, whereas traditional programs are found in folders such as "Windows Accessories".

**1** Click the Start button

**2** Select **All apps** at the bottom of the Start menu

**3** Scroll through the alphabetic listing of all available apps

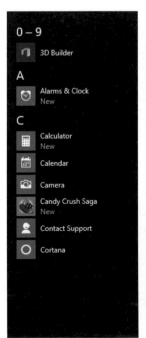

0 – 9
- 3D Builder

A
- Alarms & Clock
  New

C
- Calculator
  New
- Calendar
- Camera
- Candy Crush Saga
  New
- Contact Support
- Cortana

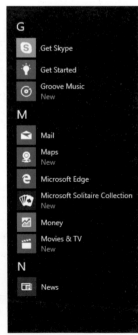

G
- Get Skype
- Get Started
- Groove Music
  New

M
- Mail
- Maps
  New
- Microsoft Edge
- Microsoft Solitaire Collection
  New
- Money
- Movies & TV
  New

N
- News

O
- OneDrive
- OneNote
  New

P
- People
  New
- Phone Companion
  New
- Photos

R
- Reader
  New

S
- Settings
- Sports
  New
- Store

T
- Twitter
  New

V
- Voice Recorder
  New

W
- Weather
- Windows Accessories
- Windows Administrative...
- Windows Ease of Access
- Windows Feedback
- Windows PowerShell
- Windows System

X
- Xbox

# Traditional apps

Traditionally, Windows has provided a number of basic, but nevertheless useful, built-in applications such as those below:

- Calculator
- Notepad
- WordPad
- Sticky Notes
- Command Prompt
- Paint
- Run
- Math Input Panel
- Steps Recorder
- Snipping Tool
- Sound Recorder
- Windows Journal
- Windows Fax & Scan
- Windows Media Player
- Character Map
- Magnifier
- Task Manager
- XPS Viewer

The Calculator app has now been reborn as a Universal Windows App but all other traditional apps are still available in Windows 10 – within the Windows Accessories, Windows Ease of Access, or Windows System folders on the **All apps** Start menu.

If you intend to use any traditional app often, it will be a good move to pin a shortcut to that app in a handy place. Locate the app in the Start menu then right-click on the item and choose **Pin to Start** (if you want it on the Start group), or **Pin to taskbar**. This is demonstrated in the example below, where we are creating a handy shortcut to the Notepad app on the Taskbar:

- Choose **Pin to taskbar** and the program will then be instantly accessible from the Taskbar on the Desktop.
- Choose **Pin to Start** and the program will then be instantly accessible from the Start group menu.

Hot tip

If you pin a lot of programs to the Taskbar, you may find yourself running out of room. Create more space by resizing the Taskbar.

We'll take a look at the reborn Calculator program and some of the traditional Windows programs in the next few pages.

# Calculator

Whilst there's no spreadsheet capability built in to Windows, it does offer a handy calculator.

 On the Start menu open **All apps**, then find **Calculator** under "C"

Click calculator buttons or press equivalent keyboard keys, to enter numbers and operations such as Add, Subtract, Multiply, Divide, Square Root, Percent and Inverse.

You can also use the numeric keypad to type numbers and operators. Press **Num Lock** if it is not already turned on.

To complete the calculation, select or press the **Enter** key

You can also store and recall numbers from memory, and the History capability keeps track of stages in the calculations.

This is just the Standard calculator. You can also choose to use the Scientific, or Programmer, version of the calculator.

In Windows 10 **Calculator** is a Universal Windows App with more functionality than the old traditional program.

Click the hamburger button and choose, for example, **Scientific**

Calculator clears the display when you switch views. You should use the memory buttons if you need to retain a number between mode switches.

The Scientific calculator includes many functions and inverse functions, including logarithms and factorials. There is also a Programmer calculator view that can perform arithmetic on binary, octal, decimal and hexadecimal values. Converter options usefully convert between many different units of measure.

# Notepad

There are several applications that provide various levels of text management capabilities. One of these is Notepad.

The program is a basic text-editing application and it's most commonly used to view or edit text files, usually with the **.txt** file name extension, but any text file can be handled.

**1** On the Start menu open **All apps**, then find **Notepad** under "Windows Accessories". Type some text, pressing **Enter** to start a new line

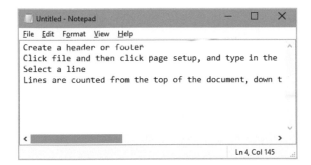

**2** Parts of the lines may be hidden, if lines are longer than the width of the window

**3** Select **Format, Word Wrap** to fit the text within the window width

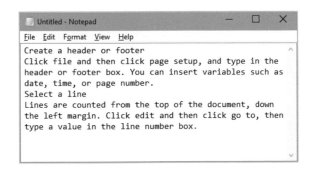

**4** Select **Edit** to cut, copy and paste text, or to insert a Time/Date stamp into the document

**5** Select **File** to save or print the document

**Hot tip**

Select **Format, Font** to choose the Font, Font Style and Size. This will apply to all the text in the whole document.

109

**Don't forget**

When you print a document the lines are wrapped between the margins, whatever the Word Wrap setting.

# WordPad

WordPad is a text-editing program you can use to create and edit documents which can include rich formatting and graphics. You can also link to or embed pictures and other documents.

**1** On the Start menu open **All apps**, and find **WordPad** under "Windows Accessories". Then type in some text

The text automatically wraps as you type, and the Enter key starts a new paragraph.

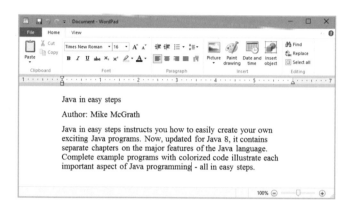

**2** Select text and use the formatting bar to change font, etc.

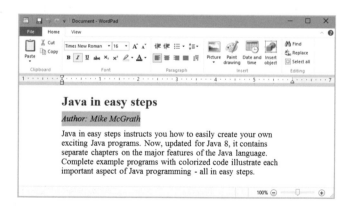

Saving as a Rich Text Document (.**rtf**), Open Office XML (.**docx**) or OpenDocument Text (.**odt**) will retain the text styling. However, the other formats save as plain text, and remove images or links.

**3** Click the **Save** button on the Quick Access Toolbar, type the file name and confirm the file type, then click **Save**

# Paint

Paint allows you to create drawings on a blank drawing area or edit existing pictures, photographs, and web graphics. Open the program as described below:

**1** On the Start menu open **All apps**, then find **Paint** under "Windows Accessories". The app launches a blank canvas

File button (for Paint Tooltip)  Quick Access Toolbar  Home tab  Ribbon  Drawing area  Color palette

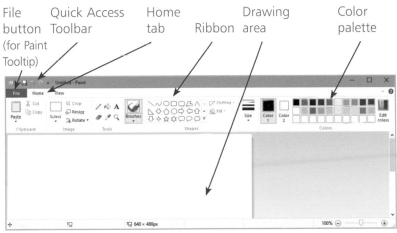

111

**2** Right-click an image file and select **Open with, Paint**

Zoom tools   View tab   Scroll bars

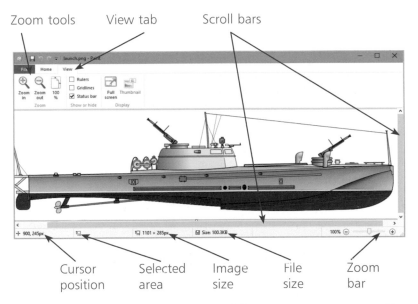

Cursor position   Selected area   Image size   File size   Zoom bar

You can zoom in on a certain part of the picture or zoom out if the picture is too large, and show rulers and gridlines as you work.

# Snipping tool

This will capture a screenshot, or snip, of any object on your screen, and you can then annotate, save, or share the image. For example, if there's a window open with information to be copied:

**1** On the Start menu open **All apps**, then find **Snipping Tool** under "Windows Accessories"

You can capture a free-form area, a rectangular area, a window or the full screen.

**2** Select the arrow next to **New** to pick the snip type, e.g. Rectangular

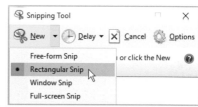

**3** Click a corner and drag to mark out the area you wish to capture

You can save the snip as file type **.png**, **.gif**, **.jpg** or **.mht** (single file .html). You can then include the saved file in documents or email messages.

**4** Release the mouse, and the snip is copied to the Clipboard and the mark-up window

**5** Highlight or annotate the snip if desired then click the **Save Snip** button, adjust the name and location and click **Save**

# Sticky Notes

## Sticky Notes

You can keep track of small pieces of information such as phone numbers, addresses or meeting schedules using Sticky Notes. You can use Sticky Notes with a tablet pen or a standard keyboard.

To create a new Sticky Note:

**1** On the Start menu open **All apps**, then find **Sticky Notes** under "Windows Accessories"

**2** The new note appears on the Desktop with the typing cursor active

**3** Type the text of the reminder that you want to record

> Microsoft Ignite
> Conference
> May 9–13, 2016
> Chicago, Illinois
> May 9, 09:00
> Keynote
> Satya Nadella |

**4** Text wraps as you type, and you can press **Enter** to start a new line

**5** The note is extended in length to accommodate text

**6** Drag a corner or edge to resize or reshape the note

> Microsoft Ignite Conference
> May 9–13, 2016
> Chicago, Illinois
> May 9, 09:00
> Keynote Satya Nadella

You can format text, add bullets to make a list, or change the text size using keyboard shortcuts.

**1** Select the text that you want to change

**2** Use the appropriate keyboard shortcut to format the text

| Ctrl+B | Bold text | Ctrl+Shift+L | Bulleted list |
|---|---|---|---|
| Ctrl+I | Italic text | Ctrl+Shift+L (repeated) | Numbered list |
| Ctrl+U | Underlined text | Ctrl+Shift+> | Increase text size |
| Ctrl+T | Strikethrough | Ctrl+Shift+< | Decrease text size |

**Hot tip**

Sticky Notes don't have to be yellow. Right-click the note and choose one of the six colors offered.

| Cut |
| Copy |
| Paste |
| Delete |
| Select All |
| Blue |
| Green |
| Pink |
| Purple |
| White |
| Yellow |

**Don't forget**

To create another note, click the **New Note** button. To remove a note, press the **Delete Note** button.

You can create or delete a note using the buttons

# Fax and scan

Windows provides software to support sending and receiving faxes, but you need a fax modem installed or attached to your computer, plus a connection to a telephone line.

There's also support for scanning documents and pictures, but you need a scanner (or all-in-one printer) attached to your computer.

To start Windows Fax and Scan:

Select **View**, then **Zoom** and you can choose a larger or smaller scale, or fit to page or fit to width, as desired.

**1** On the Start menu, open **All apps**, then find **Windows Fax and Scan** under "Windows Accessories"

**2** An example document is displayed, and this provides guidance for getting started with faxes and scanning

**3** To scan a document or photo, click the **Scan** button then click **New Scan** on the toolbar, and follow the prompts

When you have scanned a document or picture, you can forward it as an email or a fax.

# Command Prompt

All versions of Windows have included a command line feature for typing MS-DOS commands and other computer commands.

**1** On the Start menu open **All apps**, then find **Command Prompt** under "Windows System"

**2** To display a list of commands with a brief description of each, type "Help" and press **Enter**

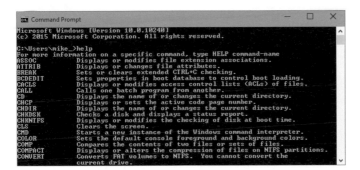

Don't forget

If the commands you use require authorization, right-click Command Prompt and select **Run as administrator**.

**3** For more details of a specific command, type "Help *Name*" then press **Enter**, e.g. "Help Convert"

**4** To adjust Command Prompt options, right-click the title bar and select **Defaults** or **Properties**

Hot tip

Select **Edit** from the right-click menu, and you can mark, copy and paste text onto the command line.

**5** To close Command Prompt, type "Exit" then press **Enter**

# Windows PowerShell

To support system administrators and advanced users, Windows provides a command-line and scripting environment, far more powerful than the old MS-DOS batch file system.

**Don't forget**

Windows PowerShell can execute "Cmdlets" (which are .NET programs), PowerShell scripts (file type **.ps1**), PowerShell functions and executable programs.

**1** On the Start menu, open **All apps**, then find **Windows PowerShell** under "Windows PowerShell"

**2** Type "Get-Command" for a list of PowerShell commands

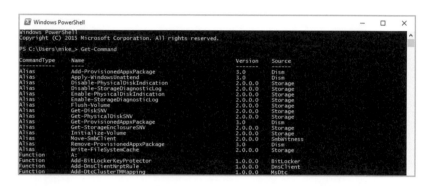

**3** Now you can discover more about any command using the PowerShell help system – for example, to discover more about a particular alias, type "help Flush-Volume"

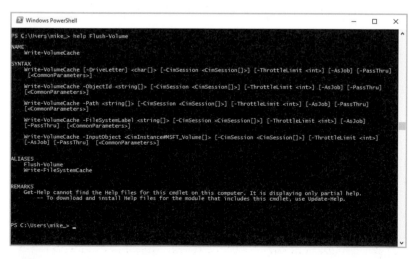

**Hot tip**

You'll find more help in the MSDN library at **msdn.microsoft.com/ library**

**4** The PowerShell help system can be updated online using the command "Update-Help" and further assistance can be found online at **msdn.microsoft.com/en-us/powershell**

# Administrative tools

Administrative tools are intended for system administrators and advanced users. To see the list available on your system:

**1** In the Control Panel, open **System and Security, Administrative Tools**

You can use the System Information tool to discover details of the hardware, components, and the software environment of your entire system.

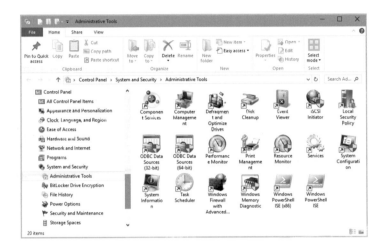

**2** Here you see a range of tools that enable you to manage the way the PC is used. For example, click **Services** and you will see a list of all services running on the PC

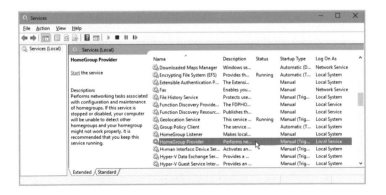

**3** Double-clicking a service reveals options for starting and stopping the service. This enables you to disable the ones that aren't necessary. A typical example is network-related services – if you don't use networking, you can safely disable these and gain a small performance boost

# Unknown file types

A problem you may come across occasionally is trying to start a program only to be greeted by the following message, or something similar:

The reason for the message is that Windows hasn't recognized the program's file type and so has no idea what program will open it.

Initially, you are offered one option – Look for an app in the Store. Clicking this will take you to the Windows Store where, if you aren't already, you will have to log in with a Microsoft account. Once done, a search is made automatically for apps capable of opening the file in question. If one is found, you are offered the option of downloading it – remember, you may have to pay for it.

If the results inform you that a suitable app hasn't been found for this type of file, you can return to the message box to retry.

If you try any of the suggested programs, make sure the "Use this application for all xxx files" option is not selected. Only do this when you are sure the program is the one you want.

Clicking the "More apps" link will reveal a list of suggested programs. However, if none of these work either, your last recourse is the internet. There are quite a few sites that provide lists of file types and the programs associated with them. For example, you could try looking online at **filext.com**

# Change default program

All files are designed to be opened with a specific type of program. For example, graphics files, such as JPEG and GIF, can only be opened by a graphics editing program, e.g. Paint, or with a web browser, such as Microsoft Edge.

A common problem that many users experience is when they install a program on their PC, that automatically makes itself the default program for opening related files. If the user prefers the original program, he or she will have to reassociate the file type in question. Alternatively, the user might want to set a different program as the default.

**1** Go to Control Panel, **Programs**, **Default Programs** then click **Associate a file type or protocol with a specific program**

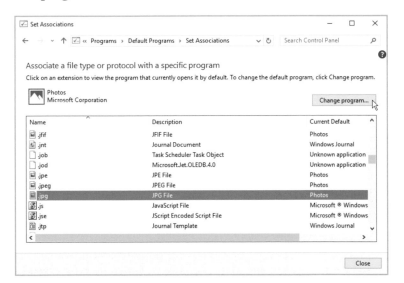

If a newly-installed program has hijacked your files, you can reassociate them with your favored program.

**2** Select the file type and then click the **Change program...** button

**3** You will now see a list of programs on the PC capable of opening the file. Select the one you want to use

How do you want to open this .jpg file from now on?

Keep using this app

Photos
Photos are easily enhanced, organized for you, and ready to edit and share.

Other options

Paint

Look for an app in the Store

More apps ↓

OK

Another way is to right-click a file and then click **Properties**. Click the **General** tab and then click **Change**. Browse to find the program you want to open the file with and select it.

When you need a certain program only temporarily, download a time-limited trial version for free.

Watch out for phishing sites that imitate those of major manufacturers and rip you off.

Software acquired from download sites can be poorly coded and thus contain bugs. These can cause problems on your computer.

# Search the web for software

There was a time when if you wanted a specific program, you either had to visit a store to buy it, or order it online – the instant downloads of today were very rare due to painfully slow internet connections. Because of this it was almost impossible to "trial" a program – you had to pay for it and hope it did the job.

Nowadays, thanks to broadband, the situation is completely different, and there are several very useful sources of software.

### Manufacturers

Without doubt, the best source of software is the manufacturers' websites. The vast majority of them allow users to download time- or feature-limited versions of their products to try out before parting with the cash.

The big advantage here is that the software is guaranteed to be the real deal, and with no unwelcome attachments in the form of viruses and malware. The downside, of course, is that once the trial period is up, you have to pay for the program if you want to keep using it.

### Download Sites

Software download sites are set up specifically to provide an outlet for the legions of small software developers. Many of these programs are free (freeware), others are time- or feature-limited, (shareware), while others require up-front payment.

Well-known download sites include **Download.com**, **Soft32**, **ZDNet Downloads**, and **Tucows**. The big advantage offered by these sites is variety – a vast number of programs of all types are available. However, you do have a risk of picking up viruses and malware hidden in the programs, and many of the freeware programs also come with irritating nag screens or ads.

### File Sharing

File sharing is a common internet activity that makes use of peer-to-peer networks. Users install a program that connects to these networks and lets them share designated files on their PC with other users.

This enables all types of data (software, video, images, etc.) to be downloaded at no cost. The practice is quite legal. However, actually using the data is often illegal. There is also a high risk of virus and malware infection.

Total items checked out: 4

**You just saved an estimated $60 by
using the Library today.**

**Thank you for visiting!**

# 8 Windows downloads

*Microsoft provides Windows Essentials, a set of free traditional applications that supplement and extend Windows, with email, messaging, photos and movie support.*

# Windows Essentials

**1** To install Windows Essentials, first browse to **windows.microsoft.com/en-us/windows-live/essentials** then click **Download now**

**2** Choose to **Run** the Windows Essentials setup program

**3** The setup program is installed and run, and you are prompted to choose the programs that you want to install

**4** If you are sure you want all programs click **Install all of Windows Essentials (recommended)**

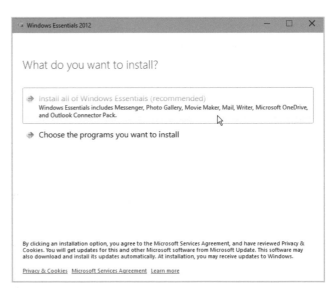

Or, if you want to select which programs to install, click **Choose the programs you want to install**

Now, uncheck any programs you wish not to install, then click the **Install** button

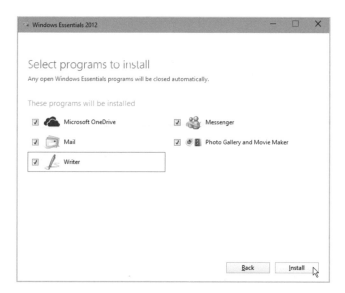

You can choose to install just some of the programs, and you will be able to install the others later if you wish.

**5** Wait while your choice of programs get installed onto your computer, then click the **Close** button

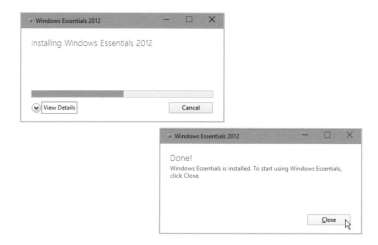

Click **View Details** for a progress report on the installation.

# Applications included

The following applications are included with Essentials 2012:

### Windows Live Mail

Mail is a comprehensive email program that can handle all of your email accounts. It provides spam and phishing filters, a search facility, storage on OneDrive, a conversation view, and a calendar.

### Photo Gallery

Photo Gallery allows users to organize their digital photos. Options here include by date, plus tags for people, keywords and locations. The program offers tools for creating panoramas, collages and slide shows. Photos can be shared via several online services, and also published to YouTube, Flickr and Vimeo.

### Movie Maker

Movie Maker offers an easy way to create and edit home movies. Videos and photos can be imported from a PC or camera, then soundtracks, transitions and various effects can be added. Completed movies can be published to sites such as YouTube.

### Windows Live Writer

Writer is a tool that enables blog posts to be created. It provides all the required formatting tools including links, images and video. A useful preview function helps ensure your blog is perfect before publishing. Writer works with many popular blog service providers, such as WordPress, Blogger, and TypePad.

# Microsoft downloads

Apart from the Essentials 2012 suite, Microsoft provides other free software for Windows.

## Office Viewers

Microsoft Office applications such as Word and PowerPoint are used on millions of PCs all over the world. For businesses, they are essential. They are, however, expensive, and occasional users may not be able to justify the cost.

There is a partial solution available for these users. This comes in the form of Office Viewers – programs that can view, copy and print Office documents. These programs are free and there are versions for Word, Excel, PowerPoint, Access and Visio.

**1** Browse to the Microsoft Download Center at **microsoft.com/en-us/download** and search for "Word Viewer", then click **Downloads** on the menu

**2** Click the **Word Viewer** link to open the "Download Center" page, then click the **Download** button

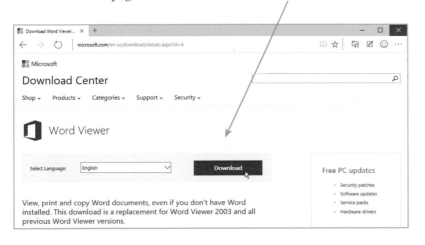

You can only view, copy and print with Office Viewers. You cannot create or save documents.

If you open a Microsoft Account, you will have access to web versions of Word, Excel, PowerPoint and OneNote. These will allow you to create documents as well as read them – all for free.

# Other downloads

There are a number of applications, not included with Windows and not supplied by Microsoft, that are used by thousands of people all over the world. They supplement the existing Windows applications or they fill in the gaps.

The reasons for their popularity are that they are free, good at their intended purpose, and generally well-behaved, i.e. they are free of bugs and malware.

There are, of course, many other programs that do the same things, but the ones we are going to highlight in the next few pages tick all the boxes – excellent performance, no malware and absolutely free to use.

**Don't forget**

For every task, there will be many programs available to choose from, for free or for a fee.

**Hot tip**

If a program offers to create a Desktop shortcut during installation, accept the option.

126

| Category | Program |
| --- | --- |
| PDF Viewer | **Adobe Reader** |
| Maintenance | **CCleaner** |
| CD/DVD Tool | **CDBurnerXP** |
| Photo Viewer | **IrfanView** |
| Text Editor | **Notepad++** |
| Office Apps | **Apache OpenOffice** |
| Photo Editor | **Paint.NET** |
| File Sharing | **uTorrent** |

**Beware**

Not every program offered on the internet is safe to use. Some are still under development; some may be infected with viruses or malware. Make sure that you check out programs at reliable sources before downloading.

All of these programs are available over the internet, ready for download and installation. In the following pages, you'll find the details needed to get started with each of the programs, including:

- Website address
- Brief description
- Installation notes
- Screenshot of application

After installation, each program can be accessed by typing its name in the Taskbar Search box.

# Adobe Reader

adobe.com/products/reader.html

Adobe Reader is the worldwide standard for viewing, printing, and commenting on PDF documents of all types.

To install the application:

**1** Browse to the website and search for "Adobe Reader" then click the **Install now** button

You may find extras such as **Google Chrome** and **Google Toolbar** being offered. You can usually uncheck these items unless you are sure they will be needed.

**2** Follow the prompts then wait while the installer downloads and installs Adobe Reader on your computer

**3** Double-click any PDF file to open it in Adobe Reader

Adobe Reader is not just for viewing documents. Select **View, Read Out Loud** to set the Reader in narrative mode.

# CCleaner

## piriform.com/ccleaner

CCleaner is a utility that cleans out the junk that accumulates over time – temporary files, broken shortcuts, and other problems. The program also protects the user's privacy by clearing the contents of the history and temporary internet files folders.

**1** At the website, click the **Free Download** button

**2** Again, choose the **Free Download** option when asked

**3** Run the Setup Wizard

**4** When the installation is complete, click the **Analyze** button to see a list of files that can be safely deleted

# CDBurnerXP

**cdburnerxp.se/en/home**

CDBurnerXP is a burning utility that enables a wide variety of disks, such as CDs, DVDs, Blu-ray and HD-DVDs to be created. Other useful options include the ability to create ISO image files and bootable disks.

**1** At the website, click the **Free Download** button

**2** Install the program by running the Setup Wizard

**3** When the program is run, you are offered various disk burner options, e.g. Data disk, Video DVD, Burn ISO image, etc.

Another free disk authoring utility with a good reputation is ImgBurn, which you can download free from **imgburn.com**

# IrfanView

*irfanview.com*

IrfanView is a very fast and compact graphic viewer for Windows that is freeware (for non-commercial use). It supports many graphics file formats, including multiple (animated) GIF, multi-page TIF and videos.

IrfanView is designed to be simple for beginners and powerful for professionals. It also provides an extremely quick way to scroll through picture folders.

**1** Visit the website and select the IrfanView **download** link

**2** Follow the prompts to download and install IrfanView

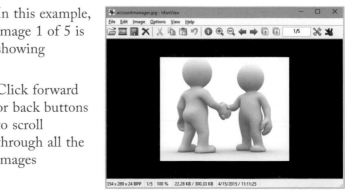

**3** On completion, the FAQ web page is displayed and IrfanView starts up

Select the download for **Plug-ins/Add-ons** to get support for the full set of file formats.

**4** In this example, image 1 of 5 is showing

**5** Click forward or back buttons to scroll through all the images

# Notepad++

notepad-plus-plus.org

Notepad++ is a free text editor and Notepad replacement that is particularly designed for source code editing and supports over 50 languages, including C, C++, CSS, HTML, Java, and Python.

**1** On the website, make sure the current version is selected on the left of the screen then click **Download**

In addition to language support, the main advantage over the built-in Notepad is tabbed editing, which allows you to work with multiple open files.

**2** Follow the prompts to run the Setup Wizard and install Notepad++

**3** The program opens with the Change Log, showing new features and fixes

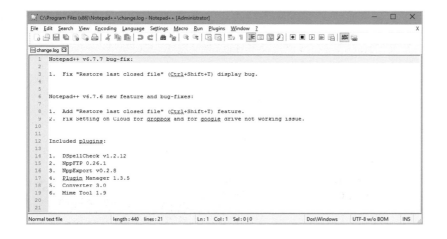

If you are interested in programming, you can download the source code for this application.

# Apache OpenOffice

**openoffice.org**

Apache OpenOffice is an open-source suite with a powerful set of applications that are very similar to those in Microsoft Office, and include techniques such as macros and templates, but have the advantage of being free to use.

This website is the entry point for all aspects of Apache OpenOffice, with help, documentation, templates and clipart, as well as installation.

You'll be invited to contribute, but it's your time and effort they want, not your money, since the product is built on user participation.

**1** Visit the website and select **I want to download...**

**2** Select **Download full installation** for your system

**3** Follow the prompts to unpack and save the installation files ready for the actual installation

**4** Provide your name and, optionally, your organization, as they are to be used in OpenOffice documents

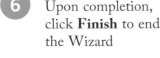

**5** Select the **Typical** setup, and click Next

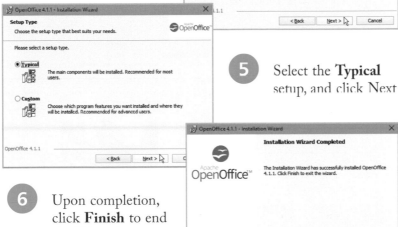

**6** Upon completion, click **Finish** to end the Wizard

**7** Click the shortcut placed on the Desktop to start Apache OpenOffice

Apache OpenOffice has these six components:
**Writer** (word processor)
**Calc** (spreadsheet)
**Impress** (presentations)
**Draw** (vector graphics)
**Base** (database) and
**Math** (formula editor)

# Paint.NET

### getpaint.net

Where the built-in Windows Paint app doesn't have the power you need, Paint.NET gives you more powerful editing facilities.

**1** Click **Download** or click the **paint.net** link

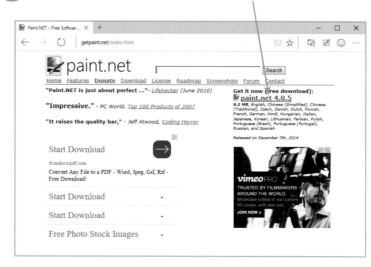

**2** Click the **Download Now** button for Paint.NET

**3** Choose to Open the compressed file Paint. NET.4.0.5.Install.zip

**4** This expands to the executable file Paint.NET.4.0.5.Install

Free Download Now:
**paint.net 4.0.5**

System Requirements

**5** Choose **Express** for the install method and click **Next**

**6** Agree terms and conditions and continue

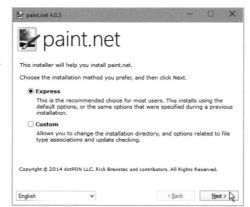

During the installation, Paint.NET will be optimized for best performance on your particular system.

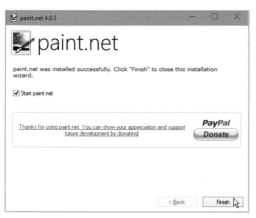

**7** Follow the prompts to complete the installation

**8** Click **Finish,** to start Paint.NET

Paint.NET is a free app, but you are encouraged to contribute to its future development.

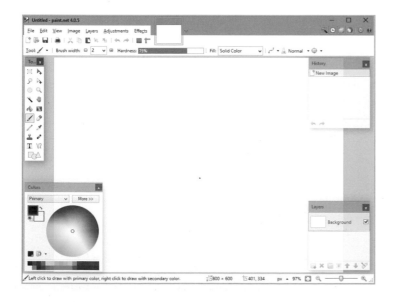

Select Effects to see the range offered; Photo, for example, with Glow, Sharpen and Soften as well as Red Eye Removal. Adjustments also applies various changes to the appearance.

# μTorrent

**utorrent.com**

μTorrent (also referred to as uTorrent) is a freeware, but closed-source BitTorrent client. The μ in its name implies the prefix micro, in deference to the program's small size, but it can handle very large downloads very rapidly.

A BitTorrent client is a computer program that manages downloads and uploads using the BitTorrent protocol. This is used for peer-to-peer file sharing for distributing large amounts of data.

136

**1** At the μTorrent website, click the **Get μTorrent for Windows** button

**2** Again, click **Get μTorrent for Windows** and a free download will automatically start

**3** Follow prompts to download and run the Setup Wizard

**4** When the installation completes, μTorrent is launched

Make sure that files you select for downloading via μTorrent are in the public domain and not subject to copyright.

# 9 Windows Store

If you need apps to run on your Windows 10 devices, the Windows Store is the place to go. This chapter shows how to access, search and navigate the Store. You will also learn how to install apps, keep them updated, and how to manage them.

# Accessing the Store

When you need apps, the Windows Store is the place to go. It is, in fact, the only place to go – official Windows 10 apps are not available from any other source. To access the Store:

**1** On the Start menu **All apps** list, click the **Store** tile

**2** The Windows Store will open

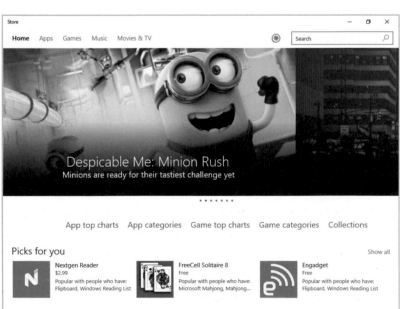

**Hot tip**

You can also click the Store icon displayed on the Windows 10 Taskbar.

The Windows Store has been redesigned to be a one-stop-shop for all Windows 10 devices.

**Don't forget**

Apps can only be sourced from Microsoft's official Windows Store.

# Store categories

The Windows Store organizes its products into these specific categories to make it easier to find what you are looking for.

| Apps | | |
|---|---|---|
| Books & reference | Lifestyle | Productivity |
| Business | Medical | Security |
| Developer tools | Multimedia design | Shopping |
| Education | Music | Social |
| Entertainment | Navigation & maps | Sports |
| Food & dining | News | Travel |
| Government & politics | Personal Finance | Utilities & tools |
| Health | Personalization | |
| Kids | Photo & video | |

| Games | | |
|---|---|---|
| Action & adventure | Platformer | Simulation |
| Card & board | Puzzle & trivia | Strategy |
| Casino | Racing & flying | Word |
| Educational | Role playing | |
| Family & kids | Shooter | |

| Music | | |
|---|---|---|
| Alternative/Metal | Kids | Reggae |
| Classical | More | Rock/Indie |
| Dance | Pop | Soundtrack |
| Folk/Blues/Country | R&B/Soul | World & International |
| Jazz | Rap/Hip-Hop | |

| Movies & TV | | |
|---|---|---|
| Action/Adventure | Family | Sci-Fi/Fantasy |
| Animation | Foreign/Independent | Sports |
| Anime | Horror | Thriller/Mystery |
| Comedy | Other | TV Movies |
| Documentary | Romance | |
| Drama | Romantic Comedy | |

**Don't forget**

When looking in a category, check to see if there are any sub-categories.

# Navigating the Store

On the Windows Store Homepage, initially, there is no obvious means of navigation. A single movement of the mouse over the Store Homepage activates a scroll bar at the edge of the window. Now you can drag the scroll bar to move up and down the page to review the featured items. Alternatively, you can use the mouse wheel to move the page up and down.

Placing the mouse over the banner at the top of the Store Homepage activates forward and back arrow buttons at each edge of the banner. Click these to scroll the banner items left and right. Selecting any banner item displays comprehensive details about that item.

Users with a touchscreen can simply swipe up or down to navigate around the page and tap any item of interest.

After a short period of inactivity the scroll bar disappears.

Select the **Home** menu item at any time to return to the Store Homepage.

Category menu      Banner scroll buttons

Page scroll bar

Move between the various categories using the menu at the top left of the Store window to review Apps, Games, Music, or Movies & TV available to download from the Windows Store.

# Exploring categories

On the Homepage, apps are presented in broad categories, which typically include **Picks for you**, **Top paid**, and **Top free**. Most of these categories offer a small selection of featured apps that can be accessed directly from the Homepage.

If you can't see what you want here then you need to dig deeper. Select a general category then refine your requirements.

**1** To open a general category, click its name on the menu, for example, select the **Games** menu category

**2** The category page will open and is laid out like the Homepage, but features only items relevant to that category

**3** The category page also provides a menu with which to explore that category further. For example, on the Games category page select the **Game categories** menu item

**4** Sub-categories are provided to refine your requirements

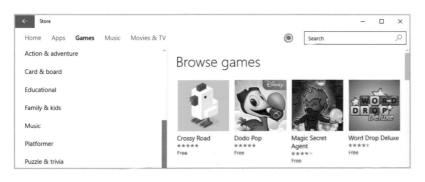

Hot tip

Use the **Back** button at the top-left of any Store window to return to previous pages.

# Search the Store

Search is an extremely important component of modern user interfaces and, currently, is one of the most common ways for customers to find things when browsing online stores.

In Windows 8, the Windows Store didn't have a Search box – you had to search using the Search charm, which many users found confusing. The revamped store in Windows 10 does provide a Search box, though, and this can be found at the top-right of any Store page, as shown below:

If you know the name of the app you want or are looking for apps by a specific publisher, enter the name into the Search box. In the page that opens, you'll see the results of your search, as in our "video" search below:

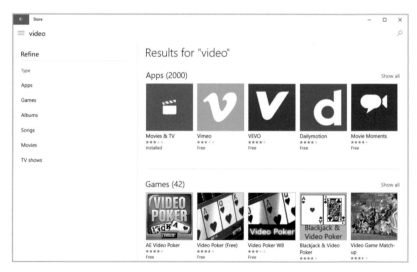

 If any of the apps shown appear to be of interest, just left-click to open it and get further details

An important aspect of the Windows 10 Search is that it is universally accessible, meaning you can search for an app no matter where you are in the Windows 10 interface – you don't need to be in the Store. We see how this works on the next page.

In the example shown below, you're using the Microsoft Edge app to browse a site about Mahjong. This triggers in you a sudden curiosity to see if there are any Mahjong apps available.

**1** Type the word "mahjong" into the Taskbar Search box

**2** Click the **Store** link on the results list

**3** A Store window opens, revealing items related to Mahjong

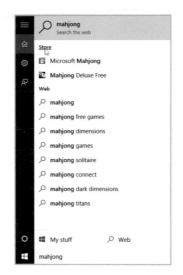

**Hot tip**

As you type in the Taskbar Search box, suggestions immediately appear in the results list.

# Select an app

To select an app, simply click on its tile. As an example, we have searched for the Amazon app as shown below:

The page begins with a brief description of the app that can be expanded by clicking the **More** link. Below the description is a download button that will display the price if the app isn't free, or "Install" if you can download the app without charge.

Moving down the page, there are five headings – **Ratings and reviews**, **Features**, **People also like**, **Additional information**, and **What's new in this version**.

**Ratings and reviews** gives you the average rating figure, the total number of ratings and the total number of reviews.

**Features** highlights the main capabilities of the app. **People also like** provides a list of similar apps that you may consider investigating. **Additional information** typically informs you what processors and languages are supported. **What's new in this version** provides any release notes for the current version.

**Don't forget**

At the risk of stating the obvious, before paying for an app it's worth checking out the reviews.

144

# Download and install

To install an app, click the Download button below the app description. If you are logged in with a Microsoft account, the download/install routine will begin immediately.

**1** Above the Download button you'll see a message that says "downloading" while the app copies to your system

**2** When the installation is complete, the message will change to "This product is installed" and the button label will change to "Open"

**3** Click the **Open** button, or click the new app item added under **All apps** on the Start menu, to launch the app

If, however, you are not logged in with a Microsoft account, you will be asked to do so:

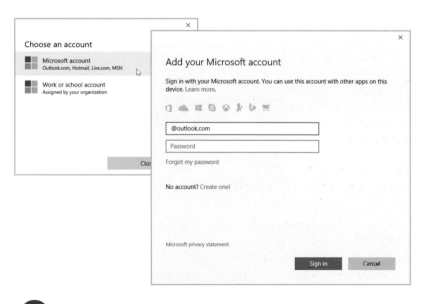

**4** Then go back to the app's page on the Store and click the Download button again to install the app

**Hot tip**

You will not be able to download an app (even a free one) unless you are logged in with a Microsoft account.

# Skype

Skype is a service that allows users to communicate by voice, video, and instant messaging. The service is available as an app for Windows 10 and can be installed from the Start menu using the **Get Skype** download link:

**1** When the app is run for the first time you will be asked to test your microphone, speakers, and webcam

Calls to other users within the Skype service are free of charge, while calls via landline and mobile networks are charged via a debit-based user account system.

**2** Next, you will see Skype's Home screen. Before you can make a call you need credit (unless you are calling another Skype user). Click the **Call phones** item in the left pane

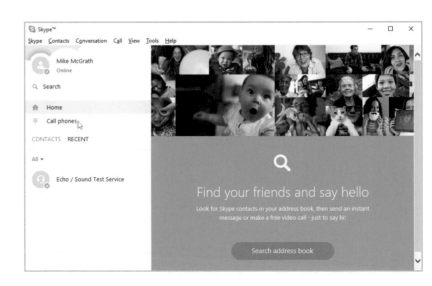

Skype provides additional features, such as file transfer, and video conferencing.

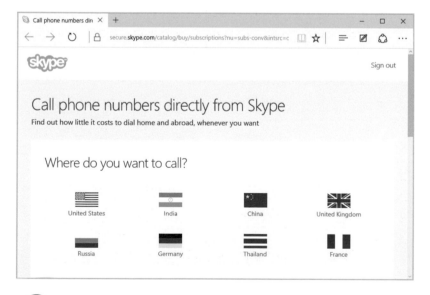

**3** At the next screen, you are offered two options – **Add Skype Credit** and **Get a subscription**. Make your choice by clicking the required option. If you select the latter, for example, a Microsoft Edge browser window will open, in which you will see the following:

The Skype app can be extremely useful when used with Windows 10's split-screen Snap feature. This enables a conversation to be had, while at the same time getting on with something else on the main part of the screen.

147

A feature of the Skype app is that it can be left running permanently without any adverse effect on the computer.

**4** Once the financial side of things is sorted out, close the browser window. You will be taken back to the app and can start using it

# App account

One of the big advantages of logging in to all of your devices with the same Microsoft account is that any apps you have bought and installed on one device can be downloaded from the Cloud and installed on another device. For example, we have bought a popular game called Hydro Thunder Hurricane and installed it on a desktop PC. To install it on a laptop, all we have to do is:

**1** On the laptop's Start menu, click the **Store** item

**2** In the Taskbar Search box, enter "hydro thunder hurricane" and click the **Store** entry on the results pane

Having paid for an app you can install it from the Cloud on any other devices you use with the same Microsoft account.

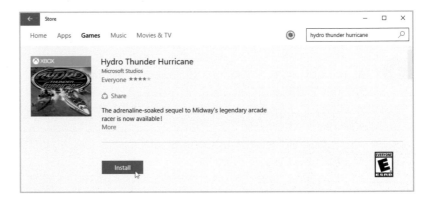

**3** When the app opens, click the **Install** button. The account password is requested

Because the app has already been paid for, the Install button is shown rather than the Buy button.

**4** Password entered and **Sign in** button clicked, the app is downloaded to our laptop and installed

# Updates

It is important to keep your system updated. This applies not just to Windows itself but also to the programs you use. App publishers sometimes update their apps to add new features and fix problems.

Windows 10 updates itself automatically. To set it up to update your apps automatically as well, do the following:

**1** On the Start menu, click the **Store** item to open the Windows Store

**2** Click your user profile icon to open the drop-down menu

**3** From the drop-down menu, select the **Settings** item

Unlike previous versions of Windows, the Windows 10 release is seen by Microsoft as "Windows-as-a-Service" – that will automatically receive free feature additions, improvements, and updates.

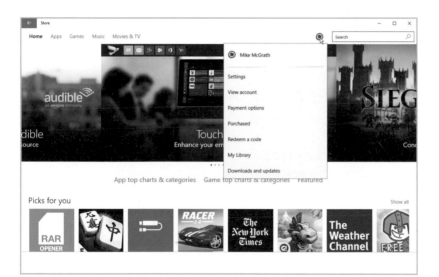

**4** On the Settings menu, slide the button to set the "Update apps automatically" option to the **On** position

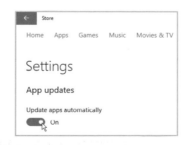

# Manage apps

App tiles on the right of the Start menu are much larger than the Start menu list items under "All apps". The more congested the Start menu becomes, the more scrolling will be necessary to get to a particular app.

### Organizing Start screen tiles

So, perhaps one of the first things a user new to Windows 10 will do is to introduce some organization into how the Start menu tiles are presented.

The most important thing is to place your most frequently-accessed apps at the top of the Start menu tile area where they will be on view by default. Do this by left-clicking on the tile, dragging it to where you want it and then releasing it.

### Create and organize groups

However, this will be a laborious way of moving large numbers of app tiles. The answer is to place your app tiles in groups, which can then be moved about the Start menu in blocks. Apart from making it easier to arrange your Start menu, having your apps in specific and related groups will make it much easier to locate them as and when required.

So, how's it done? If you take any tile and drag it across the Start menu you'll see the other tiles move to accommodate that tile within the group, as shown below. If you take any heading group bar and drag it across the Start menu you'll see other groups move to accommodate that group.

**Hot tip**

An important aspect of organizing the Start menu is placing app tiles in related groups.

The customizable Start menu is a great new feature in Windows 10.

**Hot tip**

Another thing you can do is to reduce the size of the large tiles. This will create more space on the Start menu, which reduces the amount of scrolling necessary. Just right-click on a tile, select resize and choose from the available options.

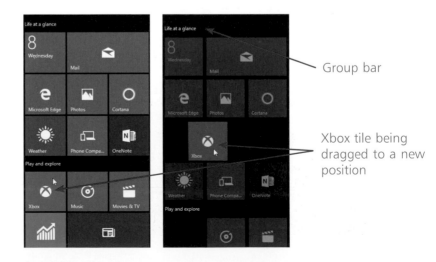

Group bar

Xbox tile being dragged to a new position

If you want to start a new group, drag an app item from the **All apps** list onto the right part of the Start menu and release it above an existing group bar – the new group is created. Add more tiles to it as already described.

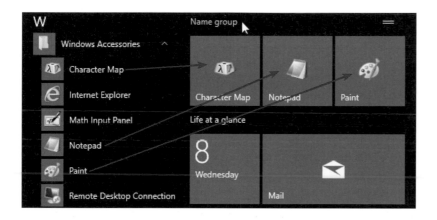

The group bar of a new group may not be visible until you place the mouse over its position.

## Name a Group

You can assign names to a group by editing its group bar:

**1** Click on a group bar to see a **Name** group box appear

**2** Type a name of your choice into this **Name** group box

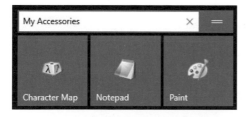

**3** Click anywhere else to apply your name to the group

You can edit the name of any existing group using its Name group box.

# Desktop apps

Although the Windows Store provides a huge range of apps, some traditional Desktop programs are not included and must be downloaded directly from the publisher's own website. For example, the popular Photoshop image editing program must be acquired directly from Adobe:

**1** Enter "adobe photoshop" in the Taskbar Search box then hit **Enter** to see the results of a Bing search

**2** Select a link from the results to visit the Adobe website

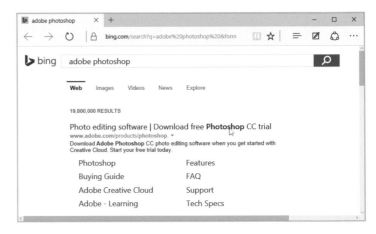

**3** Click the **Free Trial** or **Buy now** button to download and install the program directly from Adobe

When you buy a Desktop program outside the Windows Store, don't forget that updates to the app must be downloaded from the publisher's website – they won't be provided through the Store.

# 10 Search techniques

Windows provides many ways to help you find the programs, utilities and information that you need. There's a Search box in every File Explorer folder, and the Taskbar Search box is always readily available.

# Start screen search

When you need to search for something it's remarkably simple in Windows 10 – all you have to do is type what you want to find into the Search box located on the Desktop Taskbar.

Search box

By default, Windows 10 searches include the internet and Windows Store as well as the PC.

As you begin to type, the search results will instantly update, displaying the search results in a list above the Search box:

The Taskbar Search box is another great new feature in Windows 10.

In our example, we've searched for "windows". Due to its tight integration with Microsoft's Bing search engine, the results of the search are taken not just from the computer but also from the internet and the Windows Store.

# Search filters

As the default action of Windows 10's search function is to search the PC, the internet and the Windows Store (everywhere, effectively) this means that searches can bring too many results or unrelated results. To prevent this, there are two things you can do:

## Local Filter
The first is to use the local filter built-in to the Search box:

**1**    In the results, choose **My stuff** to search only your computer

Windows 10 local search lets you sort results by **Most Relevant** or **Most Recent**, and it provides seven secondary filters – Documents, Folders, Apps, Settings, Photos, Videos, Music.

155

## Internet Filter
The second is to use the web filter built-in to the Search box:

**2**    In the results, choose **Web** to have Bing search the internet

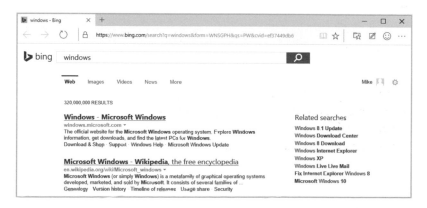

# File Explorer search

The Search utility is considered by some to be one of the best features in Windows 10 and provides quick and very comprehensive search results – sometimes too many, in fact. While secondary local filters help to narrow searches down, general and system-wide searches can produce too many results.

The Search facility provided by File Explorer is extremely useful in situations such as these, as it enables searches to be restricted to specific parts of Windows, thus producing fewer, but more relevant, results.

**1** Open a File Explorer window (it doesn't matter which)

**2** At the right, you will see a Search box. By default, searches made from this will be restricted to the contents of the folder, plus any sub-folders

**3** Clicking in the Search box also opens the **Recent searches** feature in the **Search** tab on the ribbon toolbar – here you can repeat a search or clear the search history

**4** The **Search** tab provides **Advanced options** with which to refine your search – see page 158 for more details

Results from a folder search will include any sub-folders the folder may contain.

You can change the location from any folder to search anywhere in the computer.

156

# Navigation pane

At the left of the File Explorer window, you'll see the Navigation pane. By default, this shows links for favorite folders such as Desktop, Documents, and Downloads. There are also links for OneDrive, Homegroup, This PC, and Network. These links enable any folder or drive on the computer to be accessed and thus searched. You can do this as follows:

**1** Hover over the left pane to see arrows beside the links

**2** Click a right-arrow to expand a list, or click a down-arrow to collapse a list

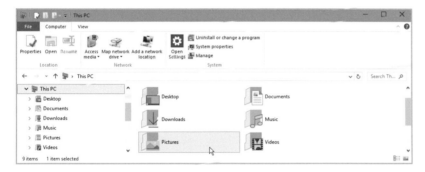

**3** Select a folder name to display its contents and find files. For example, double-click the **Pictures** folder to explore the folders and files it contains

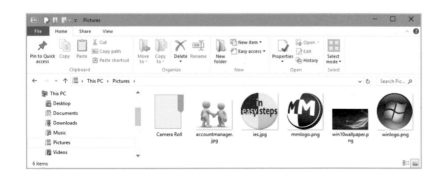

**4** At any point, you can use the folder Search box to search a particular folder

Hot tip

Double-click any name to expand that folder and display its contents with the one action.

Don't forget

Click the arrows or double-click the names to expand and collapse the entries.

# Search tools

Windows provides a number of filters with which folder searches can be made even more relevant. These can be accessed from the ribbon toolbar found at the top of File Explorer folders.

This is a toolbar that provides options related to the task at hand, i.e. it is contextual. We'll take a closer look at this later on but for now we'll see what it has to offer in the way of search options.

Open a folder you want to search and click in the Search box. The Search tab on the ribbon toolbar will immediately reveal the search tools. We'll take these as they appear on the toolbar:

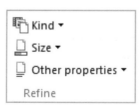

- **Current folder** – restricts the search to the current folder.
- **All sub-folders** – includes sub-folders in the search.
- **Search again in** – list of locations in which to repeat the search.

- **Date modified** – allows you to search specific dates or ranges of dates. Options provided are: Today, Yesterday, This week, Last week, This month, Last month, This year and Last year.

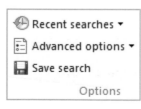

- **Kind** – choose the kind of file from a list of types, such as Movie or Program.
- **Size** – choose from a list of sizes ranging from Tiny to Gigantic.
- **Other properties** – choose from a list of properties for Date taken, Tags, Type, Name, Folder path or Rating.
- **Advanced options** – lets you change the indexed locations to search and allows searches to be limited to File contents, System files, or Zipped (compressed) folders in non-indexed locations.

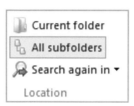

**Recent searches**, and **Save search** items are not filters.

# Favorites

The Navigation pane includes a "Quick access" section where you can keep shortcuts to the locations on your system that you may often view. To view your File Explorer **Quick access** favorites:

**1** Open File Explorer then click View, Navigation pane and ensure that **Navigation pane** is checked – to be visible

**2** Now, click on the **Quick access** item at the top of the Navigation pane to reveal your current favorites

To add a folder location to your **Quick access** favorites:

**3** Click on a folder in the Navigation pane – to select it ready to be added

**4** Next, click the **Home** tab on the File Explorer ribbon

**5** Now, click on the **Pin to Quick access** link on the ribbon to add the selected folder to your favorites

**6** Our example, Music, is added to the **Quick access** favorites

To remove a favorite location from the **Quick access** section, right-click on its folder icon and choose "Unpin from Quick access".

159

The **Quick access** favorites can also be returned to an earlier state by choosing "Restore previous versions" from the right-click context menu.

# Folder and search options

You can change the way files and folders function and how items are displayed on your computer using **Folder Options**.

**1** Open a folder, click the **View** tab, click **Options** then click **Change folder and search options**

**2** When **Folder Options** displays, select the **General** tab

From this panel you can:

- Choose to open each folder in the same window, or in its own window.

- Use double-click to open an item, or use the browser style single-click to point and select items.

- Control the operation of the Navigation pane.

- Control **Quick access** privacy.

- Restore Defaults after changes.

**3** Select the **View** tab

From here you can:

- Apply the view for the current folder to all folders of the same type.

- Reset folders.

- Apply advanced settings to files and folders.

- Restore Defaults after changes.

**4** Scroll down to reveal the remaining settings

Among these settings are options to:

- Automatically open the folders that you were using when you last shut down Windows whenever you start your computer, thus restoring your work session.

- Hide or show file tips that display when you point to files or folders.

- Use check boxes to select items.

- Hide empty drives in the **This PC** folder.

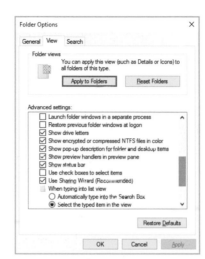

Make a note of the options that you would normally prefer, since the Restore Defaults will undo all changes, not just recent changes.

**5** Select the **Search** tab

The Search settings let you manage what to search and how to search.

- Find partial matches.

- Don't use the index when searching file folders for system files.

- Include system directories.

- Include compressed files.

- Search file names and contents.

You can click the **Restore Defaults** button to undo any changes that might previously have been applied.

# Indexing options

When you add a folder to one of the libraries, that folder will automatically be indexed. You can also add locations to the index without using libraries.

Windows uses the index for fast searches of the most common files on your computer. By default, folders in libraries, email and offline files are indexed, but program and system files are not.

**1** Go to the Control Panel and click **Indexing Options**

**2** Click **Modify** then expand the folder lists and select new locations to index, for example a USB drive, and click **OK**

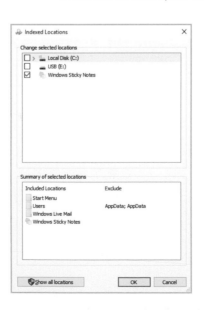

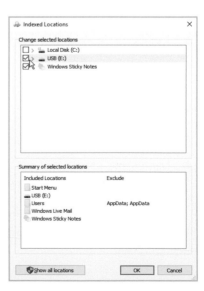

**3** The contents of the new locations are added to the index

Indexing proceeds in the background, and may slow down during periods of user activity.

**4** To make changes to the settings for indexing, click the **Advanced** button and select the **Index Settings** or **File Types** tab

You can press **Pause** to suspend indexing, but you are recommended to do this for no more than 15 minutes at a time.

You can choose to index encrypted files, ignore accents on characters for matching, change the index location, or delete and rebuild the index. You can also specify file types that are indexed by properties only or contents plus properties.

# Address bar

The address bar at the top of the folder contains the location path of the folder or library, and you can use this to check the actual folder path and to switch to other libraries and folders.

If a library rather than a folder is being displayed, you'll see a library path rather than a drive.

**1** Click the space in the address bar to the right of the location names (and left of the down-arrow)

**2** The current location is shown in the standard drive and folder path format

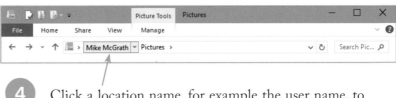

**3** Click anywhere in the folder to revert to the location path

**4** Click a location name, for example the user name, to switch to that location

Click the arrow to the right of the location name to show all the folders that are stored within that location.

**5** Click the arrow to the right of a location name, for example **Users**, to display all the folders in that location

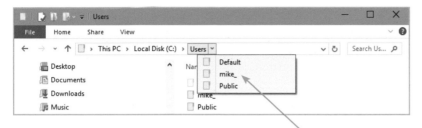

**6** When the folders are displayed, you can select any folder to switch to that location

**7** Click the back arrow to redisplay the previous folder

**8** Click the arrow at the left to see the top-level locations

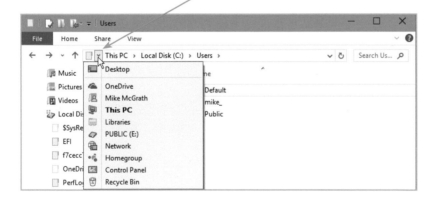

Hot tip

The libraries, user folders, network folders, etc. are included as special folders in Desktop, along with **This PC** and any Desktop icons. Note that File Explorer is also used to display the Control Panel.

**9** Select **Desktop** to see the complete structure of your system components

# Save searches

If you regularly search for a certain group of files, it might be useful to save your search. To save a search:

**1** Carry out a search as previously described

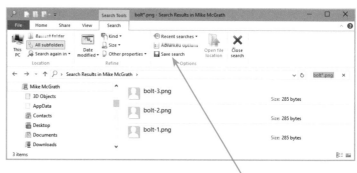

Save a search, and the next time you want to use it, you just open the saved search, and you'll see the most current files that match the original search.

**2** When the search is complete, click **Save search**

**3** Type a name for the search, and then click **Save**

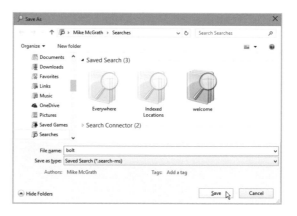

**4** The search itself will be saved in your Searches folder

# Move and copy

You can use the search results and the Navigation pane to help move or copy files and folders from their original locations.

**1** Use Search to display the items you wish to copy or move (in this case all Word files named "Minutes" within Users)

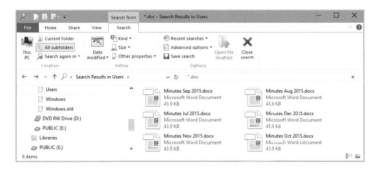

Select the first item, then press **Shift** and select the last in a range, or press **Ctrl** and add individual items to the selection.

**2** Select the items to copy, using **Shift** or **Ctrl** as necessary

**3** Expand the Navigation pane (clicking the arrows, not the folder names) to show the target folder

167

**4** Right-click part of the selection and drag the items onto the Navigation pane, over the name of the target folder

**5** Release the mouse and click **Move here** or **Copy here** as appropriate, and the files are added to the destination

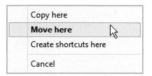

If the destination is on the same drive as the selected items, the default is Move, otherwise the default becomes Copy. However, you can still make your preferred selection.

## ...cont'd

**6** As soon as the move takes place, Windows Search adjusts the search results, in this case showing Public documents

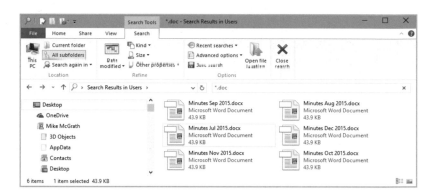

You don't have to use Search; you can Move or Copy from the original location using the same techniques.

**7** Select the target folder, and you'll see all the items added

You can simply click and drag any selected items to your preferred destination then release the mouse button to have Windows Move or Copy them there immediately, with no menu.

### Force move or copy
With either left-click or right-click, you can force the action you want, whether the same or different drives are involved:

Don't use the left-click option unless you are very familiar with it, since there's no opportunity to confirm the action.

**1** Press **Shift** as you drag, and Move becomes the default action

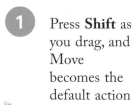
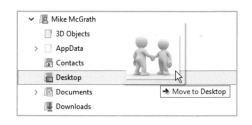

**2** Press **Ctrl** as you drag, and Copy becomes the default action

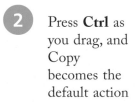
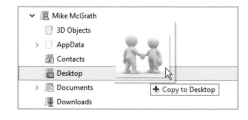

# 11

# Manage files and folders

Use File Explorer to manage your files, folders and libraries, sorting and organizing the contents and linking to the locations that hold the required datu. Windows provides libraries for documents, music, pictures and videos but you can define your own libraries for your projects or to manage information such as family history.

# Files, folders and libraries

Data storage devices are defined as blocks of fixed-size sectors. These are managed by the file system, which defines a root drive directory containing folders and files. Each folder can contain further folders and files. This gives a hierarchical structure.

Files of the same or related types will usually be stored in the same folder. For example, the **Users** folder within the root drive directory will be organized along the following lines:

Windows uses the NTFS file system for disks and large storage devices. One of the older FAT file systems is normally used for smaller storage devices such as memory cards and flash drives.

170

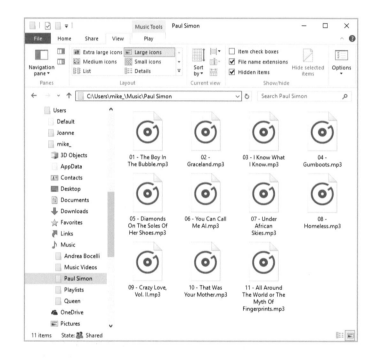

Each file has a starting block and links to the subsequent blocks, with the last link being the end of file marker. The blocks are not necessarily allocated in sequence, hence the potential for fragmentation.

The root drive directory includes the **Program Files** folder which contains applications installed on your system, and the **Users** folder which contains the folders and files associated with each user account. In your user account folder, you will see a number of folders including your **Music** folder. The example above shows the files and folders associated with a particular artist.

Windows 10 goes a stage further and associates folders with similar content into Libraries. The folders included in the library may actually be stored separately on the disk, or may be on a different disk on the computer or elsewhere on the network.

To manage the files, folders and libraries, Windows uses the File Explorer application.

# File Explorer

There are several different ways to start File Explorer or change the particular files and folders being displayed.

**1** Click the **File Explorer** shortcut icon on the Start menu, or open the Power User Menu and select **File Explorer**

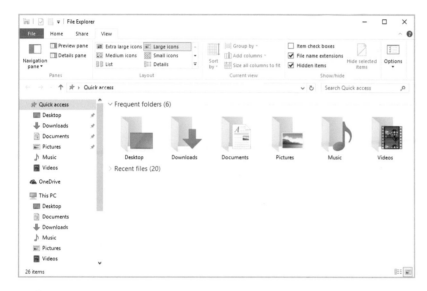

**Quick access** is new in Windows 10, replacing the classic Favorites of previous versions. You can also press **WinKey + E** to open File Explorer to see **Quick access**.

**2** The **Quick access** feature displays your **Frequent folders**

**3** Click an entry on the Navigation pane to display those contents instead, for example select the **Music** folder

*Hot tip*

If you don't want to have File Explorer start in **Quick access**, click View, Options, **Change folder and search options**, then on the General tab choose **Open File Explorer to: This PC**.

**4** To retain the current entry, and open another, right-click the newly-required entry and choose **Open in new window**

**...cont'd**

The Taskbar button for the program initially shows a single icon. When you open another window, or more, a second icon gets stacked alongside the first icon – to indicate that multiple File Explorer windows are currently open.

**1** Move the mouse pointer over the Taskbar button, and thumbnails for the open windows are displayed, as shown below:

**2** Click on a thumbnail to open that window in File Explorer

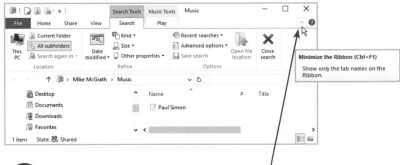

**Hot tip**

You can also open the ribbon toolbar by clicking a File Explorer tab – Home, Share, or View.

**3** Click the down-arrow to open (or up-arrow to close) the File Explorer ribbon toolbar

# File Explorer layout

This shows all the elements for File Explorer, apart from the ribbon toolbar, which we look at on page 174.

Back and Forward · Up Level · Menu Bar · Address Bar · Quick Access Toolbar · Search Box · Resize or Close

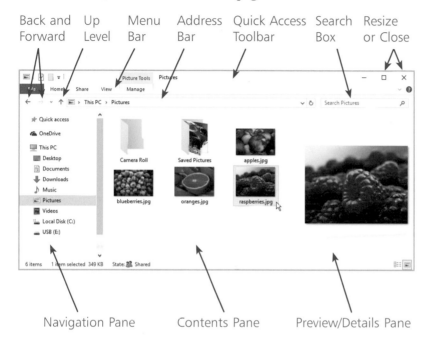

Navigation Pane · Contents Pane · Preview/Details Pane

## File Explorer preview

The type of preview displayed depends on the file type. For recognized document types you will see part of the first page.

For file types Windows does not recognize, or when a folder is selected, you will see a message saying: No preview available.

# File Explorer ribbon

The File tab offers a variety of options.

A feature in Windows 10 is the File Explorer ribbon toolbar, which is situated at the top of every File Explorer folder. By default it is hidden – to reveal it just click the down-arrow located under the red **X** close button at the top-right.

In essence, the ribbon consists of a File menu plus three core tabs – Home, Share and View – that are always visible. Other tabs include Manage, Computer and Network. The ribbon also shows colored contextual tabs, the display of which depends on the type of object selected by the user. For example, when a video folder is opened or a video file is selected, the Video Tools tab appears and provides related options, such as Play, Stop, and Pause.

This system of core and contextual tabs enables the ribbon toolbar to offer some 200 different management commands. The user gets the required options as and when required without having to wade through unrelated toolbar menus, right-click menus, etc.

Home tab

View tab

Computer tab

Share tab

Manage tab

# Folder contents

You'll also find that the way in which the contents of folders are displayed varies depending on the type of file involved.

In these example views, the Navigation, Details, and Library panes have been hidden, to put the emphasis on the Contents pane.

**Documents**
    Details view:
        Name
        Date modified
        Type
        Size

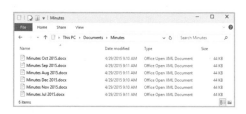

Documents and Music both use the Details view, but the fields displayed are appropriate to the particular file type.

**Music**
    Details view:
        Name
        Contributing artists
        Album
        Track number
        Title

**Pictures**
    Large Icons view

**Program Files**
    Medium Icons view

The Videos library also uses the Large Icons view, while Network and Computers use the Tiles view, the same as Libraries.

**Libraries**
    Tiles view

Since views can easily be varied, you may find the setup for some of the folders on your system may be different.

# Change view

**1** Open the folder whose view you want to change, and then right-click in an empty part of the folder

**Hot tip**

The View menu option, available by right-clicking in an open folder, provides a quick way to change a folder's view, but the **View** menu on the ribbon toolbar offers more, and more easily accessible, options.

**2** Hover the mouse on the **View** menu option and then select the required view. Using our example above, we are changing the view from **Extra large icons** to **Medium icons**. You can see how the view has changed below

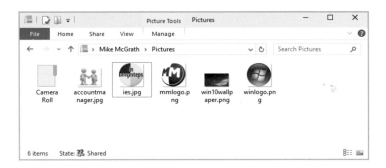

**Beware**

The information provided in the **Content** view depends on the file type. For example, Pictures has **Date taken**, and Music has **Track length**.

**3** The same commands, and more, are also available from the **View** tab on the File Explorer ribbon toolbar

# Sort contents

You can sort the contents of any folder by name, date, size or other attributes, using the **Details** view. You can also group or filter the contents.

**1** Open the folder and select the **Details** view

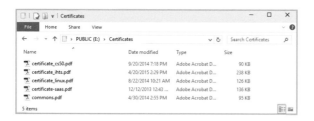

**2** Click on a header such as **Size** and the entries are sorted

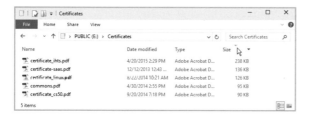

**3** Click the header again, and the sequence is reversed

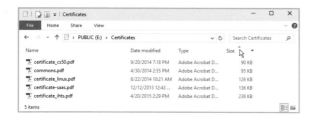

**4** Change the view, and the sequencing that you have set up will be retained for the new view

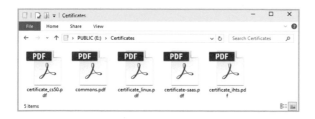

On the first selection, alphabetic fields such as Name or File Type are sorted in ascending order. Number fields such as Date or Size are sorted in descending order.

Click the arrow that appears when you hover over any header, to group the entries in ranges. By excluding some of the ranges, you can filter the contents displayed.

## ...cont'd

You can reorganize the contents from views other than Details.

**1** Open the folder, and right-click an empty part of the Contents, being sure to avoid the icon borders

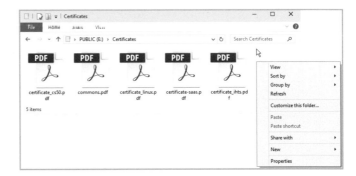

**2** Select **Sort by**, to change the sort field or sequence

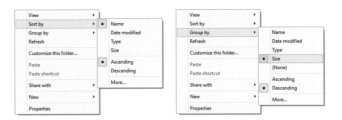

**3** Select **Group by**, and select the field (for example **Size**) by which you want to arrange the entries in ranges

**4** To remove the grouping, select **Group by**, then **(None)**

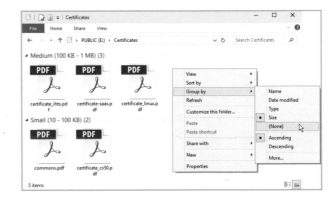

# Windows 10 libraries

Windows 10 comes with default libraries such as CameraRoll, Documents, Music, Pictures, SavedPictures, and Videos. You can add them to the Navigation pane by clicking the View tab in any folder, clicking Navigation pane and then clicking Show libraries.

**1** Click **Libraries** on the Navigation pane

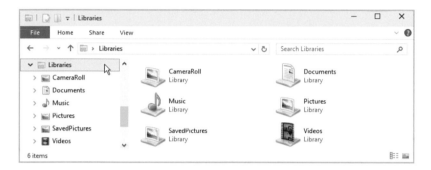

You can include other locations in the existing libraries, and you can also create your own libraries.

**2** Double-click a library, for example Pictures, to open it

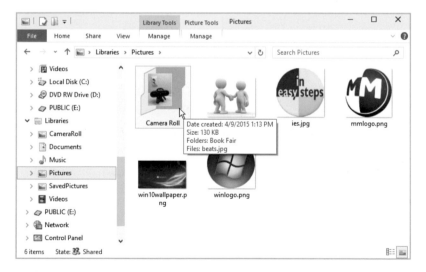

**3** Here we can see the library includes the CameraRoll location. The files and folders at that location are listed when you hover over the CameraRoll icon

# Manage library

**1** Open the Libraries folder and click the down-arrow under the red **X** close button to reveal the File Explorer ribbon toolbar

**2** In the folder contents section, select one of the default libraries, such as CameraRoll, Documents, Music, Pictures, SavedPictures, or Video

**3** Click the **Library Tools** tab on the quick launch section of the ribbon to reveal the options offered

**Hot tip**

The File Explorer ribbon Library options don't appear automatically – you have to select a library and then click the **Library Tools** tab.

**Manage library** – the Manage library link enables you to add new locations to an existing library – see pages 181-182 where we look at how to do this.

**Set save location** – this allows you to specify a default save location within a library. For example, if one of your libraries has two or more locations, you can set one of them as the default.

**Optimize library for** – the six default libraries all have different arrangement options appropriate for their respective contents. Should you create a new library, the Optimize library for link enables you to quickly set suitable arrangement options for the content of that library.

**Show in Navigation pane** – this lets you hide or show the Libraries link in the Navigation pane.

**Restore settings** – Click this link to undo all configuration changes made to the Libraries feature.

**Hot tip**

Right-click in any library and choose **Arrange by** to see its arrangement options.

# Add a location

**1** Open the Libraries folder and access Library Tools as described on page 180. Then click **Manage library**

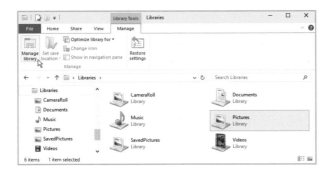

This lists the currently-defined locations and indicates the default save location, where new files would be added.

**2** Click the **Add** button next to Library locations

**3** Open the drive the required folder is located on

**4** Select the folder and then click **Include Folder**

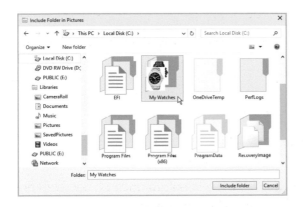

You could select folders from your hard drive, a second internal hard drive if available, or an external hard drive, as in this example.

...cont'd

**5** The selected folder becomes a new location in the library

**6** Click **OK** to see the added folder content

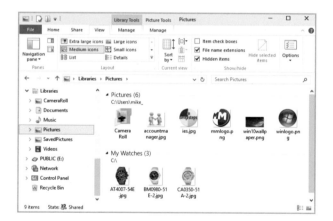

**7** Right-click on the library's icon and choose **Share with**
then select an option if you want to share this library

# Arrange library contents

Library contents are usually organized by location and folder, but you can change this.

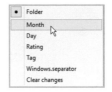

**1** Click the **Arrange by** box and select an alternative to Folder, e.g. **Month**

**2** The contents of all the folders are gathered together in groups by month and displayed as stacks

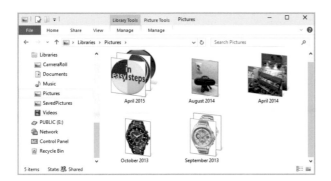

**3** Click the **Arrange by** box again and select another alternative, e.g. **Rating**

**4** The contents of all the folders are gathered together in groups by their star rating, or as "unspecified" if unrated

Files can be given star Rating and Tag names using the Details tab on their Properties dialog. Right-click on a file icon and choose the Properties item on the context menu, then select the Details tab and edit its star Rating or Tag name values there.

# Create a library

**Don't forget**

You can create a library of your own to manage other collections, for example project plans, or family history.

**1** Open the Libraries folder, right-click in the folder and select **New**, **Library**

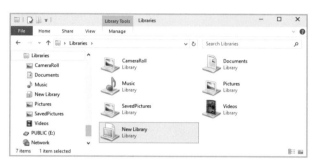

**2** Edit the library name, e.g. "Projects", and press **Enter**

**Hot tip**

The first folder that you add will be assigned as the save location, but you can change this later if you wish.

**3** Double-click the new library to open it, and you'll be invited to add folders

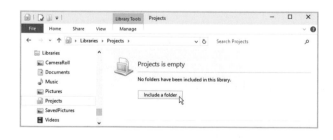

# Adjust properties

When you've added folders, the library appears on the Navigation pane and shows locations and folders, just like default libraries.

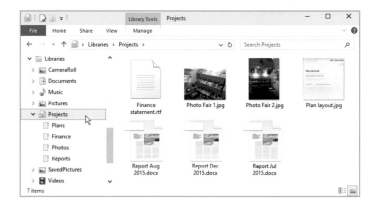

185

**1** Right-click the library name in the Navigation pane or in the Libraries folder and select **Properties**

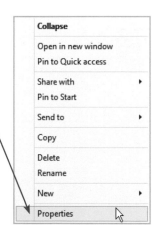

From here you can:

- Select a location and click **Set save location**

- **Add** a new folder or location

- **Remove** an existing location

- Hide or show in **Navigation pane**

- Check **Shared** status

- **Restore Defaults** after making changes

- **Apply** the changes you make

**2** Click **OK** to save your changes, or click **Cancel** to abandon your changes

From the right-click menu you can open the library in a new window, share it with other users, and hide or show it in the Navigation pane, as well as displaying properties.

By default, the library will be optimized for the type of file it contains, or for general items if the file types are mixed. However, you can choose a particular file type if you prefer.

# Customize folders

**1** Right-click the folder and select **Properties**

To customize a folder in a library, access it from your hard disk or right-click its folder and select Open file location.

**2** Click the **Customize** tab on the Properties panel

**3** To specify a folder picture, click the **Choose File** button

**4** Find and select the picture image and click **Open**

By default, the folder will be optimized for general items, but you can choose a specific file type if you wish.

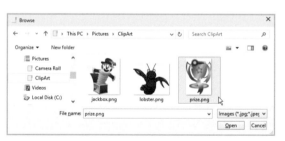

You can only add images on drives defined with the NTFS file system with its extended attributes. They cannot be added to drives defined with a FAT file system.

**5** Click **Apply, OK** on the Properties panel to add the image as the custom folder image

# 12 Email and messaging

You can use the communications tools built in or added to Windows to communicate with others, sending messages and attachments to individuals or groups of contacts. The Calendar facility helps you manage appointments and tasks. You can also receive general communications, such as newsletters and information feeds.

# Email

You can use email (electronic mail) to receive and send messages and files to individuals or groups of people. You can send messages at any time of day or night. The recipients don't have to be at their computers, since they find the messages waiting the next time they check their email inbox. However, if they are at their computer (or using their smartphone) they'd get the messages immediately and could respond straight away.

This is much more efficient than regular mail or telephone services, and it is free, no matter how far away the recipients might be. The only cost is for your internet connection, though you also need an email program or web-based email service.

### Web mail

You can register for a free web-based email service, such as Gmail, Outlook, or Yahoo! Mail. These services allow you to check your email using a web browser on your own computer, or on any computer connected to the internet, for example a friend's computer, or a computer in a public location such as a library or hotel.

### Email programs

On your own computer you can also check your email using an email program, from Microsoft or another supplier. Email programs often have more features and are faster to search mail than most web-based email services.

In previous versions of Windows, Microsoft supplied an email program as an integral component; either Outlook Express or Windows Mail. You can use the Mail app included in Windows 10 or download Windows Live Mail as part of the Windows Essentials. We will use the latter as the example product for Windows email.

### Microsoft Outlook

Microsoft also provides an email program named Outlook, which is part of the Microsoft Office system. This provides similar functions to Windows Live Mail, but it must be purchased as a separate product or as part of the Microsoft Office Suite.

To connect your computer to the internet, you must sign up with an Internet Service Provider (ISP), who provides a modem or router that gives access over phone line or cable.

An email address consists of a user name, @ sign, and the name of your ISP or web-based email provider. For instance: mike@example.com

To set up your email program you must get details from your ISP of your email address, password, and names of your incoming and outgoing email servers.

# Mail app

The Mail app provided by Windows is, like all the apps, a fairly basic affair. It lets you send and receive email but little else – it does not offer the range of features found in traditional desktop email programs.

However, one noteworthy feature that it does have is that it is integrated with the People and Calendar apps. For example, when you add an email account to the Mail app the contacts are added to People, and the meetings and other events are added to Calendar.

Set up the email app as follows:

**1** Click the **Mail** tile on the Start screen

**2** On the first page you'll see a list of email services

**3** Click the service you use

**4** When prompted, enter your email address and password in the boxes

**5** Assuming your email address and password are valid, your account will now be set up with no further input so you can read messages sent to this account in the Mail app

The Mail app is a new Universal Windows App in Windows 10.

Used in conjunction with the People and Calendar apps, the Mail app will take care of all your private communications.

If your email provider is not in the list, click **View all** in Settings. Then click **Other account**. Here, you can configure your account manually.

### ...cont'd

**Hot tip**

The Options tab can be used to mark the message importance and also check its spelling.

Folders      Message list      Reading pane

**6**   To send an email, click on **+ New mail** at the top-left

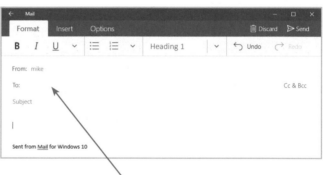

**7**   Enter the email address of the intended recipient

**8**   Add a subject heading, then type your message below

**9**   Click on the **Insert** tab to add attachments to the message. For example, pictures and a link

**Hot tip**

To insert an Emoji into your Mail message, first open the Touch keyboard

then hit the 🙂 Smiley icon key and choose from the Emoji selection.

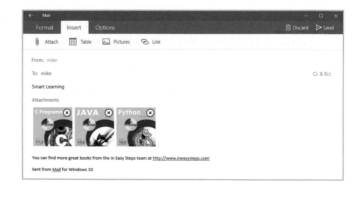

# Windows Live Mail

As already stated, Windows 10's Mail app provides few configuration options for the more advanced email user. If this is you, you will need to install a third-party program.

Mozilla, authors of the FireFox web browser, provides the free Thunderbird email client, while another free email program with a very good reputation is Eudora. Both of these are good choices and can be downloaded from the manufacturers' websites. If you do an internet search, you will also find a multitude of other email programs. This might be a good time to try out a few and see how you get on with them.

Alternatively, you can opt to stay with Microsoft. Their current free offering is Windows Live Mail, an updated version of the Windows Mail program that was provided with Windows Vista.

If you are migrating from an earlier version of Windows and used Windows Mail, you will probably decide to go with Windows Live Mail. This can be downloaded from the website at **windows.microsoft.com/en-us/windows-live/essentials**

When the installation is complete, start Mail as follows:

If you are likely to use Windows Live Mail frequently, pin it to the Start screen or Taskbar as previously explained.

**1** Under **All apps** in the Start menu, expand the "Windows Live" folder and click on the **Windows Live Mail** item to launch that application

**2** OK the license agreement by clicking **Accept** to see the Windows Live Mail startup splash screen

# Sign in to Windows Live Mail

When the splash screen closes, the "Add your email accounts" dialog box will open.

If you already have a Hotmail or MSN email address, this acts as a Windows Live ID. Otherwise, use an existing email address, e.g. Gmail, Yahoo! Mail, or an ISP email.

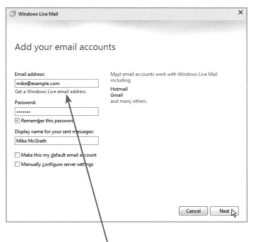

**1** Add your account if you already have an email account, or click the link to **Get a Windows Live email address**

You can also choose to create a Windows Live ID immediately, and use this in Windows Live Mail.

**2** Now sign in to Windows Live Mail, or click the **Sign up** link and fill in the web form that opens

# Add email accounts

**1** In Windows Live Mail, enter the email address and password, and type the display name for messages

Click the link to **Add another email account** if you have others you want to define.

**2** If this is a Windows Live ID, you should sign in to Windows Live

**3** Your email account will be added to Windows Live Mail

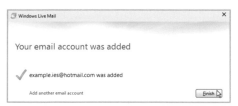

**4** Available messages will be downloaded from the server

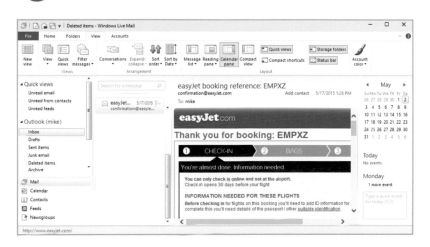

Select File, Options to discover lots of ways you can customize Windows Live Mail to suit your personal preferences.

## ...cont'd

### To add another email account:

If more accounts are required, add them as follows:

**1** Select the link to **Add another email account** or select **Accounts**, **Email** in Windows Live Mail

If Windows Live Mail does not have the server information required for the email account, you will be prompted to supply them.

**2** Type the email address and other details, and click **Next**

**3** Select the server type, and enter server addresses and other details (as provided by your ISP) then click **Next**

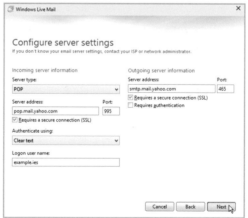

You can define three server types: POP (used for most ISP accounts), IMAP (used for web-based accounts such as Gmail) and Windows Live Hotmail (for Windows Live IDs).

**4** This email account is also added to Windows Live Mail

**5** The messages for the specified email are downloaded from the server to the Inbox for the account

The layout of Windows Live Mail in these examples has been adjusted to allow more room to display the list of messages.

**6** You may find that some messages are identified as junk email and automatically moved to the Junk email folder

**7** Some messages may be identified as phishing email, trying to deceive you into giving personal information, and these are also moved to the Junk email folder

Not all of the messages identified as junk email are necessarily invalid. One phishing message, for example, is a genuine communication that happens to be addressed to Dear Customer, which may raise a warning.

# Mail layout

**1** Open Windows Live Mail, and it typically has Mail selected, with folders, Inbox, preview and calendar

File button     Quick Access Toolbar     Title bar     Ribbon

Tabs

Email accounts

Folder list

Inbox message list

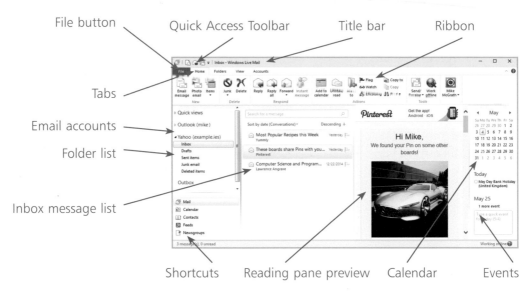

Shortcuts     Reading pane preview     Calendar     Events

The **Home** tab displays the commands on the ribbon that you require for working with messages you send and receive.

**2** Click the **Folders** tab to create, copy or move folders

**3** Click the **View** tab to change window view and layout

**4** Click the **Accounts** tab to add accounts or view properties

**Don't forget**

When you switch to Calendar, Contacts, Feeds or Newsgroups, the Home tab displays a different set of commands appropriate to the chosen function.

To change the view and layout of the Mail window:

**1** Open Windows Live Mail, select the **Mail** function and click the **View** tab

**2** Click **Reading pane**, and select **Off** to avoid showing a preview of the selected message

**3** Click **Calendar pane**, which operates as a toggle to hide or show the calendar

**4** Click **Compact shortcuts**, to show the functions as a set of icons

**5** Right-click the ribbon and select **Minimize the Ribbon**, to hide it

**6** To display the ribbon temporarily, so you can select a command, simply click the appropriate tab

# Messages

To see the messages that are available for any of your accounts:

**1** In Windows Live Mail, select **Mail** and click the account

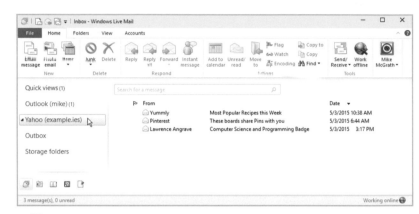

Hot tip

Unread messages are shown highlighted, and the count of unread messages appears in brackets after each account name. The count for Quick views shows the total number of unread messages across all the accounts.

**2** To see mail for all accounts defined, click **Quick views**

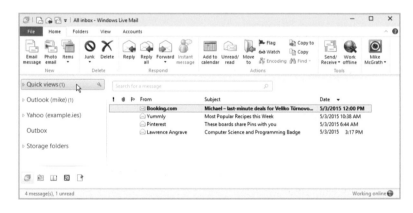

198

Don't forget

You can click the **Send/ Receive** button at any time to check if there's any mail waiting at the servers for your accounts.

By default, Windows Live Mail will check on the server for new email messages, at startup and then at 10-minute intervals.

**1** To change the delay time, select the **File** tab and select **Options**, **Mail**. Then click the **General** tab

**2** Enter the new interval required and click **OK**

To read an individual message in the account or **Quick views** list:

**1** Double-click an entry in the list (or select the entry and press **Enter**) to open the message

Don't forget

Click the white triangle next to the account name to display the folders – Inbox, Drafts, Sent items, etc.

**2** It opens in a new window

**3** Click **Reply** and type the response

Hot tip

You can reply to the sender, reply to all addressees, or forward the message to one or more other users.

**4** Click the **Send** button

**5** The reply is moved to your Outbox, from where it is sent to your mail server

**6** A copy of the reply is saved in your **Sent items** folder

Beware

You may receive a message requesting confirmation. Click the **Verify** link, or type the characters and select **OK**.

# Attachments

**1** Select and open a message with an attachment

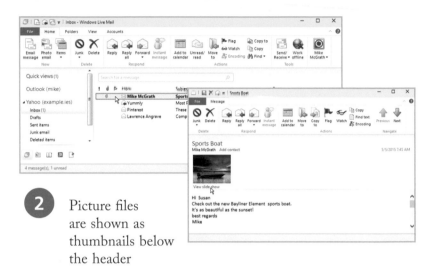

**Don't forget**

Some messages have files attached, as shown by the paperclip icon on the Inbox entry.

**2** Picture files are shown as thumbnails below the header

**3** Click **View slide show** to look at the images

**Hot tip**

When you receive other file types such as documents and spreadsheets as attachments, they will be shown as file icons.

**Hot tip**

Alternatively, you can click the Windows Live Mail button, select Save, **Save Attachments**, and choose which attachments to save.

**4** Right-click the thumbnail or file icon and select **Save as** (for just that attachment) or select **Save all**

**5** Confirm the folder location and click **Save** to write the attachments to disk

**...cont'd**

To add an attachment to your messages or replies:

**1** Type the message then click **Insert, Attach file**

**Don't forget**

Select Insert, **Single photo** to add the picture as an image in the message, positioned at the current location of the typing cursor.

**2** Locate the required folder, select the file and click **Open**

**3** The file is added as an icon below the message header

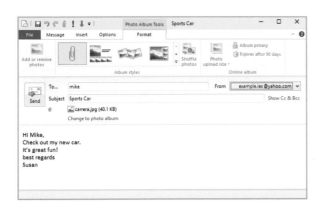

**Hot tip**

You can add other file types, for example a Word document. Click the **Send** button when you've finished typing the message and adding attachments.

201

# Contacts

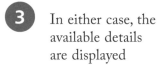 When you receive an email from a new contact, right-click the Inbox entry and select **Add sender to contacts**

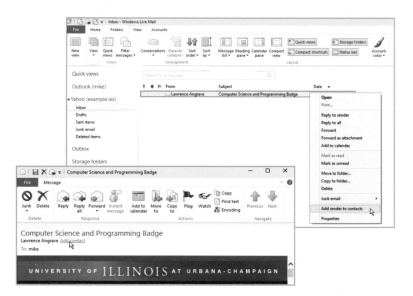

You can save contact details in the Windows Live Mail Contacts folder, which acts as an address book, with personal and business information.

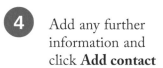 Alternatively, open the message and click the **Add contact** link next to the sender name (unless already in Contacts)

You can right-click any email address in a message and select **Add to contacts** (or **Edit Contact**, if there is already an entry).

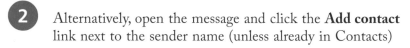 In either case, the available details are displayed

 Add any further information and click **Add contact**

Click the Contacts icon or shortcut to view the contents of your Contacts folder, and add, edit or delete entries.

# Junk email

Junk email, or spam, is unsolicited mail that is sent to lists of email addresses. Your ISP will provide filters to filter spam so that it doesn't actually reach your computer. Your antivirus program may redirect suspect mail. For spam that gets past these checks, Windows Live Mail lets you set up rules to block suspect senders and redirect junk mail.

1. Select the **File** tab, select **Options** and then choose the **Safety options** item

2. Click the **Options** tab

3. Review the option selected and adjust it if appropriate

4. You can permanently delete junk mail, but this risks deleting valid mail which has been inadvertently redirected

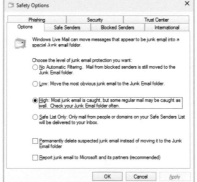

5. Decide if you want to notify Microsoft of junk mail detected

6. Click the **Safe Senders** and the **Blocked Senders** tabs, to add particular email addresses or domain names

7. Click the **Phishing** tab to enable or disable the protection against phishing attacks

8. Click the **International** tab to block messages from specific countries or in a particular language group

Hot tip

The default level of protection is **High**, but you can try a lower selling if you are the only user on the computer.

203

Beware

You may find that your email is filtered before it gets downloaded, so sign on to your account at the appropriate website and check the junk mail folder there, in case valid messages have been trapped in error.

# People app

While on the subject of contacts, Windows 10 provides three apps that are related to, or make use of, contacts (apart from the Mail app). The first of these is the People app. This is a useful contacts manager for storing information such as email addresses, phone numbers, addresses, etc.

The People app has the ability to amalgamate all your contacts across a range of different email services and social media websites. It allows you to easily call a contact from a phone, send an email to a contact, or retrieve a map of the contact address.

The People app is a new Universal Windows App in Windows 10.

**People** lets you access your contacts, regardless of where they are, from one convenient location.

**People** can link the same contacts from different networks under one profile. There is also an option that allows you to link contacts manually.

**1** On the Start menu, click the **People** item

**2** If you are signed in to the computer with a Microsoft account, the Home page will open. If not, you will be asked to connect accounts from which to gather contacts

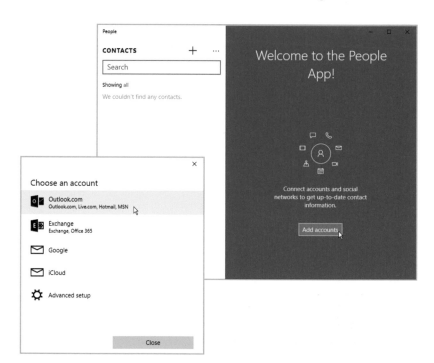

**3** Click the **Add accounts** button then choose an account. For example, choose **Outlook.com** to add that account

**4** Sign in to the account to add contacts to the People app

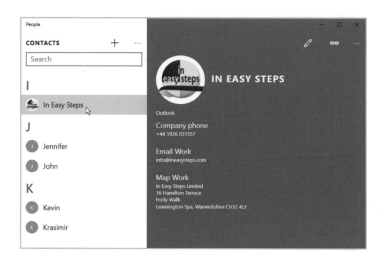

**5** Scroll down the contacts list and select any one to see their profile details

**6** Click an email address in a profile to launch the Mail app, ready to send that contact a message

**7** Click a location address in a profile to launch the Maps app, to see that contact's physical address

On a phone you can tap the telephone number in the contact's profile to call that contact.

The People app can be used with the Maps app to plan a route to a contact's address.

# Mail calendar

There's full calendar capability included in Windows Live Mail.

**1** Open Windows Live Mail and select the Calendar icon

**2** Select a date, double-click a time period and define an event start time, end time and reminder time

**3** Click **Save and close** to add the event to the calendar

**...cont'd**

By default, the calendar opens at the Month view. However, you can change this by clicking Day or Week on the View section of the toolbar at the top.

**Hot tip**

All Live mail calendars are automatically synced with browser-based calendars in Outlook, and calendars in Windows Phone devices.

If you find yourself scrolling through the calendar and can't find your way back to the current date, clicking Today will take you straight back – this is a key element of using the calendar, and is worth remembering.

The Mail calendar does not restrict you to just one calendar; you can have as many as you wish. To create a new calendar:

**1** Click the Calendar icon at the bottom-left of the screen while on the Home tab

**2** On the toolbar, click **Calendar**. The "Add a Calendar" dialog box opens, as shown below:

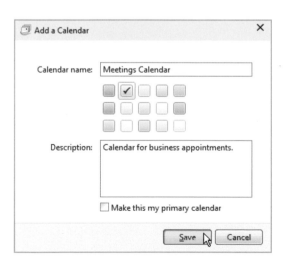

**3** Give your new calendar a name, color and description and click Save. It will now be listed under Calendars on the left when you open the Calendar view of Windows Live Mail

# Calendar app

An alternative to Windows Live Mail's calendar is the Calendar app supplied by Windows 10.

The app is powered by the Exchange ActiveSync (EAS) technology that is the backbone of Microsoft services such as Hotmail, Exchange, and Office 365. It can also connect to other EAS-based calendars, which include Google Calendar.

As with other Windows 10 apps, Calendar uses a browser-like form of navigation. When using a mouse, you'll see small navigational arrows appear near the top-left and top-right of the screen. Or you can use the keyboard – **Ctrl + left-arrow** and **Ctrl + right-arrow** to move left and right respectively.

A cool feature is that moving backwards or forwards in time is done within the context of the current view. For example, going back while in week view takes you back a week. Going forward while in day view takes you forward to tomorrow.

The Calendar app is a new Universal Windows App in Windows 10.

Calendar can show detailed information regarding your next event on the Lock screen.

**1** Click the **Calendar** item on the Start menu

**2** If you are signed in to the computer with a Microsoft account, the calendar will open in monthly view. If not, you will be asked to sign in

**3** Initially, the calendar has no entries. Create one by clicking on a day to open the "Details" page

Calendar works well when snapped to the side of another app. It provides a thumbnail view of the month and the current day's events.

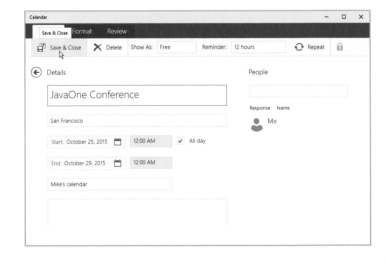

**4** Under Details there is a range of options:

● **Event name** – specify what the event is.

● **Location** – specify where the event is to take place.

● **When** – select a day, time, and duration for the event.

● **Calendar** – specify which personal calendar to add this event to.

Clicking the **More details** link reveals a list of further options, such as how often the event is to take place, reminders, status, etc.

**5** Add details of an event then click the **Save & Close** button to return to the Calendar view

**6** Ensure that the specific calendar you have chosen in Step 4 is selected, to see your event displayed in the Calendar view

You can import calendars into the Calendar app from Hotmail, Outlook and Google by clicking Settings, Accounts, then **Add an account**.

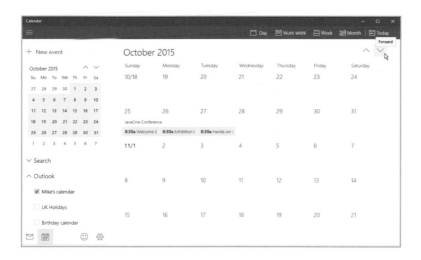

**7** To move about in the Calendar, click the up (back) or down (forward) arrows at the top of the screen

## ...cont'd

The Calendar app toolbar options let you choose to view **Day**, **Work week**, **Week**, **Month**, or **Today**, to change the calendar view as required. Changing from Month view to Week view provides rows for each hour under each day's column. This is useful for noting daily agenda schedules of events for each day. The hamburger button collapses the left pane for extra space.

The **Work week** view shows a five-day week.

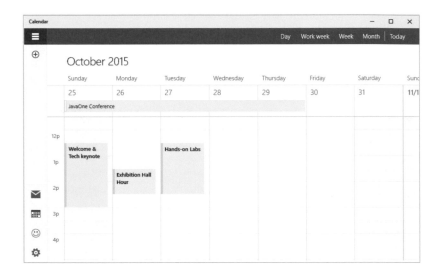

The **Today** button returns the Calendar view to the current date and retains the left-pane position – full or collapsed.

The Calendar also has icon links for the Mail app and for preferred Calendar Settings.

# Newsgroups

To take part in a discussion, you need to access the appropriate newsgroup server and subscribe to a particular newsgroup.

To specify the newsgroup server in Windows Live Mail:

**1** Choose the Newsgroup shortcut icon, then select the **Accounts** tab and click **Newsgroup** in New Account

Windows Live Mail also includes Newsreader capability, so that you can participate in online discussion groups.

**2** Supply the display name or nickname that you want others to see and click **Next**

**3** Provide your email address for personal replies

If you do mistype the address, accidentally or deliberately, you'll get a warning but will be allowed to enter the address as typed.

You could make a deliberate error in the email address, such as putting "at" rather than @. This will be obvious to a human reader, but would help avoid your email address being detected by robots that search the internet for email addresses to use for spam.

## ...cont'd

**4** Name the newsgroup server you have decided to use, for example: **freenews.netfront.net**

**5** Click **Next** then click **Finish** to add the account

**6** The names of the newsgroups will be downloaded – there are over 40,000 in the list for the example newsgroup server

**7** Type keywords related to your interest, e.g. "Bridge", to list only those newsgroups that are relevant

**8** Select a particular newsgroup, click **Subscribe** and **Go to** to open the selected newsgroup

# 13 Microsoft Edge

*Windows 10 includes Microsoft Edge as the default web browser. Here we explore its features and discover the innovations it brings to web browsing.*

The Microsoft Edge web browser app is a new Universal Windows App in Windows 10.

If you need to view a web page that uses legacy technology you can find Internet Explorer under Windows Accessories in **All apps** on the Start menu.

# Better browsing

Windows 10 introduces the next-generation web browser named Microsoft Edge. This replaces the Internet Explorer web browser that has been around for many years. Microsoft Edge is a brand new, faster, more streamlined web browser.

Microsoft Edge has a new rendering engine called EdgeHTML that replaces the Trident rendering engine used in Internet Explorer. The new browser doesn't support old "legacy" technologies, such as ActiveX, but instead uses an extension system similar to those in the Chrome and Firefox web browsers. There is, however, a version of Internet Explorer included with Windows 10 for backward compatibility. Not supporting legacy technologies in Microsoft Edge has a number of benefits:

● Better interoperability with other modern browsers.

● Enhanced performance.

● Improved security and reliability.

● Reduced code complexity.

In addition to these benefits there are several great innovations in the Microsoft Edge web browser:

● Integration with the Cortana Personal Digital Assistant for voice control, search, and personalized information.

● Annotation of web pages that can then be easily stored on OneDrive for sharing with other users.

● Compilation of web pages into a Reading List that synchronizes content between devices.

● Elimination of formatting distractions in Reading View mode that allows web pages to be read more easily.

The Microsoft Edge web browser is uncluttered in appearance, as its design intends to emphasize web page content. Browsing the web simply requires use of the familiar "navigation buttons":

Back  Forward  Reload

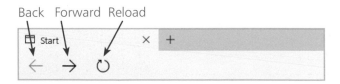

# Interface layout

When the Microsoft Edge web browser is launched it shows just the Start page and provides the interface features shown below:

Navigation buttons    New Tab button    Page content    Hub    Web Note    Share    More

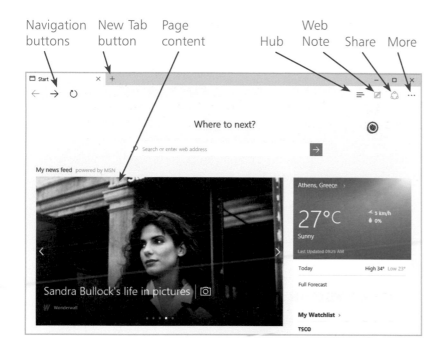

The Hub is a new feature in Microsoft Edge on Windows 10.

Beware

Additional interface features of Address Bar, Favorites button, and Reading View button are initially hidden, but will appear to the left of the Hub button as you begin to browse web pages.

215

Clicking the **+ New Tab** button opens a new tab containing a Search box and, by default, an intelligent selection of **Top sites** tiles that may be of interest to you.

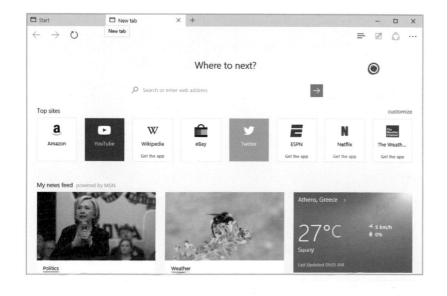

Hot tip

Use the **Customize** option on the new tab page if you wish to include your news feed or wish to exclude the top sites list.

# Search and navigation

The Search box on the Start page contains a text message inviting you to "Search or enter web address". This indicates its multi-purpose function for both web search and for address navigation:

 Type a word or phrase into the box to see a list of suggestions instantly appear

2 Now, hit **Enter**, or press the Search box arrow button, to see search engine results for the entered word or phrase

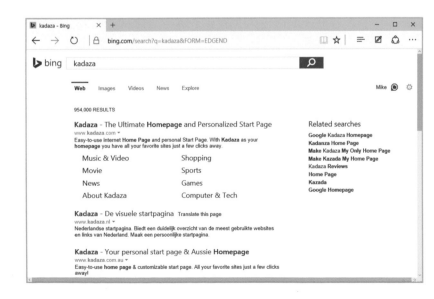

**3** Next, hit the browser's back-arrow navigation button to reload the Start page once more

**4** Then, type a URL address into the box to see a list appear containing a recognized website and search suggestions

Hot tip

Recognized websites are denoted by the world globe icon.

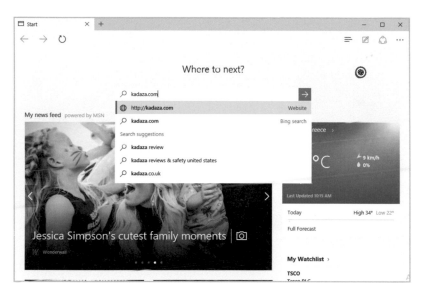

**5** Hit **Enter**, or press the Search box arrow button, to load the recognized website

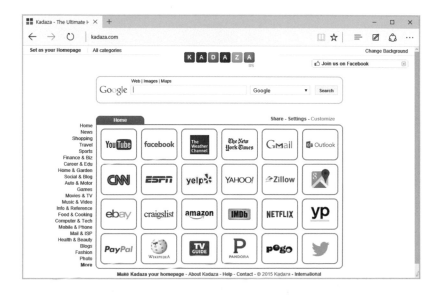

Hot tip

Click on the Address Bar to make it active then enter a search phrase or URL address – it works just like the Search box.

# Opening options

Typing a URL address or search phrase into Microsoft Edge's Search box or Address Bar will, by default, display the search results or specified website in the current window area. It is, however, often preferable to retain the current window and open search results or specified websites in other tabs or windows:

**1** Click on the Address Bar to make it active, then type in a search phrase and hit **Enter** to see the search results

**Don't forget**

If the Address Bar is hidden you can click to the right of the navigation buttons to make it appear.

**2** Now, place the mouse cursor over one of the result links and right-click to see a context menu appear

**3** Select the menu option to **Open in new tab**

**Hot tip**

The **Copy link** menu option copies the URL address of the selected link onto the clipboard.

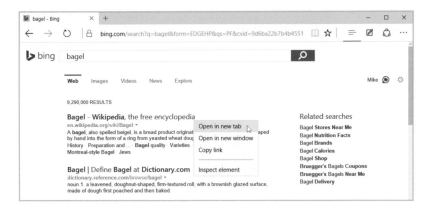

**4** Now, click the new tab that appears to see the page contents of the link displayed in that tab

**...cont'd**

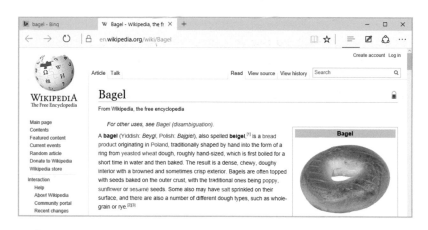

You can also use the keyboard shortcut **Ctrl + Tab** to move forward between tabs.

**5** Click the original tab to see the search results once more

**6** Place the mouse cursor over a different result link and right-click to see the context menu appear

**7** Select the menu option to **Open in new window**

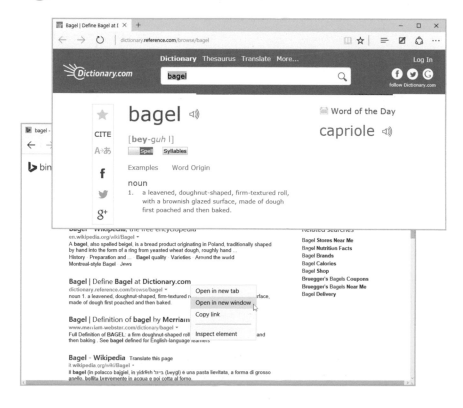

# Saving favorites

If you've found a website that you are likely to visit frequently it can be made quickly accessible as a saved Favorite:

**1** Open the website then click the **Hub** button

**2** On the Hub pane, click the **Favorites** star icon

**3** Edit the favorite Name, if desired, then choose to **Create in Favorites** and click the **Add** button

You can also use the keyboard shortcut **Ctrl + G** to see the Reading List.

The Favorites Bar is hidden unless enabled in **More actions**, Settings.

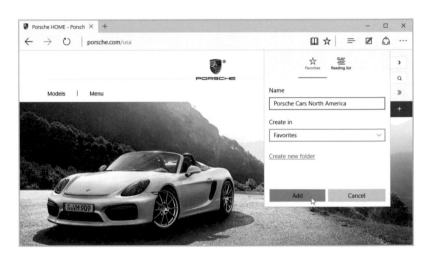

**4** To open a saved Favorite, first launch Microsoft Edge then click the **Hub** button

**5** On the Hub pane, click the **Favorites** star icon to see saved Favorites

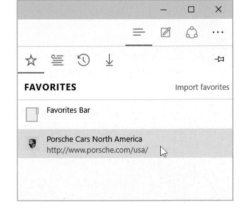

You remove a saved Favorite from the list by right-clicking on it and choosing **Remove** from the context menu.

**6** Click the saved Favorite from the displayed list to open that website once more

# Pinning websites

A website that you are likely to visit frequently can alternatively be made quickly accessible as a link pinned to the Start menu:

**1** Open the website in the Microsoft Edge browser

**2** Click the ellipsis (**...**) **More actions** button

**3** On the **More actions** menu, choose the **Pin to Start** action to create a link to the current website

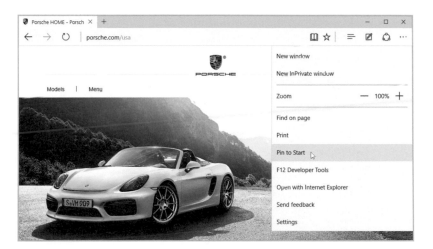

**4** To open a pinned website, open the Start menu

**5** Click on the link tile to launch Microsoft Edge and open that website once more

See page 230 for more functions of the **More actions** button.

Notice the option here to **Open with Internet Explorer** for legacy websites that do not perform well in the Microsoft Edge browser.

You can remove any tile from the Start menu, including a pinned link, by right-clicking on it then choosing **Unpin from Start** from the context menu.

# Reading articles

When you discover an article of interest that you don't have time to read right away you can save it to your Reading List for later:

**1** Open the website then click the **Hub** button

**2** On the Hub pane, click the **Reading List** icon

**3** Edit the article Name, if desired, then click the **Add** button

You can also use the keyboard shortcut **Ctrl + G** to see the Reading List.

Reading List is a new feature in Microsoft Edge on Windows 10.

**222**

You remove a saved article from the Reading List by right-clicking on it and choosing **Remove** from the context menu.

**4** To open a saved article, first launch Microsoft Edge then click the **Hub** button

**5** On the Hub pane, click the **Reading List** icon to see saved articles

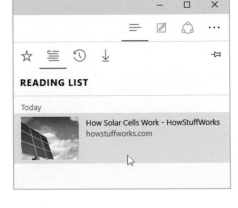

**6** Click the saved article from the displayed list to open that website once more

# Reading View

Microsoft Edge provides a Reading View option that lets you read articles in a distraction-free format that you can customize:

**1** Open the website then click the **Reading View** icon to switch to the default textual content display mode

**2** Click the (**...**) **More actions** button, then choose **Settings**

**3** Scroll down to the **Reading** section, then adjust the Reading View style and font size to suit your preferences

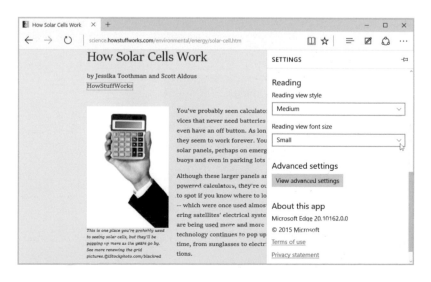

Don't confuse the Reading List (for saved articles) with the Reading View – for easy viewing.

Reading View is a new feature in Microsoft Edge on Windows 10.

Your chosen Reading settings will be used for Reading View each time you choose that option.

# Reviewing history

As you are browsing the web, Microsoft Edge automatically saves a link to each web page you visit. This means you can easily revisit any page by recalling your browsing history and choosing its link:

**1** Launch Microsoft Edge then click the **Hub** button

**2** On the Hub pane, click the clock **History** icon to see links to web pages you visited earlier

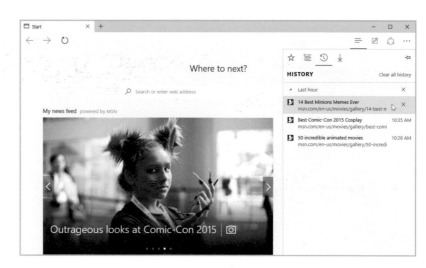

**3** Click any history link to re-open that web page

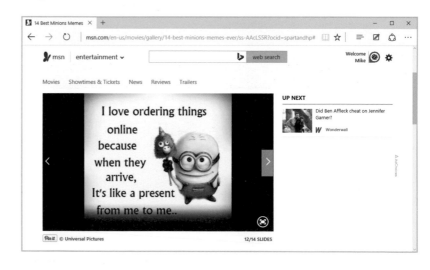

# Managing downloads

Microsoft Edge includes a simple download manager facility. This allows you to easily monitor, pause, resume, or cancel downloads from the web. Upon completion, downloaded items can be found in your Downloads folder:

**1** Start to download an item then click the **Hub** button

**2** On the Hub pane, click the **Downloads** arrow icon to see the progression of your downloading item

You can also use the keyboard shortcut **Ctrl** + **J** to see the Downloads list.

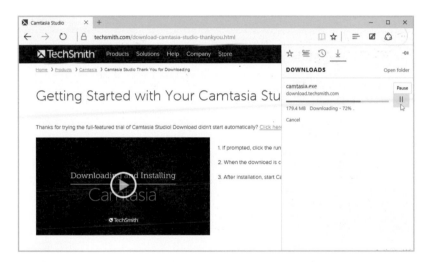

**3** Click the || button if you want to pause or resume progress of the download

**4** Click the **Open folder** link to launch File Explorer in the Downloads folder to find your downloaded items

You can click the **Cancel** link to terminate a download in progress and click the **X** button against an item to remove it from the list of completed downloads.

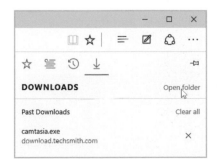

# Making web notes

Microsoft Edge lets you make notes and highlight important text directly onto web pages, creating your own "Web Notes" that can be saved and shared:

**1** Open a page in Microsoft Edge then click the  Web Note button to see the toolbar switch to Web Note mode

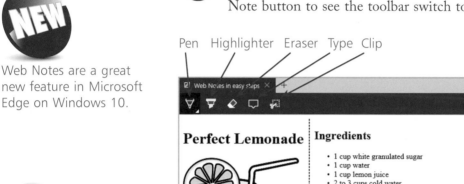

Pen  Highlighter  Eraser  Type  Clip          Save      Share

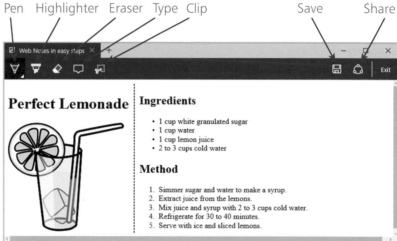

Web Notes are a great new feature in Microsoft Edge on Windows 10.

The Clip tool simply copies a selected area to the clipboard so you can paste it into another app, such as Paint.

You can double-click the Eraser icon and select **Clear all ink** to remove all highlights and pen notes.

**2** Click the Pen icon to select the Pen tool then choose a color and nib size

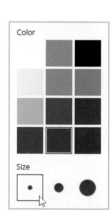

**3** Now, use the cursor to scribble a web note on the page using your chosen color and nib size

**4** Click the Eraser icon then drag the cursor across your note if you want to erase individual written characters

**5** Click the Highlighter icon to select the Highlighter tool, then choose a color and shape

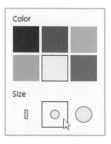

**6** Now, use the cursor to highlight any items of particular importance

**7** Click the Type icon then click on the page at a point where you want to type a note

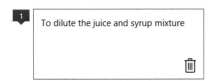

**8** Enter text into the box that appears to create a typed note

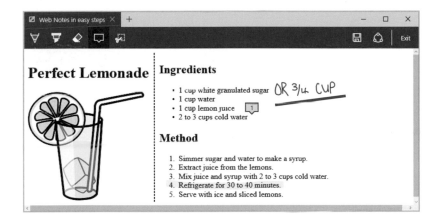

**Hot tip**

Click the numbered icon beside a typed note to collapse or expand that typed note.

**9** Click the Save icon then choose to save the complete noted page for OneNote – so it will be sent to OneDrive

**10** Open the OneNote app on any device to see the page complete with your notes

**Don't forget**

You can also save in your Favorites or Reading List, and use the Share button to send the noted page to another location.

# Sharing pages

When you want to share a web page of interest, Microsoft Edge provides the ability to share a link to that page's URL address or a screenshot of the part of that page visible in your browser:

**1** Click the ♻ **Share** button – to open the Share panel

Sharing to the Reading List just saves the link by the name you give it.

**2** Select the **OneNote** option on the Share panel

**3** Add a note if desired then click **Send** to share the link

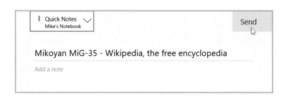

**4** Open the OneNote app on any device to see the shared link

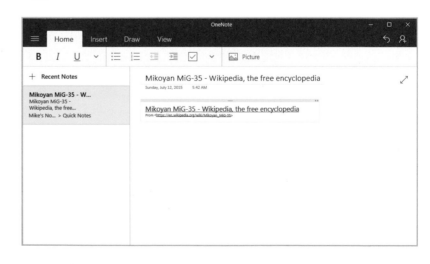

**5** Click the **Share** button again then click the down-arrow in the Share panel to reveal dropdown options

You can share a screenshot to a printer app if you want to print it out.

**6** Select the **Screenshot** option then share to OneNote again

**7** Add a note if desired then click **Send** to share the screenshot

**8** Open the OneNote app on any device to see the screenshot

# Customizing Edge

The dropdown menu from the (...) **More actions** button in Microsoft Edge provides typical options to **Zoom** the page view, **Find** text within the page, or **Print** the page. It lets you open a **New window** or, if you prefer, a **New InPrivate window** that does not store cookies, history, or temporary files on your PC. The **F12 Developer Tools** option provides a suite of tools to build or debug web pages and the **Settings** option provides several customization possibilities.

**Hot tip**

You can open the current web page in Internet Explorer from this menu if the page uses any legacy technologies not supported by the Microsoft Edge browser.

**1** Click the (...) **More actions** button then select the **Settings** option

**2** In Settings, **Choose a theme**, click the down-arrow and select the **Dark** option from the dropdown that appears

**3** Next, slide the "Show the favorites bar" toggle button into the **On** position

**Don't forget**

Here, the Favorites Bar has simply imported Bing and Bing Translator but your imported Favorites will vary.

**4** Now, click the link to **Import favorites from another browser** and select a browser from the list that appears

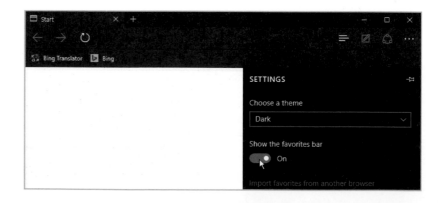

**5** In Settings, **Open with**, select **A specific page or pages**

**6** Next, select the **Custom** option from the dropdown list

**7** Now, enter the URL of a preferred start page and click **+**

You must click the X against any other listed Start page URL or Microsoft Edge will launch with multiple Start pages.

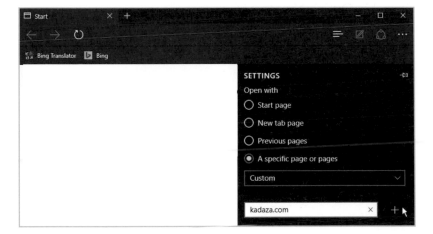

**8** Scroll down to the bottom of the Settings options to find **Advanced settings** and click the button to view them

You can also edit the Home button target by changing "about:start" to your preferred URL.

**9** Slide the "Show the home button" toggle button into the **On** position

# Selecting text

When selecting text in a web page it can be difficult to select precisely what you want without also selecting adjacent text, and objects such as images and tables, as shown below:

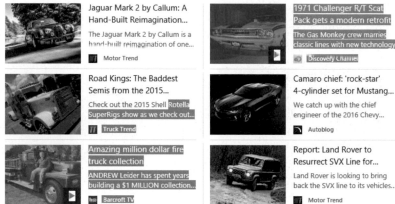

You will not be able to select text that appears within an image; you can only select actual text content in a document.

With Microsoft Edge, the Caret Browsing feature helps solve this problem. This lets you use the keyboard instead of the mouse to make selections and it offers much more precise control.

To activate Caret Browsing, press **F7**. Then place the cursor at the beginning of the text block you want to select, press and hold down the Shift key and highlight the text with the arrow keys.

Some users find this feature so useful that they may want to have Caret Browsing permanently enabled. This is very easy to do:

Hold down the **Shift** key and select characters with the **Forward/Back** keys or select lines with the **Up/Down** keys.

**1** Click the (**...**) **More actions** button then choose **Settings**

**2** Under "Advanced settings" click **View advanced settings**

**3** Slide the toggle button "Always use caret browsing" into the **On** position

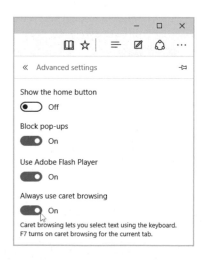

# 14 Digital images

*The computer is the ideal way to manage and organize the digital images you capture with your still camera, camcorder or cell phone. You can edit and print photos, create slide shows, or turn your photos and videos into movies that can be displayed on the TV or published to the internet, to share with your family and friends.*

# Digital images

Digital images may be created in a graphical application, using a scanner or with digital still and movie cameras. The images are defined in terms of picture elements or pixels. The location, color and intensity of each pixel is stored in the image file. The images can then be displayed, enhanced, printed and shared using software on your computer or on specialized websites.

The size of the file depends on the image resolution (the number of pixels used to represent the image) and the color depth (the number of color variations defined). For example:

| Pixel size | Bytes | No. Colors | Name |
| --- | --- | --- | --- |
| 8-bit | 1 | 256 | System |
| 16-bit | 2 | 65,536 | HighColor |
| 24-bit | 3 | 16,777,216 | TrueColor |

Another factor that influences the image size is the degree of zoom that the camera utilizes. Cameras use the capabilities of the camera lens to bring the subject closer, enlarging the image before it is stored as pixels. This is known as Optical zoom.

High-resolution cameras can take images of, say, 4000 x 3000 pixels in TrueColor. This works out at 36 million bytes per picture. Various image file formats have been developed to store such large images. These incorporate image compression algorithms to decrease the size of the file. The algorithms used are of two types: lossless and lossy.

**Lossless compression algorithms** reduce the file size without losing image quality, though they will not be compressed into as small a file as a lossy compression file.

**Lossy compression algorithms** take advantage of the inherent limitations of the human eye and discard information that does not contribute to the visible effect. Most lossy compression algorithms allow for variable quality levels (compression) and as these levels are increased, the file size is reduced. At the highest compression levels, the deterioration in the image may become noticeable, and give undesirable effects.

Don't forget

Cameras also have Digital zoom, which magnifies the picture by cropping it to select only the specific area after it has captured it as pixels. This would reduce the saved image size. However, it is usually better to edit and crop on your computer, using software supplied with the camera or included in Windows.

# Image file formats

### BMP (Windows bitmap)
This handles graphics files within Windows. The files are uncompressed, and therefore large, but they are widely accepted in Windows applications so are simple to use.

### GIF (Graphics Interchange Format)
This is limited to 256 colors. It is useful for graphics with relatively few colors such as diagrams, shapes, logos and cartoon-style images. The GIF format supports animation. It also uses a lossless compression that is effective when large areas have a single color, but ineffective for detailed images or dithered images.

### JPEG (Joint Photographic Experts Group)
The JPEG/JFIF filename extension is JPG or JPEG, and it uses lossy compression. Nearly every digital camera can save images in the JPEG format, which supports 24-bit color depth and produces relatively small files. JPEG files suffer generational degradation when repeatedly edited and saved.

### PNG (Portable Network Graphics)
This was created as the successor to GIF, supporting TrueColor and providing a lossless format that is best suited for editing pictures, where lossy formats like JPG are best for final distribution of photographic images, since JPG files are usually smaller than PNG. PNG works well with web browsers.

### Raw image format
This is used on some digital cameras to provide lossless or nearly-lossless compression, with much smaller file sizes than the TIFF formats from the same cameras. Raw formats used by most cameras are not standardized or documented, and differ among camera manufacturers. Graphics programs and image editors may not accept some or all of them, so you should use the software supplied with the camera to convert the images for edit, and retain the Raw files as originals and backup.

### TIFF (Tagged Image File Format)
This is a flexible format that saves 24-bit and 48-bit color, and uses the TIFF or TIF filename extension. TIFFs can be lossy and lossless, with some digital cameras using the LZW compression algorithm for lossless storage. TIFF is not well supported by browsers but is a photograph file standard for printing.

These are the main image file format types you will encounter in dealing with digital photographs and website images.

You should save originals in the least lossy format, and use formats such as PNG or TIFF to edit the images. JPEG is good for sending images or posting them on the internet.

# Photos app

The Photos app provides links to the photo collection on your PC, as well as your photos on OneDrive, plus any other connected PCs and devices. As with the People app, which can amalgamate all your contacts from a variety of sources, the Photos app does the same with all your pictures. So, while they may be scattered about on various websites, computers, portable drives, etc., the app pulls them all together so they can be quickly accessed.

**1** Click the **Photos** item on the Start menu to launch it

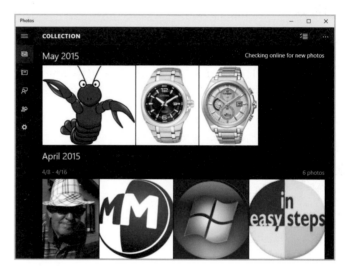

**2** Click any image to see it displayed alone

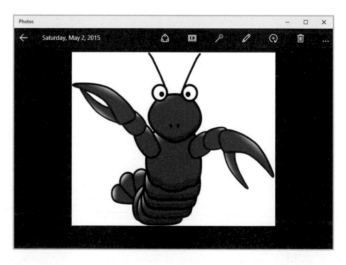

The Photos app provides a very basic photo acquisition function for importing photos.

The Photos app is a new Universal Windows App in Windows 10.

The default view of the Photos app displays your collection of images grouped by month.

**3** Click the **(...)** ellipsis at the top-right to reveal a menu of options – for example, choose **File info** for image details

Notice that this menu has options to **Copy** or **Print** the image.

**4** Now, click the **(...)** ellipsis at the top-right and choose **Set as lock screen** from the menu – that image becomes the default that will appear on the Lock screen

**5** You can use the bar to share and edit this image, or click the **Slide show** options to view all images in your collection full-screen, one-by-one

The **Share** options available to you depend on what accounts you have set up in the app, what other apps you have installed, and how they are configured.

# Import photos

There are a number of ways to import pictures into a Windows 10 PC (they can also be imported from different types of device). We'll start with the Photos app:

**1** Connect the device containing the pictures to your computer

**2** Launch the **Photos** app from the Start menu then click the **Import** button at the top-right of the window

**Beware**

If you import two or more picture folders, the folders themselves will not be imported – just the pictures. These will be "lumped together" and placed in the Pictures library.

**3** You may see a list of devices connected to your computer. Choose the one that contains the pictures to be imported

**4** A summary of all the pictures on the device is shown. Click the summary's **Import** button to copy the pictures

**Don't forget**

If only one device is connected to your computer, no list appears – the summary of pictures it contains appears right away.

...cont'd

## Import with Windows

Windows AutoPlay offers another method of importing pictures to a computer.

**1** Connect the device to the PC – a camera, for example. Click on the notification message that appears

**2** Windows AutoPlay will open at the top-right of the screen and ask what you want to do with the device. Click the option to **Import photos and videos**

The next time that you import from this device, Windows will only select new items.

**3** This opens the Photos app. Select the camera device from the list then click the summary's **Import** button

The Import process will tell you when there is nothing to transfer.

**4** The pictures are imported and saved in the Pictures folder

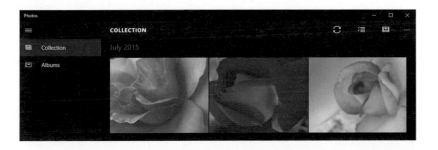

...cont'd

## Import with Windows Live Photo Gallery

Imaging applications also offer picture import options. In this example, we are using Windows Photo Gallery from the Windows Essentials 2012 suite.

**1** Connect the device containing the pictures

**2** Open Windows Photo Gallery and click **Import** at the far-left of the ribbon menu

**3** Select the required device and click the **Import** button

**4** Add tags if desired, then click **Import**

**5** The image files are transferred to the folder specified

**6** Windows Live Photo Gallery displays the contents of the folder, grouped by month and year taken

If you have Windows Essentials installed on your system, you can use Windows Photo Gallery to import your pictures.

If the pictures cover a variety of events, you can choose **Review, organize, and group items to import** prior to importing.

# Camera app

Of all the apps bundled with Windows 10, the Camera app is one of the most basic. The first thing to note here, and it's something that confuses many users, is that the app only works with webcams – connect a digital camera to it and absolutely nothing will happen.

**1** Connect your webcam to the PC

**2** Open the **Camera** app from the Start screen

**3** You may be asked to approve the app using your location

**4** When the camera is on, you see two buttons at the right of the window offering options for **Video** and **Photo**

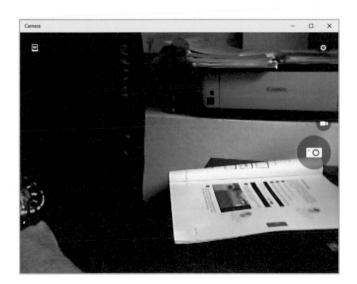

**5** Click the **Video** button to start making a video, then click it again to stop recording – the completed video will then be automatically added to your Camera Roll folder

**6** Now click the **Photo** button to take a picture – the photo will then be added to your Camera Roll folder

You cannot use a digital camera with the Camera app – it only works with webcams.

The Camera app is a new Universal Windows App in Windows 10.

To get the best picture, set up your device in Camera options.

...cont'd

**7** Before you start using the app though, you may want to change some settings. Unfortunately, the app is very limited in this respect but settings can be accessed by clicking the **Settings** button in the Camera window

**8** When you have taken some pictures or videos, back- and forward-arrow buttons appear at the edges of the Camera window. These let you view your work

**9** You can also click on the camera button at the top-left of the Camera window to view your image in the Photos app. When viewing your photos, clicking on the top of the Photos window opens an app bar that has an **Edit** button. This provides a number of editing options such as Crop, Rotate, and Enhance

Note that once taken by the Camera app, your photos are actually handled (viewed and edited as explained above) in the Photos app. But if you'd rather not use the Photos app for viewing your images, you can open them with a viewer of your choice from the Camera Roll in the Pictures folder.

Pictures and videos taken by the Camera app are saved by default in the user's Camera Roll within the Pictures folder.

# Windows Photo Viewer

By default, Windows 10 uses the Photos app to open pictures. However, there is another way to view your pictures – Windows Photo Viewer.

**1** Right-click on the picture you want to open and from the menu select **Open with,** then **Windows Photo Viewer**

**2** The picture will now open in Windows Photo Viewer

If Windows Photo Viewer is not activated on your system you can activate it with Winaero Tweaker, free from **winaero.com**

243

However, the next time you open a picture, it will again open in the Photos app as it is the default viewer. If you are happy with this, fine. If not, you need to set Windows Photo Viewer to be the default viewer.

**1** Repeat Step 1 above but this time select **Choose another app** rather than Windows Photo Viewer

**2** You will now see a list of programs on the PC that are capable of opening the picture

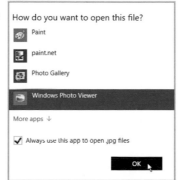

How do you want to open this file?

- Paint
- paint.net
- Photo Gallery
- **Windows Photo Viewer**

More apps ↓

☑ Always use this app to open .jpg files

OK

The options shown on this page are also available from the ribbon toolbar.

**...cont'd**

**3** Check the **Always use this app to open .jpg files** box

**4** Select **Windows Photo Viewer**

**Don't forget**

You have to associate image file types with Windows Photo Viewer individually.

Using the above example, all JPG image files will now open in Windows Photo Viewer by default. However, this won't apply to other image formats such as TIFFs and PNGs. Therefore, you will have to repeat the procedure for each file type as described above.

As a general note, Windows Photo Viewer does just what its name suggests – it lets you view pictures but little else. Features include:

- **Zoom** – move in and out of the picture

- **Previous/Next** – move backwards and forwards through a folder of pictures

- **Rotate** – rotate a picture clockwise and anti-clockwise

- **Print** – print a picture

- **Email** – attach pre-sized pictures to an email message

**Hot tip**

When you email an image file as an attachment, you can specify the size, or send it at the original size.

# Photo Gallery

The Photos app and Windows Photo Viewer are just two of hundreds of imaging programs. A free alternative is Photo Gallery, a program included in Microsoft's Essentials suite. This has the added advantage of offering many more options, which makes it a far more capable program.

**1**    Download and install it from the Live Essentials website

**2**    Right-click on the picture and select **Open with**, then choose **Photo Gallery**

If you are looking for a fully-featured imaging program to edit and organize your pictures, Photo Gallery is highly recommended.

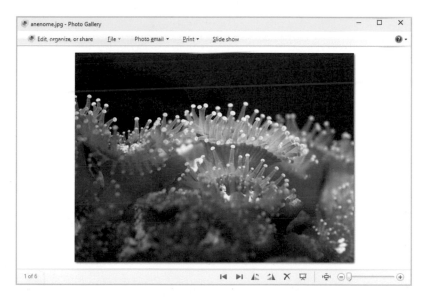

**3**    The options offered by Photo Gallery in its initial view, as shown above, are almost identical to those of Windows Photo Viewer, i.e. Previous and Next, Rotate, Zoom, etc. These are fine if you just want to view the picture

**4**    If you need more features and options, however, click **Edit, organize, or share** at the top-left of the window

**5**    A new window opens, at the top of which is a ribbon toolbar. This offers a multitude of image-related features and options. These are accessible from five section tabs – Home, Edit, Find, Create and View

...cont'd

## Home

The Home tab enables you to import pictures and videos, manage and manipulate pictures, plus organize, find, and share.

**Hot tip**

On the Home tab you will find tools that let you share your pictures with social media sites such as Facebook and YouTube.

## Edit

The Edit tab offers more managing and manipulating options, plus Properties, Quick adjustments, and Effects.

## Find

Options provided by the Find tab include a wide range of filters such as date taken, people, rated, tags, flagged, and file details.

## Create

Users looking to do something with their pictures will appreciate the options on the Create tab. These are grouped into three sections – **Tools**, **Share**, and **Publish**.

**Hot tip**

On the Create tab you will find a **Panorama** option that lets you stitch a series of photos together to create one wide panoramic image.

## View

The View tab provides various viewing options, plus image details, ratings, media type, and more.

# Edit photos

**1** Double-click the image in Photo Gallery and check that the **Edit** tab is selected

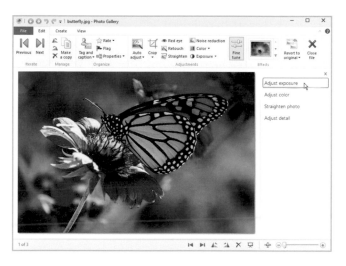

The software provided with your camera gives similar facilities to Photo Gallery. For more powerful and professional editing, use a program such as Adobe Photoshop.

**2** Select **Fine Tune**, and click **Adjust Exposure**

**3** Slide pointers either way until you get the desired effect

Successive changes may degrade the image, so you might want to click **Revert to original** to undo changes that proved unhelpful, and start over.

**4** To keep the revised image, select **Close File** and changes are automatically saved back into the folder

## ...cont'd

At any time, even after saving the changed image and closing the file, you can still retrieve the original picture.

**5** From Photo Gallery, Edit the picture and select **Revert to original**

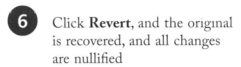

**6** Click **Revert**, and the original is recovered, and all changes are nullified

You can check the contents of the **Original Images** folder where the initial copies of images are stored:

**1** Select the **File** tab for Photo Gallery and select **Options** then click the **Originals** tab

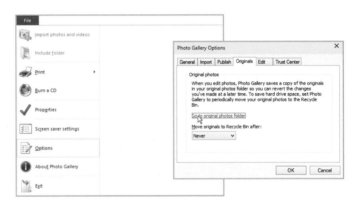

**2** Click **Go to original photos folder**, and click the Address bar to show the file path for the folder

# Print photos

**1** Open Photo Gallery and select pictures to print, using **Ctrl** or **Shift** to select multiple files

**2** Select the **File** tab, select **Print**, then click the **Print** button

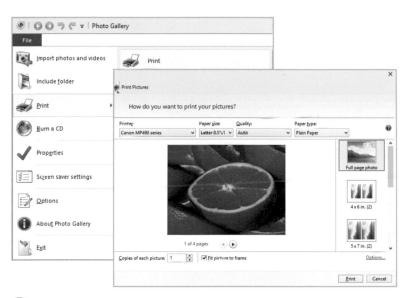

If you select Print, **Order prints...** Windows will access the internet to locate online print services in your region.

**3** The default is to print one picture per page. Scroll down to view the variety of layouts offered

**4** Check the print Quality, Paper size, and Paper type, then confirm the Printer selection and click **Print**

# Movies & TV app

As with photo viewers, Windows 10 provides two video players – the traditional Windows Media Player and the **Movies & TV** app. The new **Movies & TV** video app is what we're going to look at here. We're assuming at this point that you're signed in to the PC with a Microsoft account.

**1** Open the app by clicking the **Movies & TV** item on the Start menu. If you don't have any videos in your Videos folder, the screen below prompts you to add some

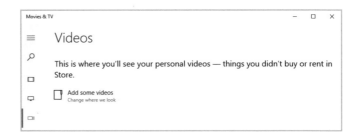

**2** Click **Change where we look** then click the + button to specify a folder other than the default Videos folder

**3** Icons will then appear for each video at your specified location – click any icon to start playing that video

Only videos placed in the Videos folder will be accessible from the **Movies & TV** app initially.

The **Movies & TV** app is a new Universal Windows App in Windows 10.

You will need to be signed in with a Microsoft account to rent or buy videos.

**4** Play, Pause, Previous, and Next controls can be accessed from the app bar at the bottom of the app window

The **Movies & TV** app isn't just about your personal videos, though. If you click the ⬜ Movies button or the 🖵 TV button on the app window you will be offered a selection of movies or television shows that you may buy or rent.

Trailers are available for most movies.

# Movie Maker

Microsoft's Essentials software suite provides a program called Movie Maker. With this, it is possible to create and edit movies.

**1** Open the program by typing "movie maker" in the Taskbar Search box and selecting it from the results. Click **Add videos and photos** on the menu bar, browse to your video clip, select it and click **Open**

**2** On the menu bar click **Video Tools**, **Edit**

From here, you can set a new start point or finish point, split the video or trim sections out of the video. When you've finished:

**3** Select the **File** tab and select **Save project as**

**4** Amend the name and click **Save**

# Create a movie from photos

Movie Maker can be used to give a professional appearance to your photos by adding transitions and effects, music and voice-overs, titles and credits. When finished, you can save the photos as a movie, and write it to DVD to watch it on the TV, or email it to friends and family, or share it on the web.

You start with your imported collections of photos.

**1** Open **Photo Gallery**, select the folder and choose the items you want to include in your movie

**2** Select the **Create** tab and click the **Movie** button

**3** A new project called "My Movie" is generated as a slide show, with a delay of seven seconds between slides, and initially with no transition between slides or other effects

Don't forget

You can include video clips (edited as desired), as well as photos to create your movie.

Hot tip

To select a range of photos, click the first one, press **Shift** and then click the last. To select individual photos, hold down the **Ctrl** key as you click. To select all the photos in the folder, press **Ctrl + A**.

253

Don't forget

Move the mouse pointer over any slide to see the settings that are currently applied.

IMG_0349.JPG
Duration: 00:07.00
Transition: None
Pan and zoom: None
Effects: None

254

**...cont'd**

**4** Move the mouse pointer over one of the **AutoMovie** themes, and you'll see the effects immediately displayed

There are seven themes – Default, Contemporary, Cinematic, Fade, Pan and Zoom, Black and White, and Sepia. Review each in turn to decide which is most effective.

**5** Click the desired theme to apply it to your movie

**6** Click the Play button to run the movie

**7** Click **Preview full screen** (or press **F11**) to see the movie full size

**8** Drag the slider to move ahead, or click the Pause button to pause the movie

**9** Select **Video Tools**, **Edit** to adjust the time delay between slides

# Save and publish your movie

**1** Select the **File** tab and select **Save movie**, then choose a setting, e.g. high definition (1920 x 1080)

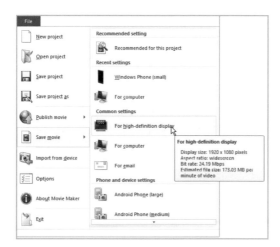

You can save the movie in the format best suited to the device where it will be played. There are formats for TV, computer and mobile devices such as Windows Phone, and lower-resolution versions suitable for email.

**2** Choose a location and video format type to include copies of all the pictures, video clips and audio files

The estimated file size is shown in the Tooltip when you hover over the menu's **Recommended setting** for each device.

**3** Select **Publish Movie** to prepare the movie for the internet

**4** Save the movie on your OneDrive or select a service, e.g. Facebook, YouTube or Flickr

Select **Add a Plug-in** to find other web services that may be made available for publishing movies online.

**5** Click **Exit** to end Movie Maker

# Photo apps in the Store

If the Photos app described on pages 236-237 does not meet your requirements, a large selection of other photo apps are available in the Windows Store.

**1** Open the **Store** from the Start menu

**2** Type "photo" into the Search box then hit **Enter**

**3** Select the **Apps** filter from the "Refine" options

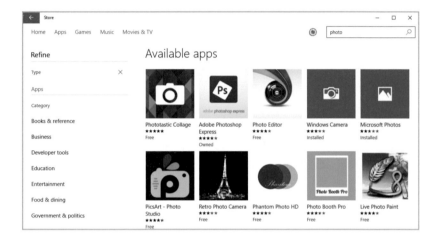

Many of these apps provide image-related options other than just organizing and sharing. For example, you will find apps that:

- Map pictures to specific locations – i.e. geotagging

- Create photo albums

- Provide editing tools

- Provide camera functions

- Import pictures from other devices

- Create slide shows

# 15 Windows games

Traditional Windows games such as Freecell Solitaire are included with Windows 10 and there are a huge number of games available in the Windows Store. We take a look at some popular ones.

# Games support

Gaming has always been a very popular use of computers and, in recognition of this, Windows operating systems have traditionally provided a selection of games with which users can amuse themselves.

However, with Windows 8 no games were included with the operating system by default, but some games are bundled with the Windows 10 operating system. The Microsoft Solitaire Collection is available on the Start menu and contains a selection of popular traditional Windows card games re-done as modern apps.

If you want to play more games in Windows 10 you can download them from the Windows Store.

Not all the traditional Windows games are available in Universal Windows App versions.

Surprisingly, the standard edition of the Microsoft Solitaire Collection supplied with Windows 10 now contains advertisements. You can, however, upgrade to the Premium edition to remove the adverts and receive other game benefits. The Menu button produces a menu that includes an **Upgrade to Premium** option.

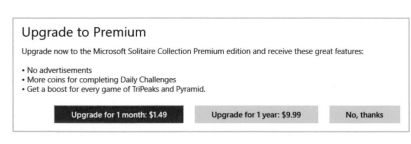

**...cont'd**

Freecell is, perhaps, the most popular Solitaire card game in the Microsoft Solitaire Collection.

**1** Open the Microsoft Solitaire Collection app then click on the **Freecell** tile to begin the game

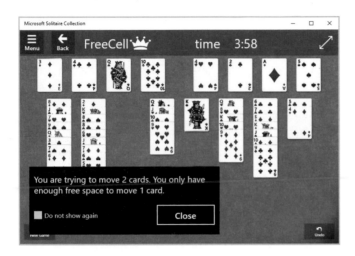

259

Hot tip

As shown here, you are notified if you attempt to make an invalid move.

**2** Click the Menu button then choose the **? How to play** option to see the game instructions

**3** Arrange the cards to create four stacks of card suits

**4** On completion you will see your game statistics

Hot tip

If you quit a game before completion it is counted as a loss in your game statistics.

# Candy Crush Saga

Windows 10 includes the highly addictive and hugely popular Candy Crush Saga match-3 game as a Universal Windows App.

 Launch the Candy Crush Saga app from the Start menu then click on the **Play** button to begin the game

2 Match three or more candies to meet the target score within the limited number of available moves

3 On success you will see and hear the phrase "Sugar Crush" then the game proceeds to the next level

# Xbox app

The new Xbox app on Windows 10 now makes Xbox features available on PCs and tablets. It allows you to keep track of friends on Xbox Live, record game play clips using its Game DVR, join in an Xbox One multi-player game without leaving your desk, and easily acquire Windows 10 games.

1. Launch the Xbox app from the Start menu then click on the 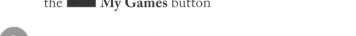 **My Games** button

2. Now, click on the **Find games in the Store** link

3. Choose a game, such as "Farmville 2 : Country Escape"

4. When the game is installed it appears in your "My games" list with a **Play** button you can click to launch that game

The Xbox app is a new Universal Windows App on Windows 10.

Xbox One consoles can stream games and media to your Windows 10 PC using the Xbox app. See pages 284-285 for details.

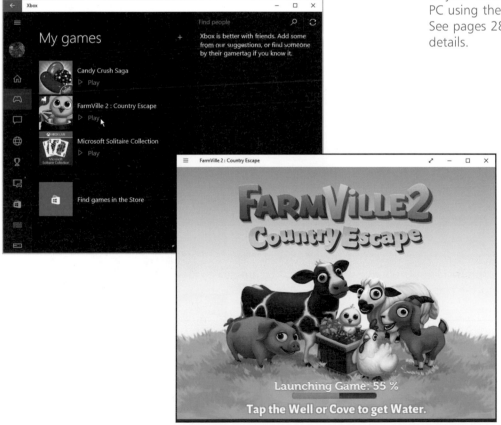

# Games in the Windows Store

The Windows Store contains some 20 different categories of software. Let's see what it has to offer to gamers.

The Store app is a new Universal Windows App on Windows 10.

**1** On the Home page is a menu of top categories – Apps, Games, Music, Movies & TV. Click on the **Games** item

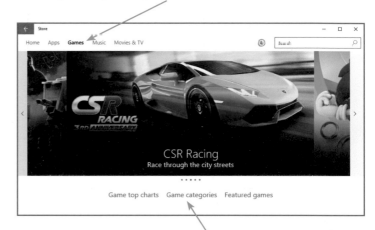

**2** Now, click on the **Game categories** link at the bottom

**3** Scroll down the left panel to select a category or choose from the list of filters to narrow your search, such as **Top Free**

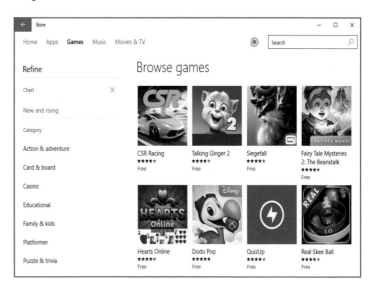

# Explore Pinball FX2

We'll take a look at some of the free games available in the Windows Store. One of the most popular is Pinball FX2, which can be played on a Windows 10 PC, on an Xbox, and online.

**1** Go to the Windows Store and type "pinball" into the Search box. Pinball FX2 will appear in the listed search results. Click to **Install** the app

Hot tip

As you click on each pinball table tile in the left panel, an overview of that table is given in the right panel.

**2** On the game's Home page you will see several tiles under **My Collection**, each of which represents a different pinball table. Some tiles are grayed out, which means they are not active, so select an active table such as "Mars"

**3** Next, choose to **Buy Now** or **Play free with ads** to launch the selected table

Hot tip

Many of the options in Pinball FX2 relate to online play.

**4** Click the "hamburger" button at the top-left of the window and select **Settings** to see a list of options including **How to Play**, **Video**, **Audio**, and **Controls**

...cont'd

**5** From the Settings options choose the **Controls** item to see the default set of controls provided. For example, the left flipper is operated with the left **Shift** key. However, if the default key for any particular control doesn't suit you, you can click on the down-arrow against the control and choose an alternative key from the drop-down list that appears

**6** Settings provides three main options – **Audio**, **Video** and **Graphics**. On the right we see the audio settings. Slide the bar to adjust volume controls for different types of sound used in the game

**7** When you are ready to play, you can choose from **Single Player** or **Hotseat** mode. The latter enables two, three or four players to play a game

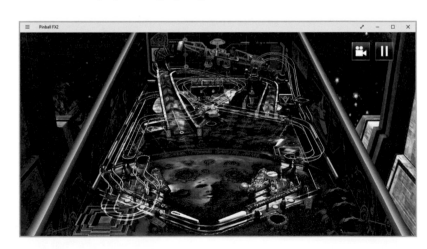

# PuzzleTouch

PuzzleTouch is all about jigsaws and is a game that will appeal to jigsaw buffs and children. A number of jigsaws are supplied with the program but it is also possible to create them from your own pictures.

1 The Homepage presents sets of puzzles, some of which are free and others which have to be paid for

2 Click on a jigsaw to open the set

If you lose your way in the jigsaw, right-click on the screen. From the app bar that opens, click Sneak peek to see a complete picture of the jigsaw.

3 You will now see all the puzzles in the set. Select the one you want and in the next screen you can choose the level of difficulty

To access the more advanced features of PuzzleTouch you will have to pay.

4 Complete the puzzle by arranging the pieces

# Mahjong Solitaire

Microsoft Mahjong is a solitaire game that can be played on the PC, a tablet or online. The purpose of the game is to remove all the tiles from the board by matching them with identical tiles.

**1** The Homepage shows a number of sections – choose from **Puzzle**, **Daily Challenges**, **Awards**, **Leaderboards**, **Statistics** and **How to Play**

**2** If you are new to Mahjong, click **How to Play**. The various options will tell you everything you need to know to play the game

**3** When you are ready to play, click **Choose new puzzle**

**4** Select your skill level. Initially, you are restricted to the first game in each level – when you have completed this, you can move up to the next one

**5** Click pairs of matching tiles to remove them from the board. Clear the board completely to win

If you play a lot, the **Statistics** section on the Homepage will be interesting.

Microsoft Mahjong has been redesigned as a Universal Windows App for Windows 10.

If you get stuck or just want to take a break, open the app bar. Clicking **Hint** will reveal a matching pair. Click **Pause** to stop for a while.

# Minesweeper

Microsoft Minesweeper is another solitaire game. The purpose is to uncover all empty squares in a grid while avoiding the mines.

**1** On the Homepage, select your skill level – **Easy**, **Medium**, or **Expert**. There is also a **Custom** option, which allows you to set your own degree of difficulty

**2** At the top of the screen are a timer and the number of mines on the board

**3** As you reveal empty squares, numbers appear on them. These indicate how many mines are touching that square and thus help you determine which squares are mined

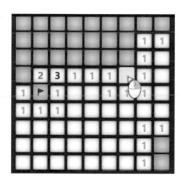

**4** If you hit a mine, that's it – the game is over

**5** When all the empty squares are uncovered, you win

267

The more difficult the skill level you choose, the more squares and mines there are on the board.

Microsoft Minesweeper has been redesigned as a Universal Windows App for Windows 10.

Right-clicking on a square that you suspect contains a mine will put a warning flag on the square.

# Compatibility Center

So far, we've looked at ways of acquiring games via Microsoft sources, i.e. the Windows Store and the Games app. One of the advantages of doing it this way is that the game is guaranteed to be compatible with Windows 10. If you're thinking of buying a game from a different source it will be a good move to check out the game before paying for it. This can be done at the Microsoft Compatibility website.

**1** Open your web browser and go to **microsoft.com/en-us/windows/compatibility**

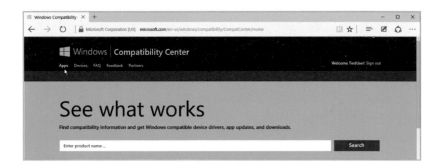

**2** Click **Apps** on the toolbar then select **PC gaming**

**3** Search for your game and see if it is listed. If it is, it will be categorized as either ⊘ Compatible, ⊗ Not compatible, ⑦ No Info, or ⊕ Action Recommended

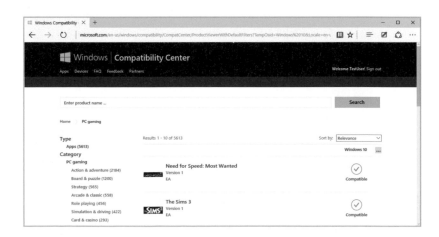

# 16 Music and sound

The sound card in your computer lets you play music, listen to internet radio or play videos with audio tracks. You can also share your media files with others on your network. With a microphone you can dictate to your computer. You need suitable software for which Windows 10 provides the Groove Music app and Windows Media Player.

# Audio connections

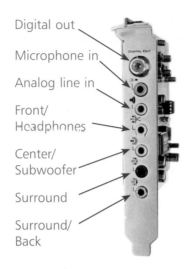

Digital out

Microphone in

Analog line in

Front/
Headphones

Center/
Subwoofer

Surround

Surround/
Back

Desktop and laptop computers are equipped with audio facilities that can produce high-fidelity audio playback. On desktop machines, the soundcard can provide the connections for various types of speakers, ranging from simple stereo speakers to multiple speaker sets with surround sound.

For a laptop or notebook the options are often limited to microphone and headset sockets, though some laptops include more sophisticated connections, such as the SPDIF (Sony Philips Digital Interface) used for home theater connections.

You may have speakers attached to your computer, or built into the casing of portable computers. To check the configuration:

**1** Go to the Control Panel, Hardware and Sound, Sound, and then **Manage audio devices** (from the Sound section)

**2** Select **Speakers** and click **Configure**, then select your configuration, click **Next** and follow the prompts to **Finish and save** the speaker specification

**Hot tip**

On a desktop computer, the soundcard may be incorporated into the motherboard or provided as a separate adapter card, as shown here.

**Don't forget**

The configurations listed depend on the features of your soundcard. To check the operation of each of your speakers, click the **Test** button. Note that some software will only use the main speakers, especially with tracks that are two-channel stereo only.

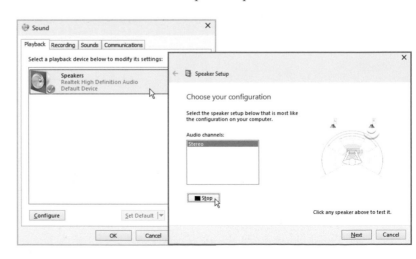

# Groove Music app

The Groove Music app in Windows 10 not only allows you to play your own music; it also lets you access a huge range of artists and genres from the Microsoft Store.

**1** The first thing to do is place all your music in the **My Music** folder. It will then be accessible in the app

**2** Open the Groove Music app and click the buttons to see your music listed as ▣ **Albums**, ⋀ **Artists**, or ♪ **Songs**

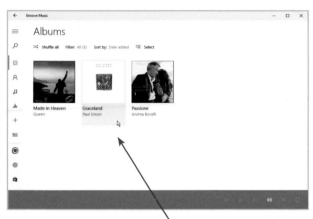

**3** Click a music tile to open an Album

**4** Double-click a music track to play it, or click the track to select it then click the Play button below the album title

**5** Explore the playback controls at the bottom of the screen

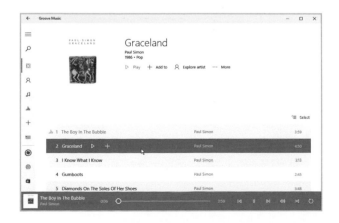

**Hot tip**

You can pin a music track to the Start menu by clicking the **More** icon at the right just under the track name.

The Groove Music app is a great new Universal Windows App on Windows 10.

**Hot tip**

The **+ Add to** option allows you to create playlists by adding tracks.

# Download media files

Due to the quantity and variety of music available through the Microsoft Store (accessible via the Groove Music app) you may find your own music taking a back seat.

**1** Open Groove Music and click the ▣ **Store** button

**2** In the Store window that opens, search for an album, artist, or song. For example, the artist "Caro Emerald"

**Hot tip**

You can use the Search box in the Groove Music app to find music you have on your computer.

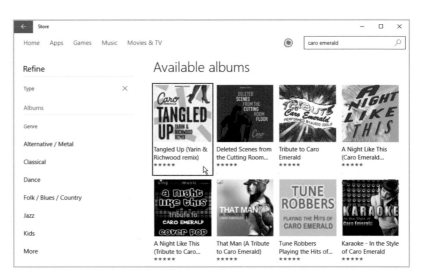

**3** Click an item of interest to discover more. For example, choose an album from the search results

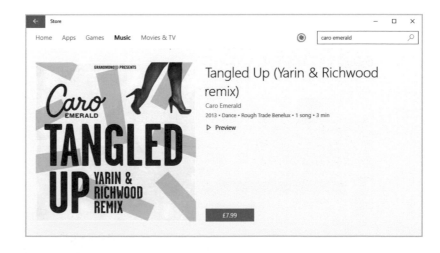

**4** Click the **Preview** button to hear a snippet off the album

**5** You can buy the album using the button showing the album price, or scroll down for alternative items

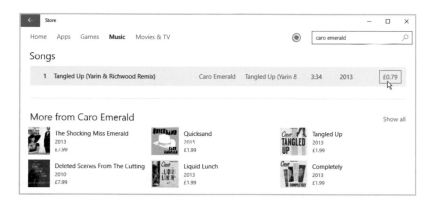

Click the artist name in the songs list to see information on the artist.

**6** Individual songs may be available from this artist that you can buy by clicking the button showing the song price

**7** You are then asked to enter your Microsoft account password or PIN code to verify your identity

**8** Finally, you are asked to choose a payment method to complete your purchase

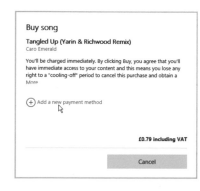

# Windows Media Player

Windows Media Player (WMP) has long been one of the best applications in Windows and the version supplied in Windows 10 is no exception. Windows Media Player can handle just about any media-related task.

Windows Media Player supports an extensive list of media codecs. This ensures it will play most types of media.

These include:

- Playing music

- Viewing your pictures

- Playing video

- Streaming media on home networks

- Ripping music

- Burning media to disks

- Downloading media files

- Listening to music on the internet

- Creating playlists

- Synchronizing media on the user's devices

- Accessing online media sources to rent or buy music

Windows Media Player features brightness, contrast, saturation and hue adjustment controls. It also provides a 10-band graphic equalizer with presets and an SRS WOW audio post-processing system.

# Play CDs

Assuming you have a CD/DVD drive on your computer, you can use your soundcard and speakers to play an audio CD.

**1** Insert the disk in the drive, and AutoPlay asks what you want to do

**2** Select **Play audio CD** Windows Media Player

The CD begins to play, as an unknown album and showing no details other than the track numbers and their durations.

If you are connected to the internet, Windows Media Player will locate and download information about the CD, and display the album and track titles. You can also change the Visualization to display the album cover image.

Hot tip

Click the box **Always do this for audio CDs** and the selected option is carried out automatically in future, whenever an audio CD is identified.

Hot tip

Right-click the window and select **Visualization** to choose the effects to display, for example Album art (cover image).

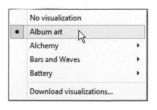

# Copy CD tracks

You can copy songs from an audio CD, an action known as "Ripping" the CD, where Media Player makes file copies that get added to your library. To specify the type of copy:

**1** Right-click the Media Player window and select **More options**

**2** Click the **Rip Music** tab

**3**

Set Format as one of the Windows Media Audio (WMA) file formats, or select the MP3 format for greater flexibility

**4** Select the bit rate – higher bit rates will give much better quality but will use up more disk space

**5** Click the **Rip CD** button to extract and compress the tracks

**6** The tracks are added to your Music library, and stored with a folder for each artist, and a sub-folder for each of their albums

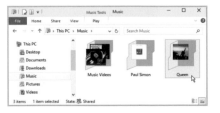

276

# Media Player library

**1** When the CD has been copied, select **Go to Library** (or click the **Switch to Library** button)

**2** Select **Music** to display the Music library, by artist and track

**3** Select **Artist, Genre**, or **Album** to group all the associated albums by your preference

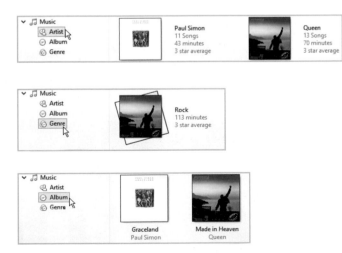

Windows Media Player library displays content of the current user's Music, Videos and Pictures libraries, plus links to the libraries of users who are online or HomeGroup members.

Click Organize, **Customize navigation pane**, to group music by other properties, such as year, rating or composer.

Double-click a group to display the individual tracks that it contains, arranged by album.

# Internet radio

The ability to listen to internet radio stations is no longer available in Windows Media Player.

The solution, therefore, is to download a third-party program. Go to the Windows Store, and search for "internet radio". You'll see a number of results. One we have tried and can recommend is TuneIn Radio, shown below:

Approximately 60,000 stations worldwide can be listened to on TuneIn Radio.

The app knows your geographical location, so when you start it the Home screen will show stations in your vicinity, together with stations recently selected. Click on these to open those stations, or browse available stations by clicking any of the filter buttons.

1   Browse by location through Europe, UK, London, then click on the **BBC Radio 2** tile to listen to that station

You can also search for podcasts of pre-recorded audio programs that are available on the internet.

2   Right-click on the screen, to open the app bar, then click the **Add** button to add the station to your favorites

3   Click the **Pin** button to pin the station to your Start menu for frequent use

# Home media streaming

Anything that you can play in Windows Media Player, you can share with other computers and devices on your home network.

**1** Open Windows Media Player, select the Library view and click the **Stream** button

**2** This should show **Allow Internet access to home media**, **Allow remote control**, **Automatically allow devices to play my media**, and **More streaming options**

With these settings, your Windows Media Player will have access to **Other Libraries**, in particular the media libraries that were shared when the computers on your network joined the HomeGroup.

**3** Select one of the computer/user combinations to see what's available – in this example Music, Videos, Pictures, Recorded TV, and Playlists

**4** Expand the Music available on the other computer, and you will be able to play these on your computer

Hot tip

These are the default settings for Windows Media Player and HomeGroup, but if necessary, turn on media streaming, and select the options to **Allow remote control** and **Automatically allow devices to play my media**.

Don't forget

You may have to wait a few moments as the list of contents is transferred from the other computer.

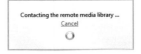
Contacting the remote media library ...
Cancel

# Play to device or computer

You can also use media streaming to play items from your computer on another computer or device on the network.

**1** Start by turning on the networked device or start Windows Media Player on the target computer

**2** Open Windows Media Player and drag a track from your Music onto the **Playlist**

**3** Hit the **Pause** button to stop playback on your computer

**4** Click the device icon's **Play to** button and select the playback target

**5** Windows Media Player contacts the device and initiates playing the selected media files. You can then control the operation from either computer

# Dictate to your computer

One way to interact with your computer is to simply tell it what you want to do, with Windows Speech Recognition.

**1** Go to Control Panel, Ease of Access, **Speech Recognition**

Speech Recognition is supported in all editions of Windows 10 and is available in the English, German, French, Spanish, Japanese and Chinese languages.

**2** Select the type of microphone that you'll be using, a headset microphone being best for speech recognition

**3** Follow the advice to position the microphone effectively then read text aloud so the microphone volume can be set

The Wizard takes you through all of the steps that are required to set up Speech Recognition on your computer.

## ...cont'd

**4** Following the prompts, choose **Manual** or **Voice activation** mode, and run Speech Recognition when Windows starts

**5** Click **Start Tutorial** to learn about the basic features and to train your computer to better understand you

When you start Windows, Speech Recognition will start up and switch itself into **Sleeping mode**, or **Turn listening off** (depending on the activation mode you have set).

**1** If it is Off, right-click the Speech Recognition bar and select **Sleep**

**2** Say "Start listening" (or click the button on the bar)

**3** Say "What can I say?" to view the Speech Reference Card

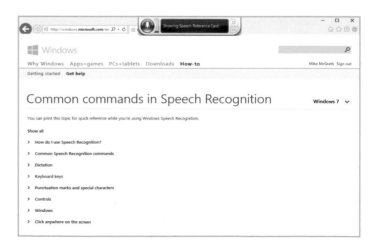

# Text to speech

You can let the computer talk to you, using the text to speech facilities of the Narrator application.

**1** Select **Narrator** from the Windows **Ease of Access** group in **All apps** on the Start menu

**2** Narrator starts up and you can configure the main settings to set up the program

From the Ease of Access Center select **Use the computer without a display** and choose **Turn on Narrator**, to have the program start automatically when you start Windows.

**3** Click **Voice** to adjust the voice settings. Adjust the speed, volume and pitch to suit your preferences and maybe select a different voice. Narrator will read the contents of the screen, including the text content of programs such as Notepad, WordPad, and Windows Help and Support

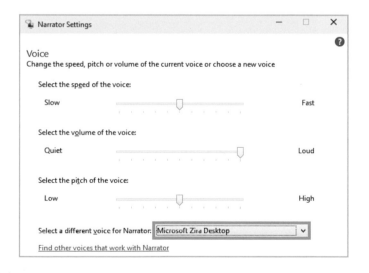

Narrator does not read the text content of all programs, so its value is somewhat limited in comparison with Speech Recognition.

**4** Click the Help icon at the top-right of the narrator window to get some useful hints

# Streaming Xbox Music

If you have an Xbox console on the same network you can stream games, video, and music to your PC:

**1** Turn on your Xbox console and controller then sign in using your Microsoft account

**2** On your PC, launch the Xbox app from the Start menu then sign in using the same Microsoft account

You must sign in to both the Xbox console and Xbox app using the same Microsoft account.

**3** Click the **Connect** button in the left toolbar when a green dot shows that the app recognizes your Xbox

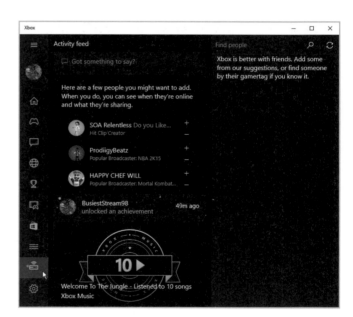

The Xbox app is a great new Universal Windows App on Windows 10 that brings Xbox gaming to your PC.

The first time you run this program, you may see Get Started setup. Select **Express** for the recommended options, or **Custom** to personalize the settings.

**4** Select the Xbox console to connect, if more than one is listed, then click the **Stream** link

**5** Your Xbox console screen now loads in the Xbox app

**Hot tip**

Xbox Music is a subscription service but you can try it free on a limited-time trial basis.

**6** Connect an Xbox controller to your PC using a USB to micro-USB cable, so you can interact with the Xbox app

**7** Use the Xbox controller to select the Xbox Music tile and choose an item to play

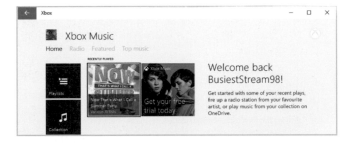

**8** Your selection will then begin to play on your PC

**Beware**

To use a wireless Xbox controller after using it on your PC you will have to re-sync the controller, using the console's sync button or a USB cable.

# Recording

To record stuff on your computer, you need a working microphone and the Microsoft Voice Recorder app that is included with the Windows 10 operating system:

The Voice Recorder app is a new Universal Windows App on Windows 10.

**1** Open the **Voice Recorder** app from the Start menu then click its microphone icon to begin recording – this starts the timer

On the playback screen use the ⊞ **Trim** button to edit recording length and the △ **Share** button to email your recording.

**2** Click the icon again to stop recording – the recording is saved as a file in your **Documents, Sound recordings** folder and gets added to the Recording list in the app screen

**3** Click an item in the **Recording** list to select it – the app screen changes to display the playback controls

You can use the ✎ **Rename** button to give your recording a descriptive title and the 🗑 **Delete** button to remove recordings.

**4** Click the ▷ play button to hear the voice recording – the play button changes so you may pause playback

# 17 Devices and printers

*Learn how to manage your devices in Windows 10. You can add various types of printers and scanners to your PC, and Windows usually provides the drivers needed to manage the devices.*

# PC settings – devices

Windows has always had a device management utility called Device Manager with which users can manage the devices on their computer. The Windows 10 interface provides a much simpler option that helps users to add and remove devices, troubleshoot device issues, and more.

**1** On the Start menu, select **Settings**

**2** In the Settings window, choose **Devices**

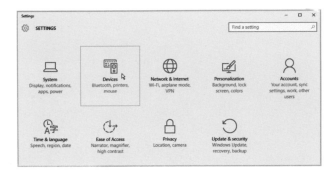

**3** Now, choose **Connected devices** and you will see a list of all the devices connected to your computer

**4** Left-clicking on a device reveals an option to remove the device

**5** Clicking the **Remove device** option uninstalls the device safely

**Hot tip**

You can also manage your devices from the Control Panel by clicking **Devices and Printers**.

The Settings menu is new in Windows 10. Here you change most of your PC's settings. More advanced tweaks may require Control Panel.

**Beware**

It is important to remove devices from your PC in the correct way. Simply disconnecting them can cause problems.

# Add a device

These days, most hardware devices are very easy to install. Simply connect it to the computer and switch on. Windows will see the device as a new addition to the system, locate the drivers from its in-built driver database, and then install it.

Things don't always happen as they should, though. If you experience any problems, try the following:

**1** Open Devices as described on the previous page

**2** Check if the device you are trying to install is listed under Devices. If it is, you may see a message that explains the problem, as shown below:

**3** If you don't see your device in the list, click **Add a Device** at the top of the screen. Windows will now look for recently-added devices

**4** You will see a list of the devices Windows has found

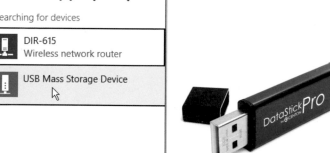

**5** If the problem device is in the list, click on it and then follow the prompts

**6** The device should then appear correctly in the list of connected devices

The most common reason for Windows not seeing a device is that it simply hasn't been switched on.

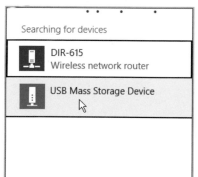

Windows 10 will first try to find a driver for the device within the system, as many device drivers are bundled with the operating system. If none are found locally, Windows will try to find a driver online if you are connected to the internet. If that too fails, you may have to visit the device maker's website and search for a suitable driver to install manually, following their instructions.

# Control Panel devices

Device management can also be carried out via the Control Panel, if you prefer.

**1** Go to the Control Panel and click **Devices and Printers** to see icons for all the devices on your computer

The Control Panel offers more management options.

**2** Click **Add a Device** to install a new hardware device. If the device being added is a printer, click **Add a printer**

**3** Left-click on a device to see its Properties, or right-click on a device to see a menu with options for that device

**4** Here, we see right-click options for a printer. Other devices will have different options

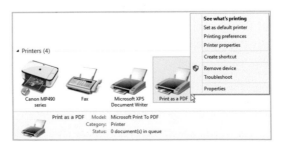

# Update device driver

To check the date for your printer driver:

**1** Go to Control Panel and open **Devices and Printers**. Right-click the printer and select **Properties**, **Hardware** tab, **Properties** and, finally, the **Driver** tab

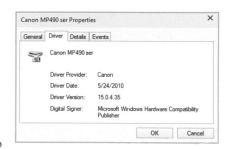

**2** In the example above, the driver is dated 5/24/2010, so it is well out of date

**3** To check for the latest driver, visit the manufacturer's website, e.g. go to **canon.com** then choose your region and select **Support & Drivers**

**4** Enter the device's model name and model number in the Search box and click **GO** to look for an appropriate driver

**5** When the results indicate that there is a more recent driver that supports this printer, click the **Download** button to grab the installer for that driver

Normally, Windows will have an up-to-date driver for the printer, but this is not always the case, so if in doubt, check with the manufacturer.

Follow a similar process at the website for your printer's manufacturer. Search **Support** for possible updates to the driver.

## ...cont'd

**6** Click the **Download** button and follow the prompts to save the driver installation file on your system

83% of mp68-win-mp490-1_05-ea24.exe downloaded     3 sec remaining     Pause   Cancel   View downloads   ×

**Don't forget**

You can run the program immediately, but if you save it to disk and then run the program, you can retain a copy for backup purposes.

**Hot tip**

You may be required to accept terms and conditions, and be asked if this is to become the default printer.

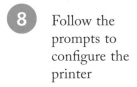

**Hot tip**

The printer will now be managed by the up-to-date driver software.

**7** Run the installation program to start Setup

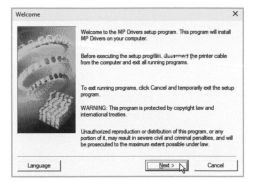

**8** Follow the prompts to configure the printer

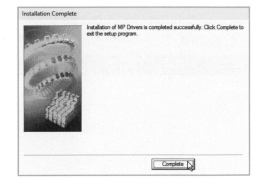

**9** The new driver will be added to Devices and Printers

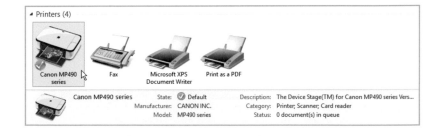

# Wireless printer

**1** Go to the Control Panel, Hardware and Sound, and click **View devices and printers**. Click **Add a Printer**

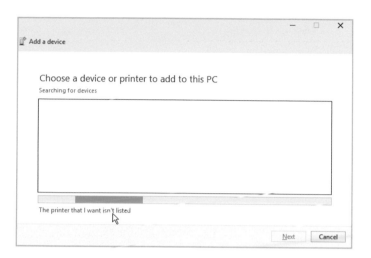

**2** Windows will attempt to find your networked printer. If it does, select it and click **Next** to install it. If it doesn't, however, you will see a blank dialog box. In this case, click **The printer that I want isn't listed**

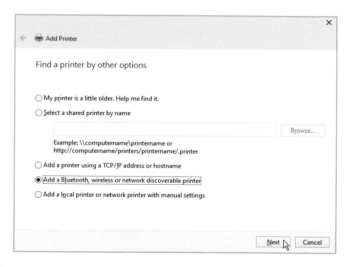

If you have a wireless printer set up on your network, you can add it to your Windows 10 computer.

**3** Select **Add a Bluetooth, wireless or network discoverable printer** and click **Next**

## ...cont'd

**Don't forget**

You may also be prompted to enter a PIN code to configure WPS (Wi-Fi Protected Setup). Refer to your printer manual on how to find the WPS PIN code for your wireless printer.

**4** This time, Windows should find the printer. Select it and click **Next** to install the printer

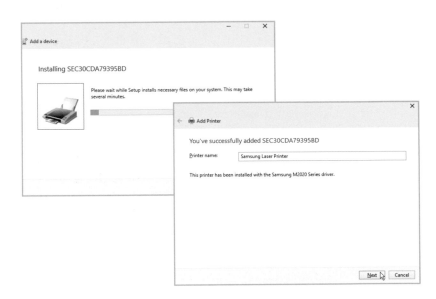

**Beware**

Adding a new printer often results in a change to the default printer, so you need to check this and ensure the right printer is specified.

**5** Give the printer a meaningful name, then click **Next** to see it added to the list of printers on your computer

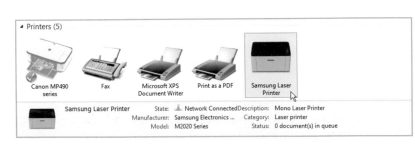

# Virtual printers

You may have some items in **Devices and Printers** that are not physical devices but are software programs that act as virtual printers. To see how these could be used:

Fax    Microsoft XPS Document Writer    Print as a PDF

1  Open a document with text and graphics in WordPad

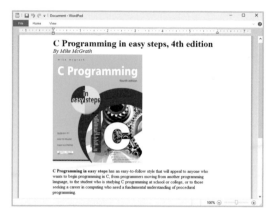

WordPad is chosen here since it supports text and graphics, but you could use almost any Windows program that prints.

2  Open the File menu and click **Print**

3  Choose one of the virtual printers, for example "Microsoft Print to PDF", as shown below. Click the **Print** button

4  You'll be asked to confirm the location and file name, and a PDF version of the document is saved

## ...cont'd

Alternatively:

**1** Select **Microsoft XPS Document Writer** as the printer

**2** Provide a name, and save in Open XPS document format

Some printer drivers pass control on to other programs:

**1** Select **Fax** as the printer and Fax Setup is started

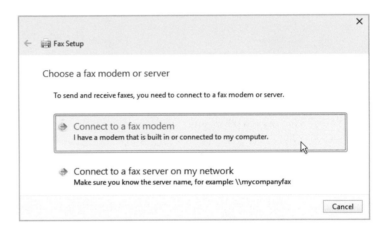

**2** Choose your setup, then complete the cover page, and send your document as a **.tif** image file

If you are not ready for Fax Setup, click **Cancel** and you can create a fax and save it as a draft to send later.

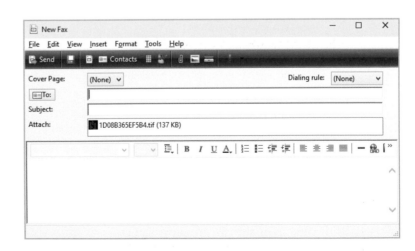

# Generic/text only printer

To create a generic/text only printer:

**1** Open **Devices and Printers**, click **Add a printer** and then click **The printer that I want isn't listed**

**2** Now, select **Add a local printer or network printer with manual settings**

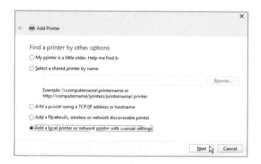

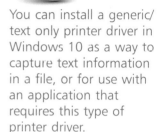

You can install a generic/ text only printer driver in Windows 10 as a way to capture text information in a file, or for use with an application that requires this type of printer driver.

**3** Select **Use an existing port** and choose **FILE: (Print to File)** then click **Next**

**4** In the Manufacturer field, select **Generic** and in the Printers field select **Generic/Text Only**, then click **Next**

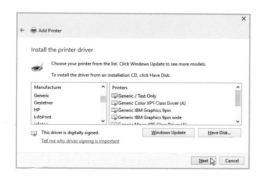

If you are creating support for an old printer, you'd choose the port it uses, **COM1** for example.

## ...cont'd

**5** Accept or amend the suggested name and click **Next**

**6** Select **Do not share this printer** and click **Next**. Ensure the printer is not set as default and, finally, click **Finish**

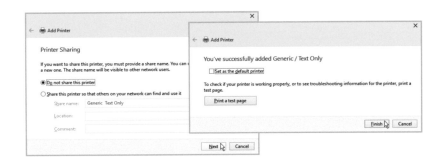

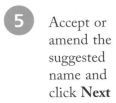
**7** The printer is added to **Devices and Printers**

To check out the operation of this printer:

**1** Create a simple plain text document using Notepad

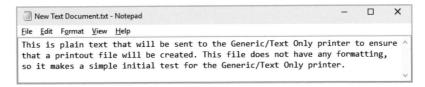

**2** Select **Print** and choose the **Generic/Text Only** printer

**3** Provide the file name (type **.prn**) and click **OK**

# Add a scanner

You can install a scanner to the **Devices and Printers** folder.

**1** To install a USB-connected scanner such as the Canon CanoScan, insert the USB cable and switch on

**2** If the driver is available, the scanner will be installed. If the driver is missing, an **Action Center** error message may be displayed, helping you to download the driver

To test the operation of this scanner:

**1** Right-click on the scanner in **Devices and Printers** then choose **Scan Properties** to open the properties dialog

**2** Select the **General** tab, then hit the **Test Scanner** button

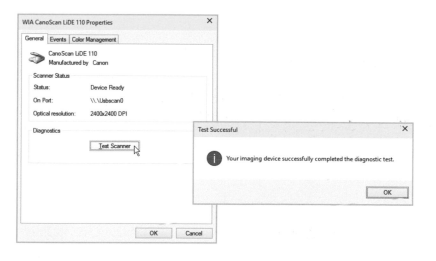

Windows 10 will have the drivers for many scanners, but may not include older devices.

Windows checks its compatibility database and identifies where to find the missing driver.

# Using the scanner

There are several ways to grab images from your scanner, such as with the traditional **Windows Fax and Scan** program. Windows also provides a new easy-to-use free app for this purpose that is simply called "Scan".

**1** Connect your scanner and insert an item to be scanned

**2** Go to the Store and get the free Windows **Scan** app

**3** Launch the **Scan** app from the Start menu then click the **Show more** link to reveal all scanning options

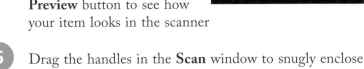

**4** Choose your preferences for file type, etc. then click the **Preview** button to see how your item looks in the scanner

**5** Drag the handles in the **Scan** window to snugly enclose your item

**6** Click the **Scan** button to save the image as a file of your specified type, color mode, resolution, and location

Image editing programs, such as Paint, provide the ability to import an image directly into the program for manipulation.

**1** Connect your scanner and insert an item to be scanned

**2** Go to the Start menu and launch the **Paint** program

**3** Click **File**, **From scanner or camera**, to open the scanner dialog box

**4** Choose your option preferences

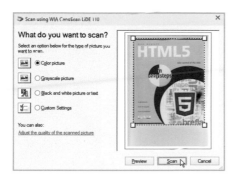

**Hot tip**

Some scanners are supplied with OCR (optical character recognition) software that can read text from a scanned document and save it as a text file.

**5** Click the **Preview** button to see how your item looks in the scanner and adjust the handles if necessary

**6** Click the **Scan** button to import the image into Paint, where you can modify it and save it as an image file

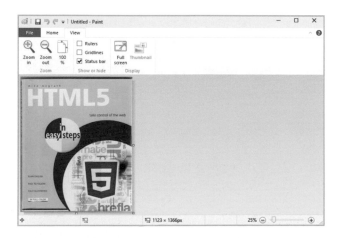

**Don't forget**

The physical size of the imported image is large for high-quality resolution – it is shown here reduced to 25%.

# Add a storage device

Adding a storage device to a Windows 10 computer couldn't be easier – Windows does the hardware configuration for you. In this example we are adding a 2.5" External Hard Disk Drive to the system.

As with most current devices, the drive uses a USB connection. If your device uses USB 3.0, connect it to a USB 3.0 socket (if available) rather than USB 2.0. (USB 3.0 is much faster than USB 2.0 so the drive will perform much better.)

**Beware**

You can run a USB 3.0 device from a USB 2.0 socket but it will not operate at its maximum performance level.

**1** Drive connected to a USB socket

**2** Switch on the drive if required

**3** Windows automatically installs the device (adding any device driver software needed)

**4** Go to **Devices and Printers** to see the device is added

**Hot tip**

If you are unsure which of your USB sockets are USB 3.0, look for any that are colored blue – these are USB 3.0; USB 2.0 are black.

# 18 Networking Windows

If you have more than one computer, even just a laptop and a desktop machine, you can connect them with cables or wirelessly, and share information between the computers. Windows makes it easy to set up and manage the network that you create. This chapter explains all you need to know.

# Create a network

A network consists of several devices that exchange information over a cable or via radio waves. A computer plus internet router forms a small network. If you have other computers, they can be added to share the internet connection and perhaps share data information with each other, creating a larger network.

To be able to connect to the network, each computer requires an Ethernet (wired) network adapter plus cable, or a wireless network adapter. The flow of data between the computers and the router is managed by Windows.

To start a new network using a wired network adapter:

**1** Install a network adapter in the computer (if required)

**2** Start (or restart) the computer and on the Start menu click **Settings** and then the **Network & Internet** icon

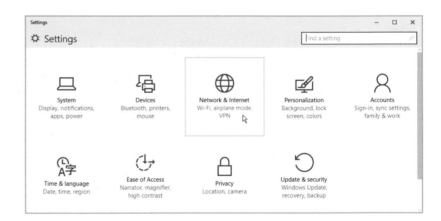

**3** Next, click on the **Ethernet** item in the left pane to see details of wired connections

**4** Now, connect the adapter to the router using a network cable (Ethernet cable)

**5** Windows will then automatically detect and identify the new network

**Don't forget**

Most routers will offer both wired and wireless connections, as well as internet access, or you may have individual devices for each of these functions.

**Hot tip**

There is no built-in option to **Create an ad hoc network** in Windows 10 but you may find third-party tools online for creating ad hoc networks, if you need to do this.

**304**

## ...cont'd

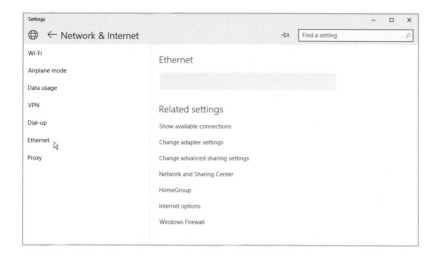

**6** Windows will ask you if you want to turn on network sharing between PCs, and connect to network devices such as printers

**7** Choose **No, don't turn on sharing or connect to devices** for networks in public places (such as coffee shops or airports), or when you don't know or trust the people and devices on the network

**8** Choose **Yes, turn on sharing and connect to devices** for home or work networks, or when you know and trust the people and devices on the network. This setting allows your computer to connect to devices on the network, such as printers

**9** Your new network is created and your computer is connected to it

The first time you connect to a network, you'll be asked if you want to turn on sharing between PCs and connect to network devices such as printers. Your answer automatically sets the appropriate firewall and security settings for the type of network that you connected to.

305

The setting formerly known as network location (Private/Public or Home/Work/Domain) is now called network sharing. You turn this setting on or off as part of the process of connecting to a network.

# Network classification

Two main types of network are possible in Windows 10 – Public and Private. If you are going to get involved in networking, it is important to understand the differences between them.

### Public

A public network is one that is directly connected to the internet. Typical examples include your computer, and airport, coffee shop, and library wireless networks. Because they use public internet Protocol (IP) addresses, devices on these networks are visible to other devices on the same network, and also on other networks.

This has advantages and disadvantages. The main advantage is that their "openness" allows data to be freely and easily shared between connected devices. This is the basis of the internet. The disadvantage is that the lack of security makes it very easy for these networks to be hacked.

### Private

Private networks tend to be smaller and much more exclusive. Examples are home networks and corporate intranets. Because members of these types of network are usually known to each other, and often are not connected to the internet, security is much less of an issue.

The most common use of private networks is in the home, since most Internet Service Providers (ISPs) only allocate a single IP address to each residential customer. In homes that need to have several computers connected to the internet, the answer is to network them so they can all share a single internet connection.

**Hot tip**

Network Location Awareness allows programs that use network connections to apply different behaviors based on how the computer connects to the network. In conjunction with Windows Firewall with Advanced security, you can configure specific firewall rules that apply only when connected to a specific network type. By default, the first time you connect to any network, the network is designated as Public unless you assign it to another category.

**1** Public network    **2** Private network

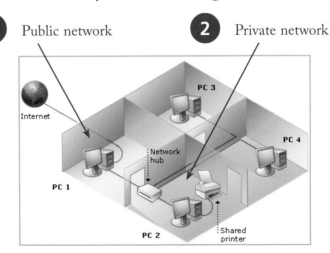

# Create HomeGroup

**1** Go to the Control Panel, Network and internet. Then click **HomeGroup**

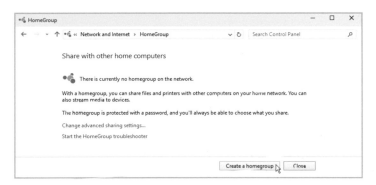

**Don't forget**

When there is already a HomeGroup on the network, you will be invited to participate.

**2** Click **Create a homegroup** and in the next window click **Next**. You'll then see the window below, from where you can choose what to share on the network

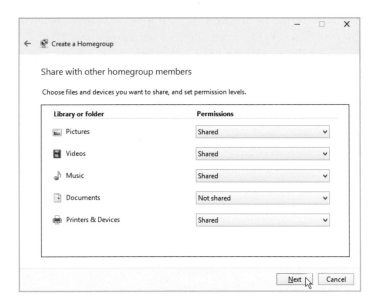

**Hot tip**

You can view or change the password from the **Network and Sharing Center** or from the Control Panel.

**3** You will now see a screen that provides the password needed for other computers to join the HomeGroup

**4** Record the password and click **Finish**. A HomeGroup has been created

# Join the HomeGroup

When you connect to a Home network which already has a HomeGroup, you are invited to join.

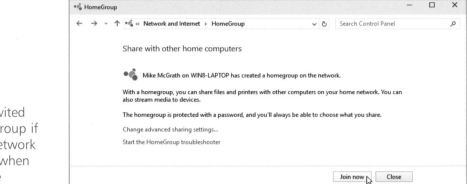

You will only be invited to join the HomeGroup if you specify your network location as **Home** when you connect to the network.

If the HomeGroup was created by another user on the network, you must be given the password to be able to participate.

Everyone on the network who joins the HomeGroup will be able to share everything that you make available.

**1**    Click the **Join now** button

**2**    Select what you want to share and click **Next**

**3**    Type the password and click **Next**

**4**    You have joined the HomeGroup

# Network settings

Settings related to networking can also be found via the network icon in the Notification area on the Taskbar.

**1** Position the mouse cursor over the network icon to see the network name and connection status

**2** Click the network icon to see connection details. In the example below, the network connection is by Ethernet cable, but there is also Wi-Fi connection available

**3** Next, click the Ethernet-connected item and choose **Disconnect** to leave the network

**4** Now, click the Wi-Fi-unconnected item and choose **Connect** to rejoin the network

**5** The buttons at the bottom of this panel indicate active states. Click the **Wi-Fi** button to close the connection, click it again to re-open the connection

**6** Click the **Airplane mode** button to disable connectivity and close connection

**7** Click the **Airplane mode** button once more to re-enable connectivity and re-open connection

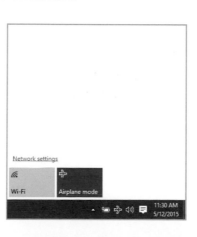

The button color indicates the active state.

Click on the **Network settings** link in this panel to open the Settings window for the current connection.

# Connect to wireless network

**1** On the Start menu click **Settings** and then the **Network & Internet** icon

**2** Next, click on the **Wi-Fi** item in the left pane to see details of wireless connections

**3** Click the network you want to join, and the **Connect** button appears

**4** Check the **Connect automatically** box, to connect whenever the network is in range, then click **Connect**

If you have a netbook or laptop PC, and your router supports wireless access, you can connect to a wireless network.

**5** You are prompted for the security key. Enter the key then click **Next** to continue

**6** Windows connects to the network and validates the security key

**7** The computer is shown as connected to the network

**8** Go to the Control Panel, **Network and Internet**. Click **Network and Sharing Center**

**9** Network information for the PC's networks is displayed

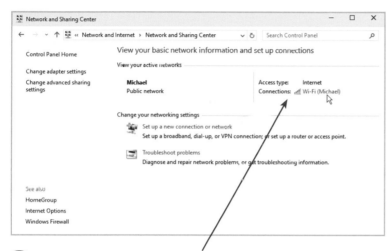

**Hot tip**

Notice the useful link here to **Troubleshoot problems** that will perform connection diagnostics if you have network problems.

**10** Click the Wi-Fi connection to display the status of the wireless network

**11** Click the **Details** button for the wireless network connection details

**12** Click **Close** then **Close** again to return to the Network and Sharing Center

# View network devices

Many networks contain a lot of devices and keeping track of them all can be somewhat tricky. To assist with this, Windows provides a location that lets you view all the devices on your network.

**1** Open any File Explorer window and select **Network** at the bottom of the Navigation pane

**2** The Network location opens

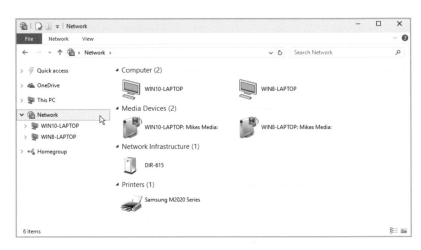

Here, you will see all the devices in your network. In the very basic network shown above, at the top are the two networked computers. Click on either of these and you see all the files on the respective computers that have been designated for sharing.

Below are media devices, a wireless router, and a printer.

Right-clicking on the various devices reveals related options. For example, right-clicking on a computer provides an option to pin it to the Start menu for quick access. Right-clicking on the router reveals an option to open the device's configuration web page.

At the very top, you can open the ribbon toolbar. This provides further network-related options.

# View HomeGroup

Another way of seeing what is being shared on the network is by viewing the networked computers in HomeGroup.

**1** Open any File Explorer window and select **Homegroup** on the Navigation pane

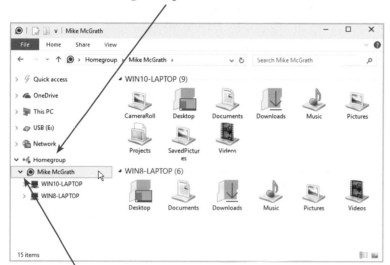

**Hot tip**

By clicking the arrows in the Navigation pane, you can access the contents of a networked PC without leaving the current folder.

**2** Click the arrow before the HomeGroup creator's name to reveal the computers in the network and see what they are sharing

**3** Click on a networked computer to browse its contents

# Network and Sharing Center

**Hot tip**

Select the Network location, in this case Private network, if you need to switch to an alternative network location.

**1** Right-click the **Network** icon in the Notification area and click **Open Network and Sharing Center**

> Troubleshoot problems
> Open Network and Sharing Center

**2** Your basic network information is displayed

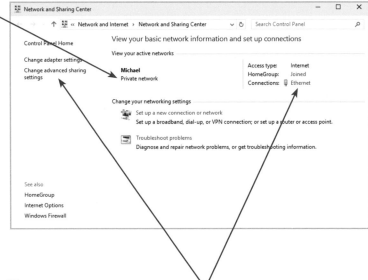

**3** Click the HomeGroup connection status link, or select the link to **Change advanced sharing settings**

**Hot tip**

Select **View or print the homegroup password**, if you need a reminder or if you want to share it with another user on the network.

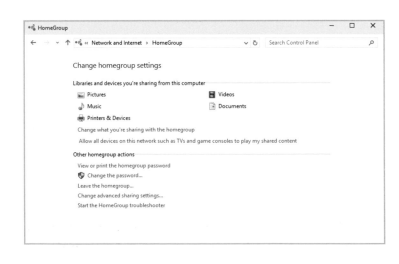

**4** For detailed information, click the **Ethernet** link

**5** The connection status is displayed. Click the **Details** button for Network Connection Details, including addresses

The **Status** dialog shows the adapter speed and the amount of data transfer activity. The **Details** dialog shows the addresses for the adapter and router components.

**6** Click **Close** to return to the Center then click **Change adapter settings**, on the left-hand menu

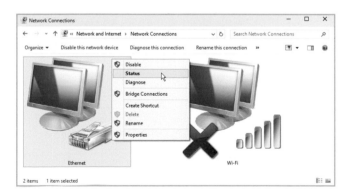

You can also view the local area connection properties from the **Status** dialog.

**7** Click the toolbar buttons, or right-click the adapter icon to select one of the options or to view the properties

# PC settings

HomeGroup and network sharing options are available from the Windows 10 **Settings** interface:

**1** Launch **Settings** from the Start menu then choose the **Network & Internet** icon and select **HomeGroup**

**2** Here, you can view or change the HomeGroup password, choose to leave the HomeGroup, or change sharing settings within the HomeGroup

**Hot tip**

If someone wants to join the network they will need its password.

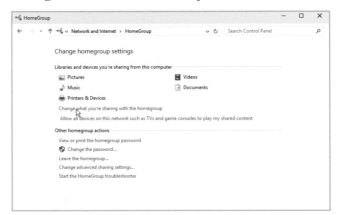

**3** Click the link to **Change what you're sharing with the homegroup**

**4** Sharing can be turned on and off for Documents, Music, Pictures, Videos, and Printers & Devices. To do this, just click in the drop-down boxes

**Don't forget**

If you are not part of the network you will not see these options but simply be invited to join.

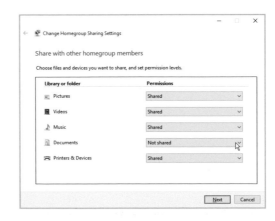

# Monitor network

Windows provides several tools to monitor the activities on your network.

**1** Right-click on the Taskbar and select **Task Manager**

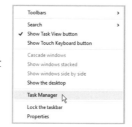

**2** Select the **Performance** tab to see activity charts for the network adapter or adapters (wireless and wired)

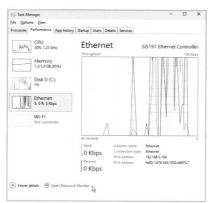

**3** At the bottom of the window click **Open Resource Monitor**

Network monitors can help you identify the causes of unexpected or excessive network activity on your system.

**4** Comprehensive tables and charts are displayed, giving a real-time view of all of the networking activity

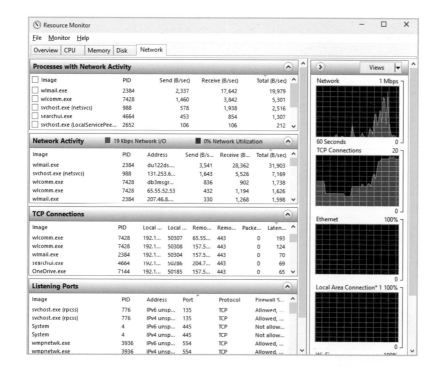

# Sharing folders

If you want to share a file or folder that is not in a library, or if you want to share with computers running other operating systems, you need the File Sharing Wizard.

**1** Open **File Explorer** and locate the folder or file to share

**2** On the ribbon toolbar, click the **Share** tab and select the appropriate share option

The HomeGroup makes it easy to share libraries and printers with other computers on the network, but there are some situations it doesn't cover.

**3** Type a username and click **Add** to include that user

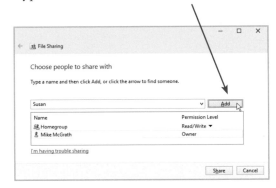

**4** Click the usernames to change the permission from the default **Read** to **Read/Write** (or **Remove**)

**5** Click the **Share** button to assign the folder permissions granted

You can type a username that you know is defined on the computer, or click the down-arrow and select from the list.

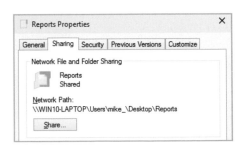

**6** Right-click on the file/folder and choose **Properties** then confirm on the **Sharing** tab that this is now shared

# 19 Control Panel and Mobility Center

# Start Control Panel

The Control Panel is a part of the Windows interface that enables users to view and adjust system settings and controls via applets. For example, adding and removing hardware and software, managing user accounts, and changing accessibility options.

You can open the Control Panel in several ways:

**1** While on the Desktop, right-click the Start button and then click **Control Panel**

**2** In the Taskbar Search box, just type "control panel"

**3** On the Start menu, click **Control Panel** in the "Windows System" group

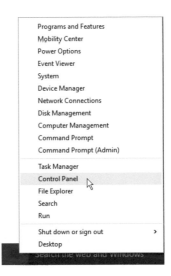

Programs and Features
Mobility Center
Power Options
Event Viewer
System
Device Manager
Network Connections
Disk Management
Computer Management
Command Prompt
Command Prompt (Admin)

Task Manager
Control Panel
File Explorer
Search
Run

Shut down or sign out        >
Desktop

If you are likely to access the Control Panel frequently, you can pin it to both the Taskbar and the Start menu.

**4** Find the Control Panel launcher, using step 2 or 3 above, and then right-click on it. You will now see options that allow you to **Pin to Start group** and **Pin to taskbar**

We recommend that all users take a look at the Control Panel – many useful options and features are available here.

# View by categories

There are some 50 applets in the Control Panel, so locating the one you want can take a while. For this reason, by default, the Control Panel typically opens in Category view, as shown below:

321

If you are interested in applets of a specific type, e.g. the internet, the category view allows you to just see related applets.

In this view, there are eight categories:

- System and Security
- Network and Internet
- Hardware and Sound
- Programs

- User Accounts
- Appearance and Personalization
- Clock, Language, and Region
- Ease of Access

Hover the mouse over the green category headings to open a pop-up that gives a brief description of what the applets do. If you click on the headings, you will see a complete list of the applets within the category. Below the category headings are blue links that lead to the more important applets in the category.

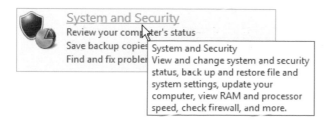

# View by icons

If you want to view all the Control Panel's applets in the same window, you need to switch to an icon view. To do this, click the **Category** link at the top-right of the window. You are given two options: **Large icons** and **Small icons**.

**Hot tip**

Right-clicking on some Control Panel applets provides options of **Pin to Quick access**, **Pin to Start**, and also to **Create shortcut**.

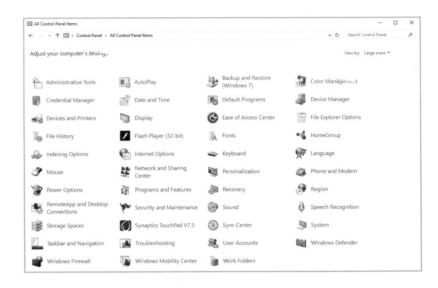

**Hot tip**

If you cannot find what you want in the Control Panel, try doing a search from the Search box at the top-right of the window.

In either view, hovering the mouse over an applet opens a pop-up window that provides a brief description of what the applet does.

# User accounts and Family Safety

Windows allows the setting up of any number of user accounts, each of which can be individually configured in many ways. For example, users can personalize their computing environment with different wallpaper and colors, they can install software that's only accessible from their account, and even hardware.

The ability to do this is particularly useful in a home environment where several family members all use one PC. By giving each their own account, which they can customize to suit their specific requirements and tastes, a single PC can be used sensibly and without conflict.

It can also be useful in a single-user environment by enabling a user to create accounts for specific purposes. For example, one account can be set up for photo-editing with shortcuts to all the relevant programs placed on the Desktop or Start screen. Another account can be set up as a home office, etc.

Another useful application of user accounts is to password-protect the main account and then create Child accounts for the children. They can use the PC but won't be able to compromise its security or performance due to the limitations placed on Child accounts.

The internet is a minefield that can expose naïve and trusting children to many different types of threat. All responsible parents will want to minimize, if not eliminate completely, the risks their children are exposed to. User accounts play a big role here. By creating a separate account for each child and setting up software to monitor and restrict their activities while using their accounts, an element of protective control can be introduced.

There are many commercially-available programs for this purpose, such as Net Nanny, CyberPatrol, etc. The best of these applications enable parents to control and monitor literally every aspect of what the typical child might want to do on a computer and the internet.

Before you try any of these, though, take a look at the Family Safety utility provided by Windows 10 – see page 327.

**Hot tip**

When two or more accounts are created, one of them must be an administrator account. The person running this account will be able to set restrictions on what other account holders can and cannot do.

**Hot tip**

A Windows 10 computer must have at least one administrator account.

**Don't forget**

Doing your day-to-day computing with a standard account will help protect your PC from viruses and malware.

# Change account type

When Windows 10 is installed on a computer, an administrator account is created by default. However, the user has the option of creating and using a standard account instead. Let's take a look at both types and see what the pros and cons are:

### Administrator

The administrator account has complete access to the computer and can make any desired changes.

Most people use it for two reasons:

● It's already there

● It allows them to do whatever they want on the computer

Note that any program that is run on an administrator account also has complete access to the computer. This is how malware, viruses and rootkits get on to a user's system. It is also possible for the user to cause unintentional damage to their system due to having access to system tools like the Windows Registry and the System Configuration utility.

### Standard Accounts

Standard accounts are much safer as they do not allow users to make unauthorized changes that affect the system. If a standard account user tries to install a program for example, they will get a User Account Control (UAC) prompt to provide an administrator password before being allowed to do so.

However, while they may not be able to install programs, make changes to global settings, etc., they will be able to do just about anything else. Therefore, on a day-to-day basis, using a standard account will present no problems to the average user.

The ideal setup then, is to create a standard account for daily use. This helps protect the user from viruses and malware as they are not allowed to run. Should the user need to make a change that requires administrator permission, they don't even need to log out and then log back in as an administrator – they simply provide the administrator password in the UAC dialog box that appears.

It is also possible to run programs under the administrator account by right-clicking the file to be run and select **Run as administrator** from the context menu.

## ...cont'd

Before you can use a standard account, you need to create one.
Do it as described below:

**1** Go to the Start menu and open Settings, Accounts, and
then click **Family & other users**. In the new window
click **Add someone else to this PC**

**2** Select the option right at the bottom **Sign in without
a Microsoft account (not recommended)**. In the next
screen, select **Local account**

**3** Enter the username
and password and
password hint

You must complete all
fields in the **Add a user**
screen, including the
**Password hint** box.

**4** The new account is
created. By default
it is a standard
account

## ...cont'd

You may, at some point, wish to change an administrator account to a standard account, or vice versa.

**1** Go to Settings, then click Accounts, **Family & other users**

**Hot tip**

Standard account holders cannot make changes in to other user accounts.

**2** Select the account you want to change and then click **Change account type**

**Hot tip**

In this example "Richard" is now an administrator.

**3** Select **Administrator** and click **OK**

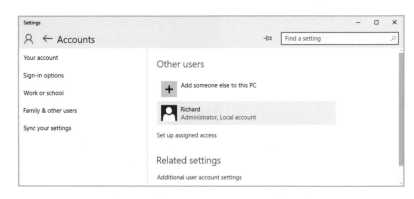

# Set up Family Safety

With Windows 8, child protection was achieved by creating a standard account and then activating the Family Safety utility for that account. Windows 10 simplifies the procedure by offering a Child account option, which is simply a standard account for which the Family Safety utility has already been activated.

**1** Go to the Start menu and open Settings, Accounts, and then click **Family & other users**. In the new window click **Add someone else to this PC**, as on page 325

**2** But now, select the option to **Add a child's account**

**3** Enter the child's existing email address, sign up for a new address, or choose **Add a child's account without email**

Existing standard accounts can be converted to Child accounts.

**4** Enter the username and password and password hint

**5** The new Child account is created and Family Safety begins monitoring it automatically

You can monitor and control your children's internet activities remotely by accessing the Family Safety website at **account.microsoft.com/family**

# Add Bluetooth

You can connect to an external device that supports Bluetooth wireless technology, such as a Beats Pill speaker, using a Bluetooth USB dongle and the Control Panel in Windows 10:

**1** Insert a Bluetooth dongle into a USB socket on your PC

**2** Switch on your Bluetooth device and make it discoverable

**3** Open the Control Panel and select **Add a device** in the "Hardware and Sound" category to look for devices

**4** When Windows finds your Bluetooth device, click **Next** to install the drivers for your device

**5** Open the Control Panel and select **View devices and printers** in the "Hardware and Sound" category to that see your Bluetooth device is now connected and ready to use

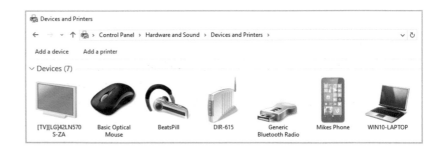

**Hot tip**

After installing the drivers you can control connection using the

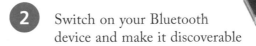 Bluetooth tile that appears in the Action Center when you insert the Bluetooth dongle.

# Ease of Access

Windows 10 provides a number of accessibility options designed to help users see, hear, and use their computers. These options are all available in the **Ease of Access Center**.

**1** Go to the Control Panel and click **Ease of Access Center**

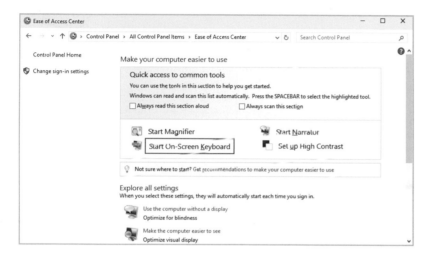

Ease of access tools are not just for those with disabilities. PC users with no impairments may find some of these tools useful in everyday computing.

**2** Click **Get recommendations to make your computer easier to use**

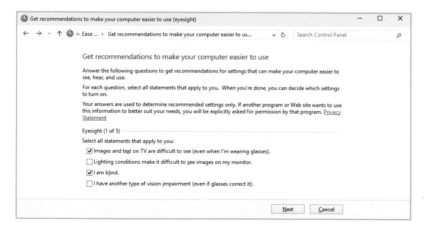

Mouse keys are a particularly useful tool. They can also keep you going if your mouse stops working for some reason.

**3** A Wizard will open and it will walk you through five screens in which you are asked questions about your eyesight, dexterity, hearing, speech, and ability to reason

...cont'd

**4** When the Wizard is finished, click **OK**. You will then be presented with a list of settings that Windows thinks will help you to use the computer

**Hot tip**

Another useful tool is Magnifier. This gives you an enlarged view of specific elements on the screen.

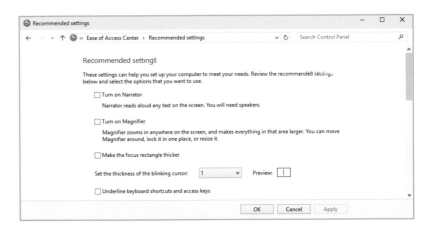

**5** None of the suggestions are actually implemented – it's up to you to read the list and select the ones you want

**6** If you don't need advice from Windows, just choose from the available options on the Home screen. These include using the PC with a display, without a keyboard or mouse, using text alternatives for sounds, and more

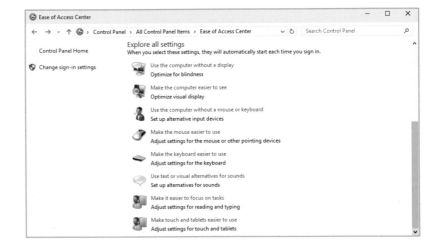

# Start Mobility Center

You'll find Windows Mobility Center (WMC) on any portable computer, though not usually on a desktop or all-in-one computer. The utility is basically a control panel that provides all the Windows options specific to portable computers in one easily-accessed location.

There are several ways to open Windows Mobility Center. These include:

**1** Press **WinKey + R** to open the Run box. Type "mblctr" then hit **Enter**

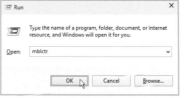

**2** Go to the Control Panel, Hardware and Sound. Then, click **Windows Mobility Center**

**3** You get a link to Windows Mobility Center when you right-click the battery icon in the Notification area

**4** When the utility opens, you will see the following window:

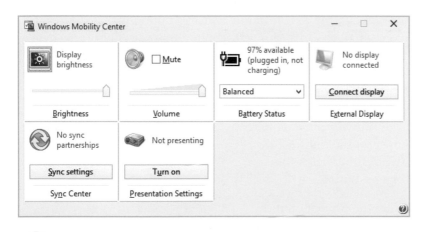

**5** The options offered depend on the type of computer and the hardware it is using

If you are using a desktop PC, Windows Mobility Center will not be accessible.

The options in Windows Mobility Center may differ from PC to PC.

# Screen management

Windows Mobility Center provides several options related to screen management.

### Brightness

The first is display brightness. This is an important setting with laptops as the higher it is set, the quicker the battery will run down. The Mobility Center provides a quickly-accessible way of adjusting the setting. If you click on the icon, you will open the computer's **Power Options** utility, from where you can make changes to various settings including the display brightness.

### Volume

As with the brightness setting, the higher the PC's volume level, the greater the load on the battery. You can adjust it with the slider, check the Mute box, or click the icon to open the **Sound** utility for more options.

### External Display

The External Display option allows you to connect your laptop to a different monitor, duplicate the display, or extend the display.

Click the icon, and the **Screen Resolution** utility will open. If you click **Connect display**, you will open **Project** options in the Windows interface. Both offer the options mentioned above.

### Presentation Settings

Laptops are often used in business to give presentations. With this in mind, the **Presentation Settings** option makes it possible to pre-configure a laptop's settings in terms of volume, screen saver, and background so that they will not detract from the presentation. To do this, click the icon and make your adjustments as shown on the right. Click **OK**, and then click the **Turn on** button.

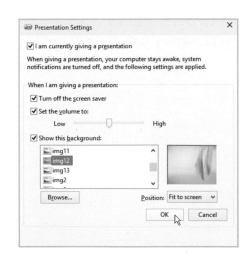

When the presentation is finished, you can revert to the normal settings by clicking the **Turn off** button.

**Hot tip**

Many people connect their laptops to the main PC monitor to take advantage of the larger, and usually better, displays these offer.

# Battery status

The main drawback with portable computers such as laptops is the constant need to conserve battery power. To this end, the Windows Mobility Center provides options that help to manage this aspect of portable computing.

All the settings described on page 332 affect to some degree the length of time the battery will last. Users looking to conserve battery power will benefit by lowering these settings as far as possible.

A related option provided by Windows Mobility Center is battery power monitoring, or status. This tells the user the percentage of power remaining in the battery.

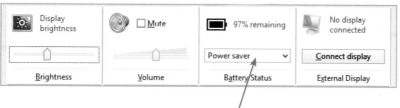

The drop-down box provides three basic options:

- **Power saver** – this option will extend battery life

- **High performance** – this option reduces battery life

- **Balanced** – this option is a compromise between performance and battery life

Clicking the battery icon opens the **Power Options** dialog box, which provides settings with which to fine-tune the **Power saver**, **High performance** and **Balanced** options.

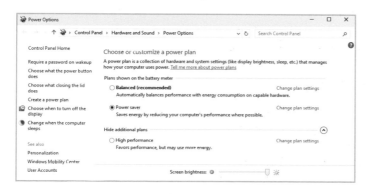

Hot tip

You can also see the battery status from the battery icon in the Notification area. If the battery is fully charged, the icon will look like this:

If it is running low, it will look like this:

Hover over the icon and you will see the percentage of power remaining:

333

Power plans set the idle time after, which the display is turned off or the computer put to sleep. For **High performance**, the setting is **Never**.

Not all computers support Hibernation, so this option does not always appear.

# Power options

This feature is provided for all types of computer, though it takes on particular significance for battery-powered PCs.

On a mains-powered computer, such as the HP TouchSmart 610:

**1** Go to the Control Panel, Hardware and Sound. Then click **Power Options**

**2** You can select one of the power plans offered, or create a power plan (based on an existing power plan)

**3** Select the action **Choose what the power button does**, to specify Do Nothing, Hibernate, Sleep or Shutdown when you press the power button on your computer

**4** On some keyboards there is a Sleep button, for which you can specify Do Nothing, Hibernate, or Sleep

# 20 Troubleshooting

# Windows error reporting

Windows 10 constantly sends data over the internet to check your PC for security and maintenance problems and sends back a message when a problem is discovered. Windows' User Account Control also notifies you when potentially harmful programs attempt to make changes to your computer. Additionally, the Windows SmartScreen feature warns you before running any unrecognized apps and files downloaded from the internet.

You can set the level of reporting you want for each one of these:

Windows identifies errors and problems and attempts to find solutions for you.

**1** Go to Control Panel then select **Security and Maintenance**

Security and Maintenance
Review recent messages and resolve problems with your computer.

**2** Here, you can review messages and resolve problems

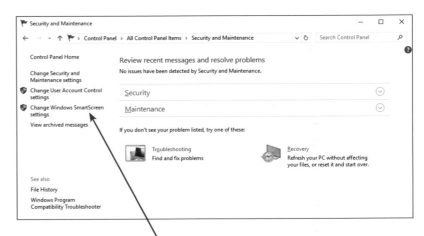

**3** From the menu on the left, select **Change Windows SmartScreen settings** then choose an option to set the reporting level for unrecognized apps

If you are concerned about the information being sent, click the link to review the **Privacy statement** to see how the information you send is managed and protected.

**...cont'd**

**4** Next, select **Change User Account Control settings** then choose an option to set the notification level for potentially harmful programs

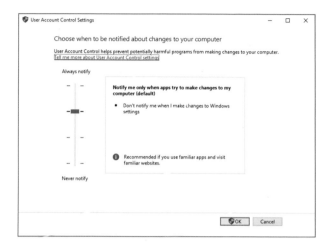

The settings shown here for Windows SmartScreen, User Account Control, Security and Maintenance, are the default (recommended) settings.

**5** Now, select **Change Security and Maintenance settings** then choose the items for which you would like to receive messages when problems are discovered by Windows

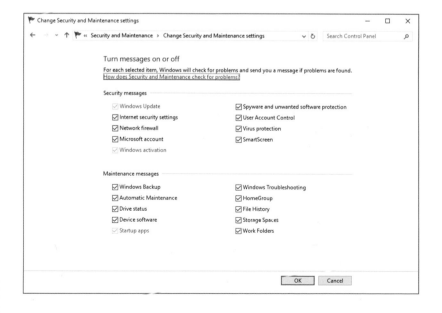

Security and Maintenance monitors security issues as well as the maintenance and troubleshooting issues discussed in this chapter.

# Troubleshooting settings

**1** Expand the **Maintenance** section, to review the status of the monitoring that is being applied

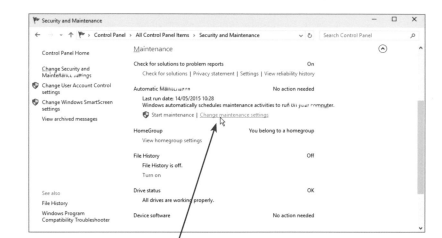

**Don't forget**

Entries will only appear here when there are problems that Windows has identified and for which solutions are available.

**2** Click **Change maintenance settings** to specify the scope of problem analysis and maintenance allowed on your system

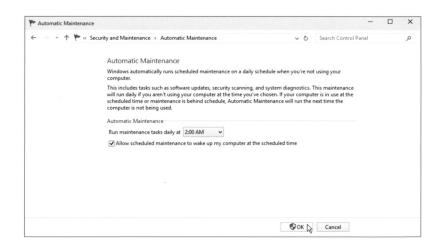

**Hot tip**

You may want to turn off these options for a system that is being operated by an inexperienced user, so they won't have to deal with troubleshooting responses.

**3** By default, Windows will remind you when the System Maintenance troubleshooter can help fix problems, and will also allow users to browse for online troubleshooters

# Windows troubleshooters

**1** Open **Security and Maintenance, Troubleshooting**

**2** This lists categories and the troubleshooters available within these to handle common computer problems

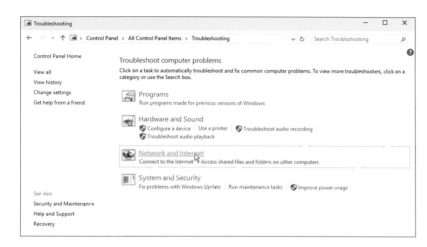

If you encounter a problem, and find no related messages in **Security and Maintenance** you can try the troubleshooters provided by Windows.

**3** Select a task that appears to match the problem you have

**4** If there's no suitable task, click the most appropriate category

**5** Windows searches online to find any troubleshooting packs in that category

**6** The troubleshooters are listed by their sub-categories

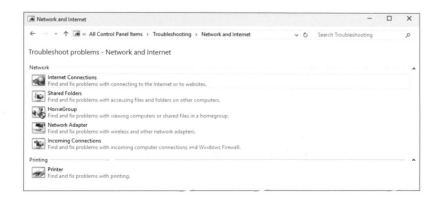

Depending on the category you select, you should find one or more troubleshooters online, ensuring that you have the latest support for the problem area.

# Troubleshooter in action

**1** To illustrate, select **Connect to the Internet**, in the **Network and Internet** category

**2** Click **Next** to run the troubleshooter, which carries out a series of checks to detect any internet connection issues

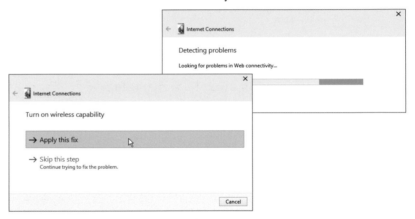

**3** In this case, the problem is identified as no wireless capability. You are offered the option to have Windows attempt to fix this problem

**4** Click **Apply this fix** to see if Windows can resolve the problem

**5** Confirmation that the problem is fixed is displayed

# Problem Steps Recorder

If troubleshooting doesn't help, and you need to report the problem, you can use Problem Steps Recorder to automatically capture the steps you take, including a text description of where you clicked and a screenshot during each click. You can save the data to a file that can be used by a support professional or a friend helping you with the problem.

To record and save the steps:

**1** Open Control Panel and type "record steps" in the Search box. Then click **Record steps to reproduce a problem**

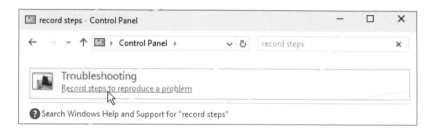

**2** When the Problem Steps Recorder has opened, click its **Start Record** button

**3** Go through the steps to reproduce the problem. You can pause the recording at any time, and then resume it later

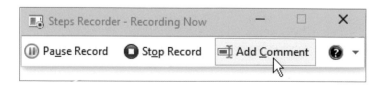

**4** Click **Add Comment** whenever you want to make notes about any step in the process you are recording

Beware

Some programs, for example a full-screen game, might not be captured accurately or might not provide useful details.

Hot tip

If you want to record any activities that need administrator authority, you must run the Program Steps Recorder as an administrator, in elevated mode.

**...cont'd**

**5** Type your comments in the box that opens at the bottom-right of the screen

When you record steps, anything you type will not be recorded. If it is relevant to the problem, use the comment option to note what you type.

**6** Click **Stop Record** when you finish all the steps

**7** Pick a name and folder for the report then click **Save**

**8** The report is saved as a compressed ZIP file in the folder

# View the report

**1** Double-click the compressed ZIP file, then double-click the MHTML document (**.mht**) that it contains

**2** The report opens

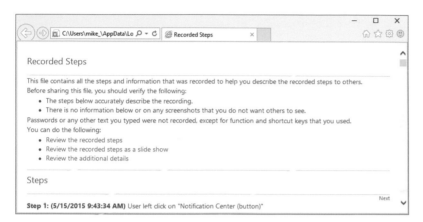

**3** Each step has a description of the action taken, plus a screenshot of the full screen at that point

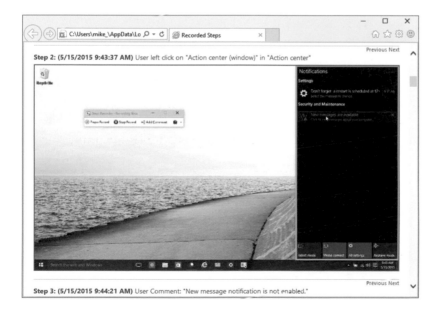

# Get help from a friend

**1** Go to the Control Panel. Click the **Troubleshooting** category, then select the **Get help from a friend** link

You can ask a friend to look at how your system is working, even if they are away from you, by connecting your computers.

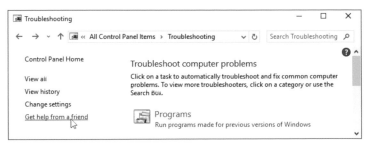

**2** Click the option to **Invite someone to help you**

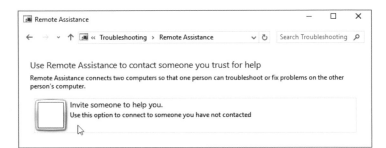

**3** Select, for example, **Use email to send an invitation**

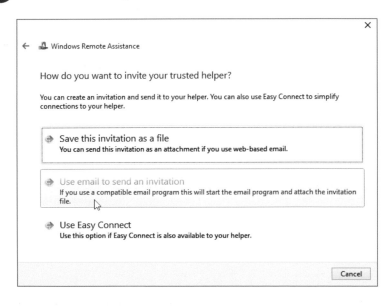

**4** Amend the message, adding the helper's name and email address, and click the **Send** button

You can change the contents of the message however you wish, to make it appropriate for the person you are contacting.

**5** Windows Remote Assistance provides a password for you to share, then waits for an incoming connection

**6** Your helper receives and opens the message and, if willing to help you, double-clicks the attached invitation file

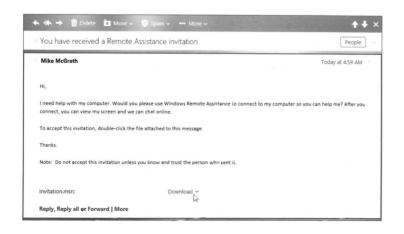

You'll need to tell your helper the connection password, perhaps via a separate email message, or via instant messaging.

# Send and respond

**1** Your helper opens the invitation file and enters the connection password

**Beware**

When your computer is connected this way, you are giving full access, so you should be sure it is a trusted friend that you have contacted.

**2** You are notified of the acceptance, and asked to confirm you will allow the helper to connect to your computer

**3** Your helper can now see your Desktop on his/her monitor, and observe any actions

**4** Your helper can click **Request control**, asking to operate your computer using his/her mouse and keyboard

**...cont'd**

**5** When you receive the request, click **Yes** to allow your helper to share control of your Desktop

Click the **Yes** button to allow your helper to respond to User Account Control prompts.

**6** Now, either you or your helper can operate the computer using mouse and keyboard

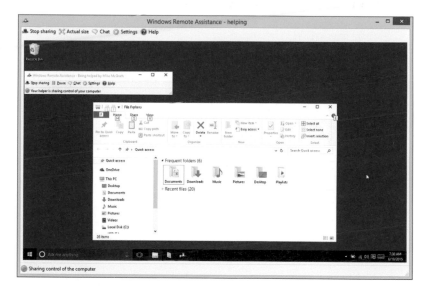

Click **Pause** if you want to temporarily stop the remote assistance session, for example to carry out a separate task.

**7** Click **Chat** to communicate via instant messaging, or click **Stop sharing** to return full control to you alone

**8** Close Remote Assistance when you have finished

# Use Easy Connect

**1** Invite someone to help you (see page 344) and select **Use Easy Connect**

If you believe you are likely to connect with the same computer on a frequent basis then you can try the Easy Connect method.

**2** Remote Assistance will generate an Easy Connect password which you must supply to your helper

**3** Your helper will open Troubleshooting and select **Offer Remote Assistance to help someone**, then select **Use Easy Connect** and enter the password provided

If you have problems connecting, such as issues with the firewall or router, try the Troubleshooting option at either computer for suggestions, or switch to the Invitation method.

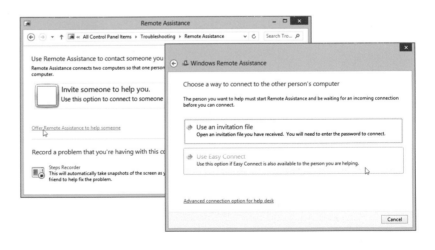

When the connection is made, contact information is exchanged between your computer and your helper's computer that will allow you to quickly connect in the future without using the password.

# System Restore

If problems arise due to recently added drivers or updates, you can use System Restore to return the computer to an earlier position.

**1** Go to Control Panel, System and Security, **Security and Maintenance** then select **Recovery**

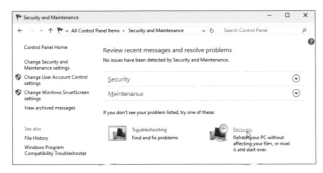

System Restore will suggest the option to undo the latest change to your system. Choose this if problems have only just appeared. You can still try another restore point later.

**2** Click **Open System Restore**, then click **Next**

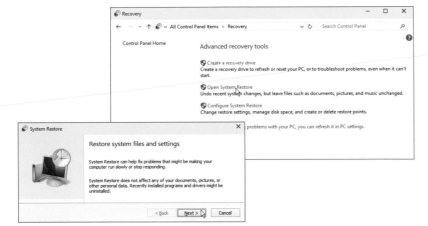

If you've displayed more restore points, select the one that immediately pre-dates the problems, then click **Next**.

**3** Choose the recommended restore, or choose a different restore point to go back to an earlier state, and click **Next**

**...cont'd**

**4** Confirm your restore point and select **Finish**

**Beware**

If System Restore is being run in safe mode or from the System Recovery Options menu, it cannot be undone.

**5** Click **Yes** to continue and carry out the System Restore

**6** Windows will close down and restart, and the system files are restored to the required versions

**7** If this does not fix the problem, you can **Undo System Restore**, or **Choose a different restore point**

**Don't forget**

Once started, you must allow System Restore to complete. You can then Open System Restore and select Undo, if you want to revert to the initial state.

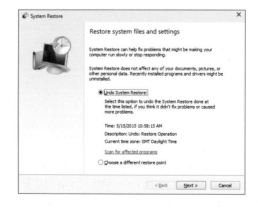

# Start in Safe Mode

**1** Open Settings, then select **Update and security**

**2** Click **Recovery** on the left

**3** Under "Advanced start-up" on the right, click **Restart now**

Hot tip

**4** The computer will reboot and ask you to "Choose an option" – choose **Troubleshoot**

Troubleshoot
Refresh or reset your PC, or use advanced tools

Safe Mode starts Windows with a limited set of files and device drivers, without the usual startup programs and services. This validates the basic settings.

**5** In the "Troubleshoot" screen, choose **Advanced options**

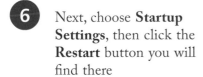
Advanced options

**6** Next, choose **Startup Settings**, then click the **Restart** button you will find there

Startup Settings
Change Windows startup behavior

351

**7** When the "Startup Settings" screen appears, press the **F4** key or the number 4 key to select Safe Mode. The computer will now reboot into Safe Mode

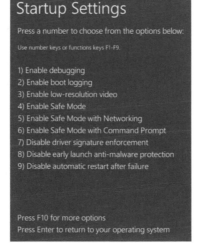

Startup Settings

Press a number to choose from the options below:

Use number keys or functions keys F1-F9.

1) Enable debugging
2) Enable boot logging
3) Enable low-resolution video
4) Enable Safe Mode
5) Enable Safe Mode with Networking
6) Enable Safe Mode with Command Prompt
7) Disable driver signature enforcement
8) Disable early launch anti-malware protection
9) Disable automatic restart after failure

Press F10 for more options
Press Enter to return to your operating system

Don't forget

Safe Mode cannot be initiated by pressing the F8 key as with previous versions of Windows.

Note that Startup settings replaces the advanced boot menu found in earlier versions of Windows. Unlike the advanced boot menu, Startup settings cannot be initiated while the PC is booting by pressing the **F8** key. It can only be initiated from within Windows as described above, from a Windows 10 installation disk, or a Windows 10 Recovery drive. Also, **Startup Settings** options cannot be selected with the mouse or keyboard – a specific key is allocated to each option.

NEW

**Hot tip**

Another way of applying compatibility settings is to right-click the program's executable (setup) file. Click **Properties** and then open the **Compatibility** tab. From here, you can choose an operating system that the program is known to work with.

**Hot tip**

If a program won't install at all, the method described on the right won't work. In this case, do it as described above.

**Hot tip**

Once a program has been successfully set up, it will use the compatibility settings every time it is run.

# Program compatibility

When you install programs on your Windows 10 PC, you may come across one or two that refuse to run – this could be due to an incompatibility issue with Windows 10. A possible solution is the Program Compatibility Troubleshooter. This will recreate the Windows environment for which they were designed and may get them running.

**1** Go to Control Panel, Programs, then click on **Run programs made for previous versions of Windows**

**2** Click **Next**, and after a few moments you will see a dialog box showing you a list of all the programs on the PC

**3** Select the one you're having trouble with and click **Next**, then select **Troubleshoot program**

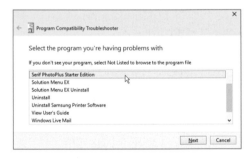

**4** Choose the appropriate problem from the list and click **Next**

**5** Windows will try to fix the issue. If the problem hasn't been resolved, click **No, try again** with different settings to repeat the procedure with other possible causes

# 21 Backup and recovery

*You need to keep copies of your data so if you have problems you can recover your system. Windows provides ways to make backups and helps you restore the copies, should it be necessary.*

# Sync settings

An important feature in Windows 10 is the ability to synchronize your settings across all your devices. This means that when you change your Desktop background, for example, the change is replicated on all your devices.

Because your settings are stored on the Cloud, not only are they synchronized, they are thus also automatically backed up. Furthermore, the backup is dynamic as it is done in real-time.

The synchronization feature is enabled by default, so you may wish to review exactly what is being synchronized, and thus backed up.

**1** Open Settings, Accounts, then click **Sync your settings** in the left panel

**2** In the right panel, you'll see all the settings on your PC that can be synchronized. At the top, under "Sync your settings" you can turn synchronization on or off altogether

**Hot tip**

With synchronization turned on, your data is accessible on all devices logged into with a Microsoft account. Your settings, such as Wallpaper, can also be replicated on all devices.

In Windows 10, sync settings are consolidated in the Accounts category.

**Beware**

If you have critical or confidential files on OneDrive, you may want to think carefully about synchronizing passwords.

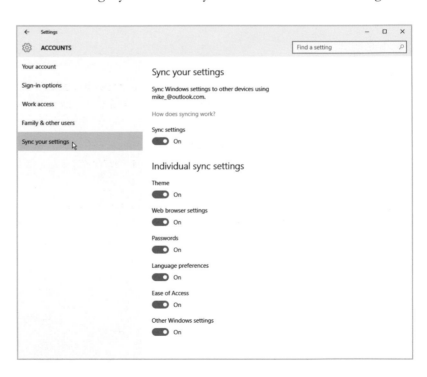

**3** You can toggle individual settings on and off by clicking on them

# Sync to OneDrive

While the synchronization feature makes it possible to automatically back up your settings, it cannot back up your files and folders. For this, you need the OneDrive feature that is built into Windows 10.

**1** Open any File Explorer window and at the left, you'll see a OneDrive item in the Navigation pane

**2** Click on the **OneDrive** item to see all your folders whose contents are stored as duplicates on "the Cloud"

The OneDrive folder works like any other folder – files can be added, deleted, renamed, etc.

**3** You can keep this selection of folders as they are, add more, delete them, or create your own folder structure

**4** To back up a file or folder just save it within OneDrive – it will be automatically duplicated on the Cloud

**5** You can save files to the OneDrive folder from a program's **Save As** menu

Some programs provide a Save to OneDrive menu option. An example is Microsoft Office 2016.

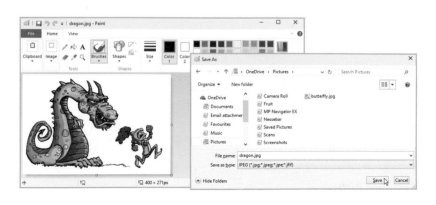

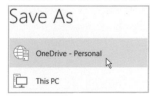

# Copy data

When you create documents or other files on your computer, it is wise to take precautions to protect your work in case problems arise with the original version.

To illustrate the options and the considerations, we'll look at an example computer:

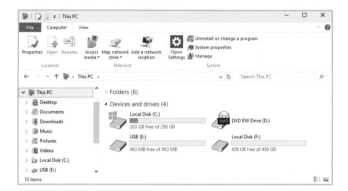

**Don't forget**

Protecting your files can be as simple as copying the files onto a USB flash drive, but there are more sophisticated methods available.

**1** Press **WinKey + X** and select File Explorer, then choose **This PC** to view the storage devices:

- Local Disk (C:) containing the system and the library files

- A second hard drive Local Disk (F:) which is empty

- USB Drive (E:) which is empty

- A DVD RW Drive (D:) is available, but with no media

**Beware**

The standard user accounts have no password assigned. As administrator, you could select the accounts from this panel and create passwords for them.

**2** Go to the Control Panel, **User Accounts** then click the **Change account type** link to see the accounts

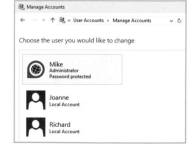

- Mike (administrator)

- Joanne (standard user)

- Richard (standard user)

# ...cont'd

To make a copy of a file on the USB drive:

**1** Navigate to the folder containing the file

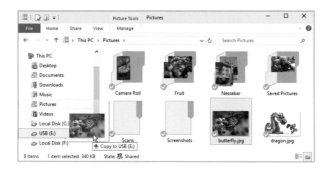

**Don't forget**

You could also right-click
a file or folder and select
**Copy**, then right-click
the destination drive and
select **Paste** (or use the
**Ctrl + C** and **Ctrl + V**
keyboard shortcuts).

**2** Left-click and drag the file onto the drive name in the
Navigation pane, and release it there

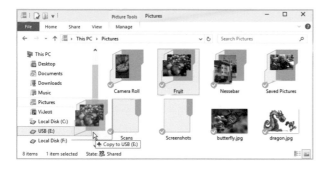

**3** You can also drag a folder to copy the whole contents

### Repeated copies

Note that a repeated copy
at a later date to the same
removable drive would
over-write the initial
copy. To keep a history of
changes, you need to copy
to a folder, perhaps named
as the copy date, or use a
separate removable drive
each time.

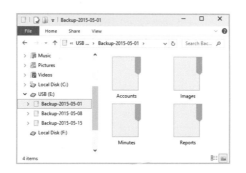

**Beware**

If you right-click as you
drag, you will Move
rather than Copy the files
to the destination drive.

# Copy libraries

Suppose you want to save the whole contents of your libraries:

**1** Open the Libraries in **File Explorer** (see page 179)

**2** Rather than drag-and-drop, right-click the **Libraries** folder and select **Copy**

**Don't forget**

On the ribbon choose View, Navigation pane, **Show all folders** – to display the Desktop and the Libraries folder in the Navigation pane.

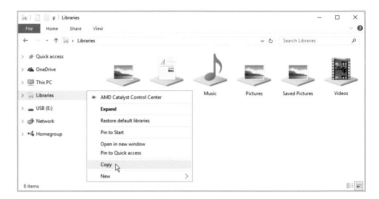

**3** In the Navigation pane, select the removable drive to open it

**4** Right-click the Contents pane and select **Paste**

**Beware**

Dragging and dropping the Libraries folder creates a link to the original folder, rather than making actual copies of the files and folders.

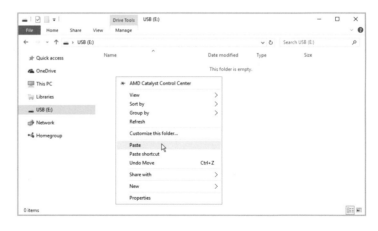

**5** The contents of the libraries then begin copying to the removable drive – click **More details** to see the progress

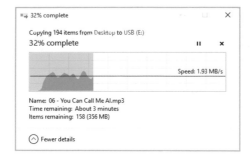

**6** Expand the Navigation pane entry for the removable
drive, and you'll see how the contents are arranged

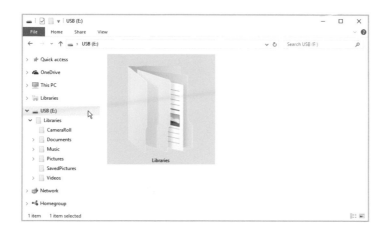

Note that each library folder on the copy contains the merged
contents of the Current user and the Public libraries. This can lead
to difficulties when restoring files and folders.

When you copy libraries, you'll also have problems with over-
writing older copies with new copies.

## Other users

You may encounter problems accessing user folders, if you are
required to make backup copies on behalf of other users with
accounts on your computer.

# Refresh your system

Like many things in life, Windows depreciates with use. It develops faults, slows down and may become unstable. Windows 10 provides a utility that will quickly restore it to an "as new" condition.

**1** Go to Settings, **Update & security**, then choose **Recovery** in the left pane

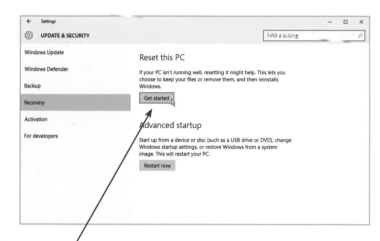

**2** Now, in the right pane, under "Reset this PC", click the **Get Started** button

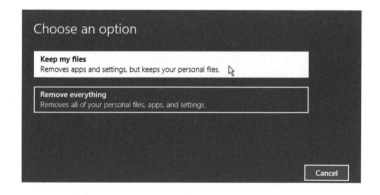

You are then asked to choose an option. If you choose the option to **Keep my files,** here is what's about to happen:

● **Your files and personalization settings won't change** – this means that your data will not be deleted, and that any changes you have made to the default personalization settings will be retained. The former is the big plus here as it means you do not have to make a backup of your data and then reinstall it afterwards.

● **Your PC settings will be changed back to their defaults** – this means that Windows 10 will be deleted and replaced by a new copy. Any configuration changes made to Windows settings will be lost.

● **Apps from Windows Store will be kept** – Windows 10 apps installed from the Windows Store will not be deleted.

● **Apps you installed from disks or websites will be removed** – All third-party software will be deleted.

● **After the refresh, a document will appear on the Desktop** – Listing the applications that have been removed.

One advantage of the refresh process is that it will reinstall Windows in less time than taken for the original installation.

**3** Having read and understood what the utility will do, click **Keep my files**

### Your apps will be removed

Many apps can be reinstalled from the Store, but the following apps will need to be reinstalled from the web or installation discs. This list will be saved to the desktop after you reset this PC.

µTorrent
AMD Catalyst Control Center
Microsoft SQL Server 2005 Compact Edition [ENU]
Microsoft Visual C++ 2012 Redistributable (x64) - 11.0.50727
Skype™ 7.7
Synaptics Pointing Device Driver
Windows Live Essentials

[ Next ]   [ Cancel ]

You may want to make a note of the applications to be deleted.

**4** You'll now see a list of applications that will be deleted during the refresh procedure. Click **Next**

...cont'd

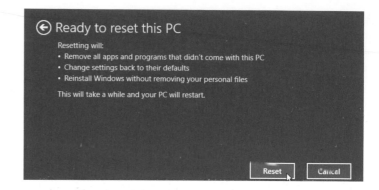

**Hot tip**

The refresh process will install a new copy of Windows 10 while retaining the user's Windows apps, data and personalization settings. Everything else will be deleted.

**5** At the next screen, click **Reset**. The computer will reboot and the refresh procedure begins

**Beware**

The big drawback is that users will probably have to reinstall/reconfigure most of their software, and reconfigure various Windows settings.

**6** When the computer has been refreshed, Windows begins its setup routine. When that's done, you're back in business

# Reinstall your system

The traditional method of completely restoring a Windows PC to its factory settings is to do a clean installation. This wipes the drive clean of all data, after which a new copy of Windows is installed. The procedure is done by booting the PC from the installation disk and is something many will be wary of trying.

Windows 10 provides a much simpler method of restoring Windows to its factory settings. This is courtesy of its Reset utility. It works as described below:

The Reset utility also provides an ideal way of securely deleting your data on a computer you are going to sell or scrap.

**1** Go to Settings, Update and Security, and choose **Recovery**

**2** Under "Reset this PC", click the **Get Started** button

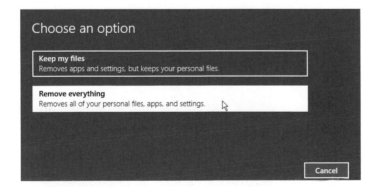

**3** You are then asked to choose an option. Choose the option to **Remove everything** to completely reset Windows 10

...cont'd

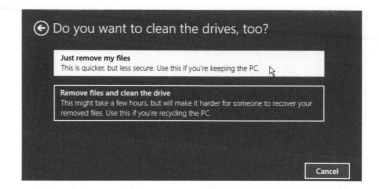

The **Remove files and clean the drive** option does the same as **Just remove my files** but also wipes the drive securely so the data cannot be recovered later.

**4** You are presented with two options as shown above. Choose the first one, **Just remove my files**, if you just want to start again from scratch. All the data you have put on the PC will be deleted, leaving you with an "as new" copy of Windows

**5** Click the **Reset** button to begin the procedure

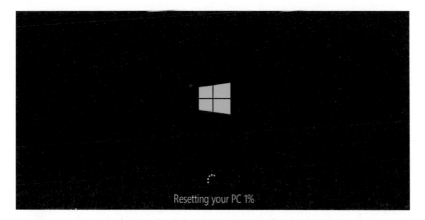

**6** The computer will now reboot and you will see the screen above as the Reset procedure begins. A progress bar keeps you updated

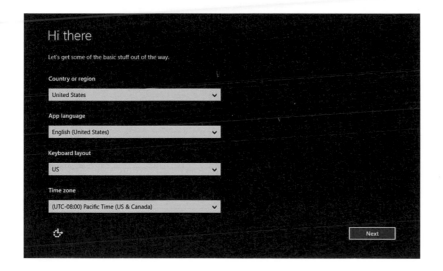

**7** When the Reset is done, Windows goes through its setting-up routine, just like the first time it was installed

At the end of the Reset, your computer will be exactly how it was when you first installed Windows 10.

# Enable File History

Windows 10 provides some very useful backup utilities. One of these is File History, which can be accessed in the Control Panel. With it, users are able to quickly restore individual files that have been modified, damaged or even deleted.

It works by making automatic backups (every hour by default) of all files stored in the following folders – Contacts, Desktop, Favorites, and the Documents, Music, Pictures and Video Libraries. By default, File History is turned off. Enable it as follows:

**1** Go to the Control Panel, **System and Security**, then click **Save backup copies of your files with File History**

System and Security
Review your computer's status
Save backup copies of your files with File History
Find and fix problems

**2** The utility will search your computer for a suitable backup drive. If it doesn't find one, you'll see the following:

> No usable drive was found. We recommend that you use an external drive for File History. Connect a drive and refresh this page, or use a network location.
> Select a network location

**3** Connect a second drive to your computer. This must be a separate drive to the main system drive and can be of any type – an external hard drive, a USB hard drive or a USB flash drive. Once done, run the utility again; this time your second drive will be recognized, as we see below:

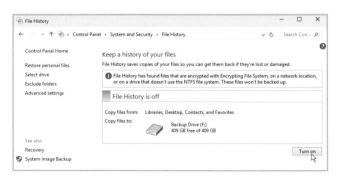

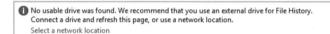

File History

← → ↑ > Control Panel > System and Security > File History

Control Panel Home

Restore personal files

Select drive

Exclude folders

Advanced settings

Keep a history of your files

File History saves copies of your files so you can get them back if they're lost or damaged.

File History has found files that are encrypted with Encrypting File System, on a network location, or on a drive that doesn't use the NTFS file system. These files won't be backed up.

File History is off

Copy files from: Libraries, Desktop, Contacts, and Favorites

Copy files to: Backup Drive (F:)
409 GB free of 409 GB

See also

Recovery

System Image Backup

Turn on

**4** Click the **Turn on** button

All files in the Contacts, Desktop, and Favorites folders and the Documents, Music, Pictures and Video Libraries will now be automatically backed up every hour.

Note that existing backups are not over-written by new ones – each backup is kept so over a period of time, a file history is created. This enables a file to be restored from a backup created at a specific time and day.

## File History options

If you have two or more drives in your system, you can set which one to use for File History by clicking the **Select drive** link on the left of the main window.

You will need to connect a second drive to your PC before you can use File History.

If you want to exclude some of the default folders to be backed up, click the **Exclude folders** link. Click the **Add** button in the new window and browse to and select the folders to exclude. In the example below, we have excluded Library folders.

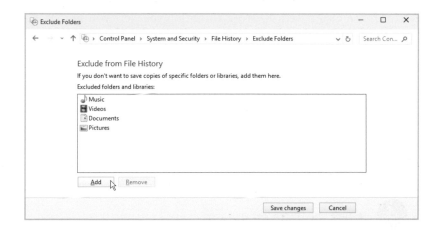

...cont'd

Going back to the main screen, you'll also see an **Advanced settings** link. This provides several options:

"Save copies of files" lets you specify how often your files are backed up – from every 10 minutes to Daily. Consider this option carefully, as the more frequent your backups, the more space is used on your backup drive. "Keep saved versions" lets you specify how long your backups are kept – from one month to forever.

By default, backups are made every hour. However, this can be changed in **Advanced settings**.

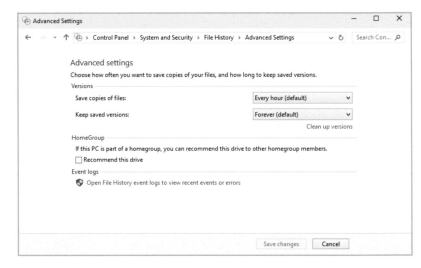

### Restoring personal files

To restore a file or folder, click the **Restore personal files** link back on the main screen. This opens a window showing all your backed-up folders. To restore the contents of a folder, right-click on it and select Restore. If you just want to restore a specific file within a folder, open the folder, right-click on the file and click Restore. You also have a **Restore to** option that lets you restore a file or folder to a different location.

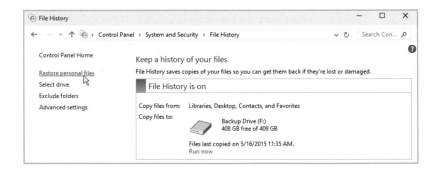

# Create a system image

A system image is an exact copy of a drive and, by default, it includes the drives required for Windows to run. It includes Windows and your system settings, programs, and files. If desired, it can be configured to include other drives as well.

Should the imaged computer subsequently develop a problem that cannot be repaired, it can be restored from the image.

There are many third-party utilities of this type; a well-known one being Acronis True Image, but Windows 10 provides its own.

**1** Go to Control Panel, **System and Security**, then click **Save backup copies of your files with File History**

**2** Next, click the **System Image Backup** link that appears at the bottom-left of the window, as shown below:

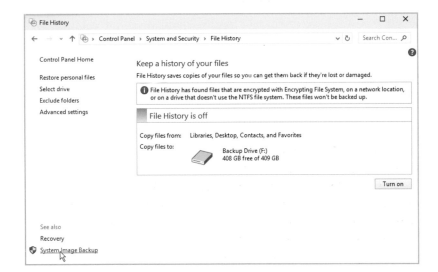

**3** Now, click the **Set up backup** link and the utility will search your computer for suitable backup mediums. These have to be separate to the main system drive and can be internal hard drives or removable media drives such as external hard drives, or USB flash drives

A system image will restore the PC to the state it was in when the image was built.

Any type of medium can be used for the image backup. It has to be separate to the main system drive, though.

## ...cont'd

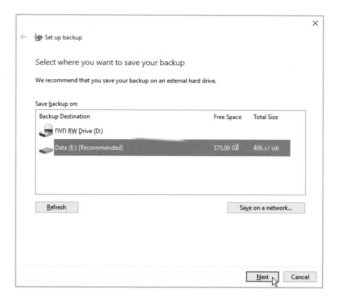

**Don't forget**

A system image of Windows 10 will be at least 15GB or so in size, so if you use a USB flash drive make sure its capacity is adequate.

**4** If you have a separate hard drive in your system, the utility will automatically select it as the recommended backup medium, but you can choose the DVD drive or network location. When you have chosen, click **Next**

**5** When asked "What do you want to back up?" opt to **Let Windows choose (recommended)**, then click **Next**

**Don't forget**

The image can include any number of drives.

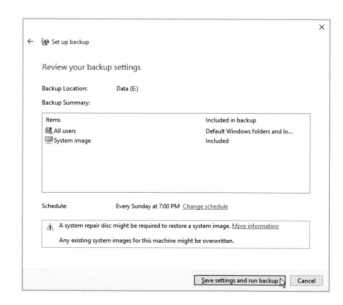

**6** Review your settings. Note the warning that states any existing images might be overwritten, before commencing the procedure by clicking **Save settings and run backup**

**7** Windows creates the system image; this can take a while

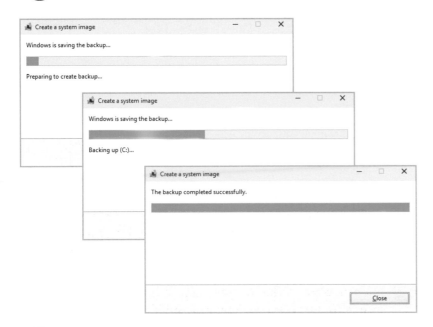

Beware

Images cannot be saved on the boot disk (where Windows is installed). You must use a different drive or partition.

**8** The image is added as a folder in the separate drive

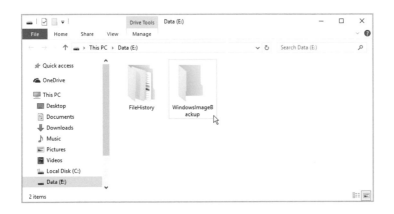

Hot tip

If you don't have a second drive, you can create a second partition on your C: drive for the image.

If you can't get Windows to start, you'll need a recovery drive to restore your system from an image.

Create a system recovery drive now – if you leave it until you need it, it will be too late.

...cont'd

### Restoring your system from an image

When you use an image backup to restore your system, be aware that, when done, your system will be exactly the same as when the backup was made. Any changes made to the computer after the backup was made will be lost – this includes files, settings and applications.

How you go about restoring depends on your reason for doing it. If it's because your system is so damaged that you cannot get Windows to start at all, you'll need the aid of a Recovery drive, as we explain on pages 375-376. If it's for some other reason and Windows is working, you can do it from within Windows, as we explain below:

**1** Go to Settings, **Update & security**, then choose **Recovery** in the left pane

**2** Now, in the right pane, under "Advanced startup", click **Restart now**

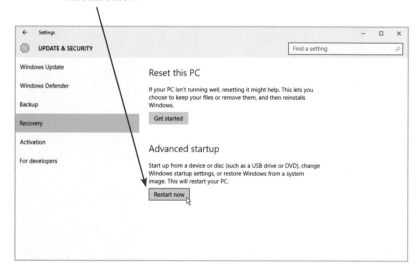

**3** When asked to "Choose an option", choose **Troubleshoot**

Advanced options also includes System Restore, Start-up Repair, Command Prompt and Start-up Settings. These can all be useful depending on the circumstances.

**4** On the "Troubleshoot" page, select **Advanced options**

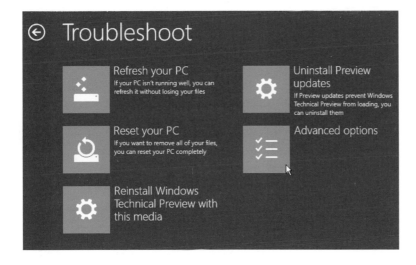

The restore procedure cannot take place while Windows is running.

…cont'd

**5** Now, select **System Image Recovery**. The PC will reboot and the recovery configuration procedure will begin

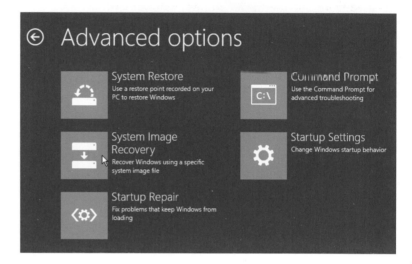

If you have several image backups, by default, Windows will select the most recent one.

**6** Select the required image – if you only have one, Windows will select it automatically

**7** Click **Next, Finish**. Your system will now be restored from the image backup

When the image has been restored, the computer will restart and boot into your newly-restored Windows.

# System recovery drive

There will be occasions when it is impossible to get into Windows for some reason – damaged startup files is a typical example. For this reason, recovery and troubleshooting utilities have to be accessible from outside the Windows environment.

To be able to use the Windows utilities in this type of situation, they have to be first placed on removable media.

**1**    Go to the Control Panel and open **File History**

**2**    In the File History window, click the **Recovery** link at the bottom-left of the window

**3**    Now, choose the option to **Create a recovery drive**

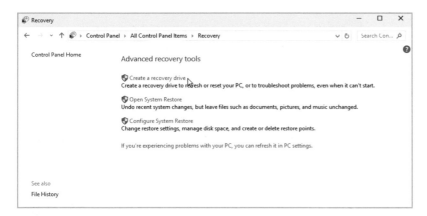

**4**    Follow the prompts to create a Windows recovery drive

Note that you will need a USB flash drive for this procedure. Also, it will erase anything already stored on the drive. So either use an empty drive or make sure you transfer any important data to another storage device.

### Using your recovery drive
The time to use your recovery drive is when you are unable to boot your computer into Windows. When you find yourself in this situation, do the following:

All the backups in the world are no good to you if you cannot get into the system. Make your recovery drive now.

...cont'd

**1** Connect the recovery drive to your computer

**2** Start the PC and go into the BIOS where you need to set the recovery drive as the boot drive – see page 43, where we explain how to do this. The procedure here is the same, apart from the fact that you want to set the recovery drive as the boot drive rather than the CD/DVD drive

**3** Restart the computer

**4** When the "Choose an option" screen opens, select **Troubleshoot**. This opens "Advanced options"

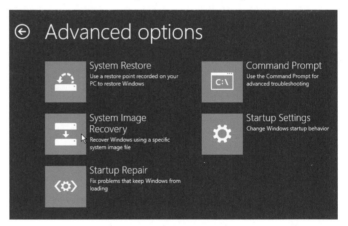

Here, you have five troubleshooting and recovery tools that will enable you to resolve most of the issues that are likely to occur.

The first option, **System Restore**, will undo any changes made to a system by installing software. So, if you've inadvertently downloaded a virus or malware, System Restore will fix it.

**System Image Recovery** we've already looked at on pages 372-374, while **Startup Repair** will fix issues that prevent Windows from booting.

**Command Prompt** is an advanced troubleshooting tool and will only be of use to people who know how to use it.

Finally, **Startup Settings** enables you to start Windows in various troubleshooting modes that can help you fix a range of problems.

# 22

# Security and encryption

*If your system or your storage devices contain sensitive information you can protect the data, even if the device is lost or stolen, using the various encryption facilities that are included in Windows 10.*

# User account management

There are several ways to manage user accounts on your computer. The primary option is User Accounts in the Control Panel. This is used to create or remove user accounts, change the account types, add or change passwords, or change the pictures associated with accounts.

**Don't forget**

The regular **User Accounts** applet is in the Control Panel.

**Beware**

This alternative **User Accounts** is very powerful and should only be used with caution.

If you have several users sharing your computer, you may want to enable Secure sign-in. To set this up, you need the alternative User Accounts dialog.

**1** Press **WinKey + R** to open the Run box

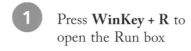

**2** Type the command "control userpasswords2" and press **OK**

**3** Select the **Advanced** tab to show **Secure sign-in**

**Hot tip**

Setting **Secure sign-in** guarantees that the sign-in prompt is genuine, not an external program trying to discover your password.

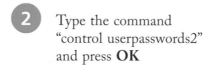

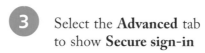

**4** Check the box that will **Require users to press Ctrl + Alt + Delete**

**...cont'd**

In the Pro and Enterprise editions of Windows 10, you can manage user accounts with the Local Users and Groups policy editor. There are several ways to display this. For example:

**1** From the "Advanced" tab of the second User Accounts option, click the **Advanced** button

**2** Press **WinKey + R**, type "lusrmgr.msc" then hit **Enter**

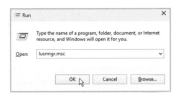

**3** When the panel opens, click **Users** and you will see an extra user, **Administrator**, not shown in User Accounts

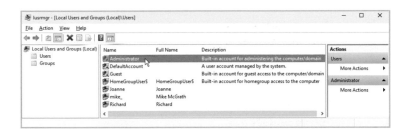

**4** Double-click user account **Administrator** to display its Properties, and you'll see it is disabled by default

This is a built-in account that is automatically created but not normally used. If you do choose to use it, make sure to set a password.

**5** If you do enable this account, make sure to select **Action**, then **Set password**

# Set password to expire

By default, your password can remain the same forever, but you are recommended to change it on a regular basis. Windows can be set to ensure that this happens.

 Open "Local Users and Groups" (see page 379), select your username and click **More Actions**, **Properties**

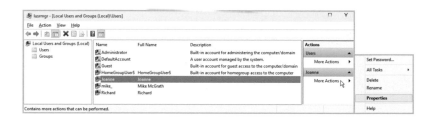

**2** Clear the box for "Password never expires" and click **User must change password at next logon**, then **Apply**, **OK**

**3** Close Local Users and Groups, then open "Local Security Policy" (see page 382) and expand **Account Policies**

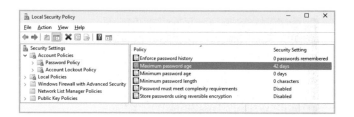

**4** Select **Password Policy**, then **Maximum password age**

**5** When you next sign on to the computer, select your account name as usual and enter your current password

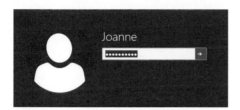

**6** Your password needs to be changed. Click **OK**

**7** Enter your existing password, then the new password and then confirm the new password and continue

**8** Windows changes the password and confirms the change

**9** Click **OK** and Windows starts. The password is reset, and future sign-ons will proceed without interruption

When you enter a new password, Windows reminds you that you can create a password reset disk. However, it is only needed once, not every time you change your password.

When the specified period has passed, Windows will again notify you that the password has expired and require you to provide a new password.

# Hide user list

Whenever you start Windows, or switch users, the "Sign on" screen lists all usernames defined for that computer by default.

**Don't forget**

You'd make changes like this if you have to leave your computer unattended, for example when running a presentation at a meeting or show.

You might feel it would be more secure for the names to remain hidden, especially if you are using your computer in a public area. You can do this using the Local Security Policy.

**1** Press **WinKey + R** and type "secpol.msc", then hit **Enter** to open "Local Security Policy"

**2** Expand **Local Policies**, select **Security Options** and locate **Interactive logon: Do not display last user name**

**Don't forget**

Local Security Policy is in Windows 10 Pro and Windows 10 Enterprise editions, but not available in the Windows 10 Home edition.

**3** Double-click the entry to display the Properties, select **Enabled**, and then click **OK**

**4** The entry will now be shown as Enabled, so click **File**, **Close** to save the change

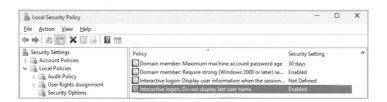

**5** The next time you start Windows, or switch users, the "Sign on" screen is displayed without usernames

**6** Type your username and your password to sign on

**7** If you make a mistake, you are just told the username or password is incorrect, and you must click **OK** and try again

If you have other users on the computer with administrator accounts, they can, of course, view the list of users in **User Accounts**, or make changes to Security Options to reverse the setting.

There's no user picture, and no **Switch Users** button. If you enter a wrong value, there's no clue and the password reminder is not offered, to preserve the security.

Anyone getting hold of a copy of the files won't be able to access their contents. Even another user logged on to your computer is unable to access the files.

TPM hardware will normally be found on business machines rather than home computers. However, a USB flash drive can be used in place of TPM.

You need a system partition in addition to the Windows volume. This system partition is normally set up when Windows is installed.

# Encrypting files

You might be storing personal, financial or other information on your computer that you wouldn't want others to read. Some editions of Windows include encryption tools that can help protect confidential data. There are three components:

- **Encrypting File System (EFS)** – with this, your sensitive files and folders can be encoded so that they can only be read when you log on to the computer with the associated user account.

- **BitLocker Drive Encryption** – this is used to encrypt an entire hard disk volume. The encryption is linked to a key stored in a Trusted Platform Module (TPM) or USB flash drive.

- **BitLocker To Go** – this provides BitLocker encryption for removable media.

## Windows editions with encryption

EFS is available in the Pro and Enterprise versions of Windows 10, 8.0 and 8.1, and the Professional, Enterprise and Ultimate editions of Windows 7. You must have Pro and Enterprise versions of Windows 10, Windows 8 or 8.1, Windows 7 Enterprise or Windows 7 Ultimate to use BitLocker or BitLocker To Go.

There are no facilities to encrypt files in the Home Premium, Home Basic or Starter editions. However, when you encrypt a USB flash drive with BitLocker To Go, you can add, delete, and change files on that drive using any edition of Windows 7.

Systems running Windows XP and Windows Vista can, with the appropriate authentication, open and read the files on an encrypted drive using the reader program that is included on the drive itself. However, files cannot be changed or added.

## Hardware requirements

For Bitlocker drive encryption of the whole system, the Windows partition and the System partition must both have NTFS format.

You can use BitLocker to encrypt additional fixed data drives, and BitLocker To Go to encrypt your removable data drives. These drives must have at least 64MB of available space and can be formatted using FAT or NTFS (unless intended for Windows XP or Windows Vista, where FAT will be required).

# Using EFS

You can encrypt individual files, whole folders, or entire drives using EFS. However, it is best to encrypt by folder (or by drive) rather than by individual file. This means that the existing files would be encrypted, and new files that get created in that folder or drive will also be encrypted – including any temporary files that applications might generate.

To encrypt the contents of a folder on your hard drive:

**1** Locate the folder in File Explorer then right-click the folder icon and select **Properties**

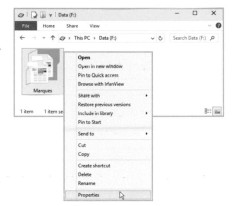

**2** Click the **Advanced** button on the **General** tab to see Advanced Attributes

**3** Select **Encrypt contents to secure data**, then click **OK**

**4** Click **OK** in Properties to apply the change

**5** Select **Apply changes to this folder, subfolders and files**, then click **OK** to continue

If you allowed encryption of individual files in a folder, temporary files created there would be unencrypted, even though they could contain copies of the information you are trying to protect.

If the folder is on a drive that is not formatted as NTFS, there will be no **Advanced** button, and EFS encryption will not be available.

If you choose **Apply changes to this folder only,** only new files will be encrypted – not existing files.

**...cont'd**

 Your encryption
certificate is created,
and the folder and
its contents are
encrypted

When encryption completes, check the folder in File Explorer,
and you'll see the name text for the folder and its files have been
re-colored in green, whether you display the contents as Tiles,
List or any other view.

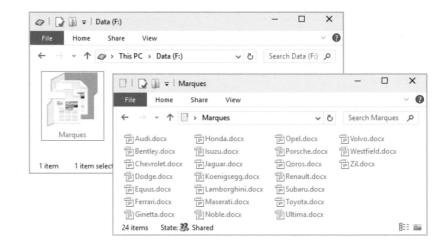

When you work with encrypted files from your user account,
that's the only visible difference. Windows will decrypt your files
as you use them and will re-encrypt them when you save, and it is
all fully automatic.

Another user logging on to your system may be able to see the
folder and open it to display the contents. However, any attempt
to access the files will give an error message from the associated
application, saying that access is denied.

Similarly, copying or moving of
encrypted files will be denied.
Even administrator user
accounts will be denied access.

# Backup encryption key

**1** Press **WinKey + R**, and enter "certmgr.msc"

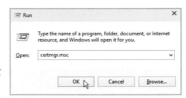

**2** Expand **Personal** and select **Certificates**

If you lose the certificate, perhaps due to a hard disk failure, you won't be able to use your encrypted files. That's why you are advised to create a backup.

**3** Select the certificate for the Encrypting File System

**4** Select **Action** and choose **All Tasks, Export**

**5** The Certificate Export Wizard starts. Click **Next**

**6** Click **Yes, export the private key** with the certificate, then click **Next**

You'll need a removable device such as a USB flash drive, which is not encrypted and which can be kept physically secure.

**7** Select the Personal Information Exchange (**.PFX**) file format, and click **Next**

## ...cont'd

**8** Provide a password, and re-enter it to confirm. Click **Next**

**9** Click **Browse** to choose the destination drive

**10** Select the storage device, enter the file name, and click **Open**

**Hot tip**

You could use the same device as you used to create a password reset disk, since it has the same security requirements.

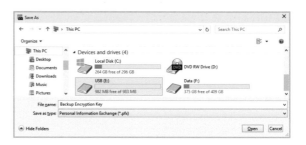

**11** Click **Next** to confirm name and location

**12** Click **Finish** to complete the Wizard

**Beware**

Remove the storage media and store it in a safe location, since it can enable anyone to access your encrypted files.

To restore the certificate, you'd insert the backup media, run **certmgr.msc** to open Certificate Manager, select Personal, Action, All Tasks, Import, then follow the Certificate Import Wizard.

# BitLocker To Go

To encrypt a removable drive with Windows Pro or Enterprise:

**1** Connect the drive and press **WinKey + X** to open the Power User Menu. Select **File Explorer**

**2** Right-click the drive icon and select **Turn on Bitlocker**

**3** Choose how you want to unlock this drive – password or smart card

*Hot tip*

Large organizations use smart cards for network authentication and have computers with smart card readers that can access the cards and store information there.

**4** Select **password** and enter your password, enter it again to confirm, then click **Next**

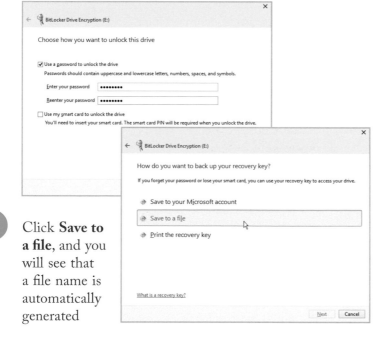

**5** Click **Save to a file**, and you will see that a file name is automatically generated

*Hot tip*

A good choice might be the USB flash drive being used as the password reset disk and for your EFS certificate.

**6** Specify the drive and click **Save**

## ...cont'd

**Hot tip**

The **Next** button is grayed out until you save or print the recovery key, then it is enabled and becomes ready to use.

**Beware**

If, for any reason, you need to remove the drive before completion, click **Pause** to interrupt the processing, or else files could be damaged.

**7** You can also choose to print the recovery key. When the key has been saved or printed, click **Next**

**8** Choose how much of the drive to encrypt, then click **Next**

**9** Click **Start encrypting** and the files on the removable device are processed

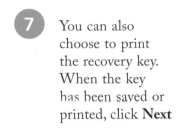

**10** Click **Close** when encryption completes

**11** Open **File Explorer** and you'll see the Lock symbol on the drive icon which indicates it is protected by encryption

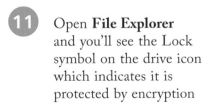

# Access the encrypted drive

To access the drive:

**1** Insert the removable device and BitLocker will tell you the device is protected

**2** Click on the message to open the password screen

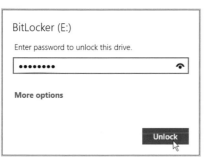

Click **More options** (see Step 3) and you will be able to select **Automatically unlock on this computer** from now on. Windows will remember the password for you.

391

**3** Unlock the drive by entering the password and clicking the **Unlock** button

**4** If you cannot remember the password, click **More options**. Then, enter the recovery key

**5** The drive opens. You can open, edit and save files or create new files on this drive, and they will be encrypted

**6** Once you have access to the encrypted drive, further options are available by right-clicking on the drive icon

Remember to always use **Safely Remove Hardware** before removing a USB drive.

**7** Choose **Manage BitLocker**, and click **Turn off BitLocker** if you want to decrypt the drive, back to its original state

# Whole system encryption

**1** Go to the Control Panel, **System and Security**, and open **BitLocker Drive Encryption**

**2** Select **Turn on BitLocker** for the system or data drive and then follow the prompts to encrypt the drive

Hot tip

To totally protect your computer and prevent access to your data, you can use BitLocker to encrypt the Windows boot drive and internal data drives.

**3** Any problems with the computer setup will be detected

Beware

You can enable TPM in the BIOS, or you can configure BitLocker to use a USB drive instead. However, problems with BitLocker could make your system inaccessible, so only proceed with this if you have adequate technical support.

**4** Press **WinKey + R**, and enter "tpm.msc" to run TPM (Trusted Platform Module) Management, and you may find the TPM module cannot be found

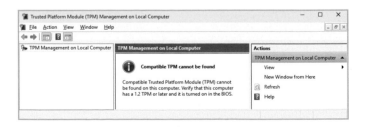

# 23 Command Prompt

*Most users won't need it, but Command Prompt in Windows can be very useful in certain situations. There's an administrator mode when necessary for the tasks being run.*

# Open Command Prompt

All editions of Windows 10 include the Command Prompt environment, where you can run commands, batch files and applications by typing statements at the command line.

There are a number of ways to start a Command Prompt session:

**1** Press **WinKey + X** to open the Power User Menu. Select **Command Prompt**

**2** Press **WinKey + R** to open the Run box. Type "cmd.exe" then click **OK**

**3** In the Taskbar Search box enter "cmd.exe" or simply enter "cmd"

**4** On the Start menu click **Command Prompt** in "Windows System" group

**5** Double-click any shortcut to the **cmd.exe** program

All these methods will start a Command Prompt session, open at the path location **C:\Users\\*username*** ready to accept commands.

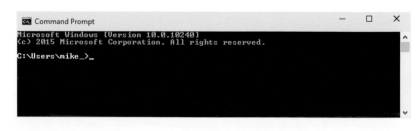

**394**

**6** You can open additional, independent Command Prompt sessions, using the same methods

**7** Alternatively, from an existing session, type **start cmd** on the command line and press **Enter**

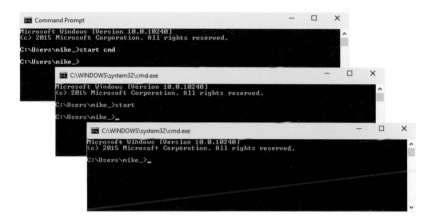

You might use multiple sessions to compare the contents of two or more folders.

**8** The new sessions are given the program path and name as title, and they open in your *username* folder

You can also open a Command Prompt window from the folder located at **C:\Windows\System32**.

If you just enter "start" it is assumed you want to start **cmd.exe**, so this also opens a Command Prompt session.

**1** Open the folder **C:\Windows\System32** and click the **cmd.exe** program icon

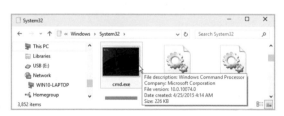

If you have a different folder or drive specified for your Windows system, folder paths will be adjusted accordingly.

# Select a folder

You can switch folders in the Command Prompt session using the CD (Change Directory) command. For example, to open the current user's Pictures folder, starting from System32:

**1** On the Command Line, type these four CD commands, pressing **Enter** after each command:
**cd \    cd users    cd "john smith"    cd pictures**

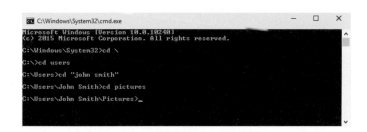

Note that case does not matter. When there are spaces in the file or folder names, you should enclose those names within quotation marks.

To avoid problems with long or complex file names, you can open a Command Session directly at the required folder.

**1** Open File Explorer and use the normal Windows methods to find the desired folder – from either the Contents pane or the Navigation pane

**2** Press and hold **Shift**, then right-click the folder

The Command Prompt session is opened and switched to the required folder.

**3** From the extended right-click menu displayed, select the entry to **Open command window here**

# Open as administrator

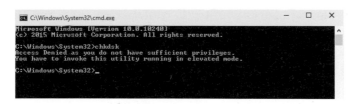

The Command Prompt session opened has, by default, the standard user level of privilege. If some commands that you want to run require administrator privilege, you can open an elevated session using the following methods:

**1** Open **C:\Windows\System32**, right-click **cmd.exe** and select **Run as administrator**

**2** Enter "cmd" in the Taskbar Search bar then right-click on Command Prompt and select **Run as administrator**

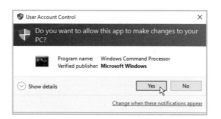

**3** Click **Yes** in the **User Account Control (UAC)** dialog box – to start a Command Prompt session with an "Administrator" window title:

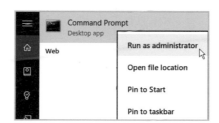

If you click the **Command Prompt (Admin)** entry from the Power User Menu (**WinKey + X**), you get a Command Prompt session, entitled "Administrator: Command Prompt". This also opens at the System32 folder, not the user's folder.

Commands that have system-wide effect are restricted to run only in the elevated administrator mode.

You can also type **start** or **start cmd** on the command line of an existing administrator session to get another administrator session – no UAC required.

397

# Administrator shortcut

You can configure a shortcut to **cmd.exe** to always start in administrator mode:

**1** Create a shortcut to **cmd.exe** (at **C:\Windows\System32\cmd.exe**)

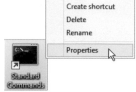

**2** Right-click the shortcut and select **Properties** from the menu

**3** Select the **Shortcut** tab and click the **Advanced** button

**4** Check the box **Run as administrator** and click **OK**, then **OK** again

**5** Right-click the shortcut icon, select **Rename** and give it a meaningful name

**6** For example, you could rename "Standard Commands" to "Elevated Commands"

**7** Double-click the renamed shortcut to start the administrator session

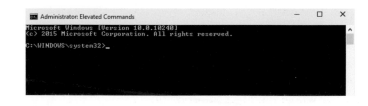

# Adjust appearance

You can adjust the Properties shortcut to control the appearance of the Command Prompt window that is launched by that shortcut:

**1** Right-click the shortcut icon and click **Properties**

**2** Select the **Options** tab

From here, you can adjust the size of the flashing cursor, change how the command history is managed, and change edit options.

**3** Select the **Font** tab to choose a different font

You can also adjust the properties from the Command Prompt window - right-click on the title bar then choose **Properties** from the context menu.

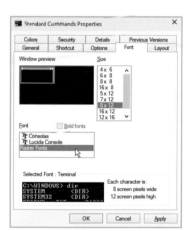

**4** The recommended font is Consolas, since this is a ClearType font that will be more readable in the window

The fonts for the Command Prompt window must be fixed-pitch.

**5** Select **Layout** to change the buffer size and screen size

Adjust the width if the default 80 characters is not enough, and change the height (in this case from the default 25 lines to 10 lines).
A vertical scrollbar allows you to view the whole buffer of information.

## ...cont'd

**6** Select the **Colors** tab, to change the colors used for the screen text and pop-up text and their backgrounds

You choose color values between 0 and 255, for the Red, Green and Blue components.

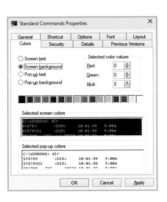 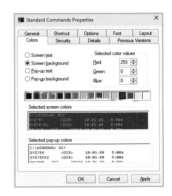

**7** Select **Screen Background** and **Screen Text** and choose from the color swatches, or enter the required color values

**8** Select **Apply** to apply any changes immediately, and **OK** to complete any changes and close the Properties dialog

**9** Double-click the shortcut icon to display the Command Prompt session and see all the changes in effect

When you make such changes to the shortcut Properties, your new settings will be retained and applied whenever you start a Command Prompt using that shortcut.

Repeat the process to adjust the Properties for a shortcut used for a standard-level Command Prompt. You might choose Blue text on a Yellow background, to distinguish the standard sessions from White text on Red background administrator sessions. Double-click the Standard Commands shortcut to view the effect.

# Changing window properties

**1** Select Command Prompt using any of the methods covered

**2** Right-click the title bar and select **Properties**

This displays the tabs Options, Font, Layout, and Colors for the shortcut Properties. Any changes you make here are for the current session and any future settings started using the same method. Similarly, if you start a session via a shortcut the changes apply for that shortcut only.

**3** To make changes that will apply to future sessions, right-click the title bar and select **Defaults** from the menu

**4** This opens the Console Windows Properties

The changes you make will not affect the current session but will be applied for all future sessions (except for those launched from a shortcut whose properties have been customized).

These changes also affect future sessions in character-mode, MS-DOS-based applications that do not have a program-information file (PIF) or store their own settings.

You can also make changes to the properties when you have a Command Prompt session already started.

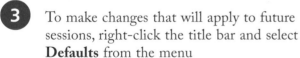

Command Prompt has been improved in Windows 10 to allow direct copy-and-paste from the clipboard to the command line, and you can find new features on the Options tab.

# Using the Command Prompt

You'll use the Command Prompt to carry out tasks that are not easily achieved using the normal Windows functions. A typical example is to create a text file containing the names of all the files of a particular type in a folder:

To list a different type of file, just change .jpg to the required file type, e.g. .doc. You can also list more than one file type, for example:
dir *.jpg *.tif > filelist.txt

**1** Open a prompt at the required folder, using the Shift + right-click menu option **Open command window here**

**2** Put the following on the command line and press **Enter**:
**dir *.jpg > filelist.txt**

**3** Open the folder and you will see a file called "filelist"

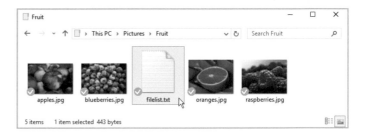

To see a list of files but no attributes, you'd enter
dir *.jpg /b >filelist.txt

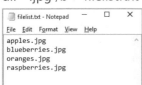

**4** Open the file and you'll see a list of all JPG files in the folder, the date and time they were created, and their file size

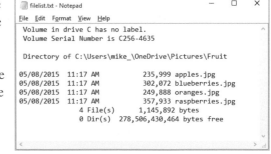

**...cont'd**

If your Command Prompt session is already open, you need to switch directories to get to the required folder. Here, you can use Windows features to assist the Command Prompt operation.

**1** Open the required folder in File Explorer

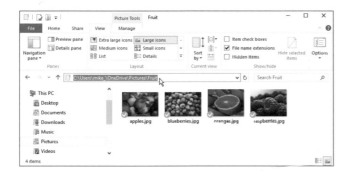

**2** Click the Address bar to show the path and press **Ctrl + C**

**3** Switch to the Command Prompt and type the command **cd** (followed by a single space)

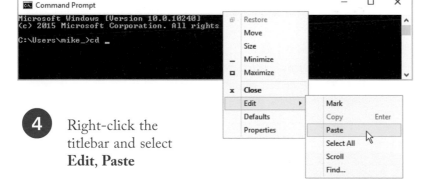

**4** Right-click the titlebar and select **Edit, Paste**

When you select Paste, the contents of the Clipboard are copied to the command line, thus completing the CD command already started.

**5** Press **Enter** to run the command and switch directories

# Command line changes

There are lots of aids you can take advantage of when working on the Command line. This example session illustrates some of these.

**1** To switch to a parent directory, enter the command **cd ..**

**2** Press the up-arrow and press **Enter** to repeat the command

**3** At **C:\Users**, type **cd** then press **Tab** until the required user name appears, then press **Enter**

**4** Open a "Trial" folder and type **copy** (followed by space)

The Tab key displays the files and directories in the current directory in alphabetic sequence, displaying the next one each time it is pressed.

When you make an error in a command, the up-arrow lets you redisplay it and you can insert or delete characters as needed for correction.

The right-arrow copies the command, letter by letter. Tab inserts the next file name, and then you copy the new name, amending where necessary.

**5** Right-click the titlebar, select **Mark** and highlight the path for Sample Pictures, then Copy and Paste – quote marks are needed, since there are blanks in the path, so just press Up then edit the command as needed

**6** Type a **ren** Rename command, and press **Tab** to insert the first of the file names in the directory

**7** Use the right-arrow and **Tab** to copy/amend the command

# (24) Update and maintain

You need to regularly update Windows and other applications on your PC, to ensure the system keeps working effectively and to incorporate the latest security and performance features. Windows Update automates this process.

# Windows Update

The Windows operating system requires frequent updates to keep it secure and fully operational. Updates are provided on a regular basis for Windows 10 and should be applied when available.

To see what the update situation is for your computer:

1 Go to the Start menu and click **Settings**

You can alternatively type "settings" into the Taskbar Search box to open the Settings window.

2 In the Settings window, click **Update & security**

Unlike previous versions of Windows, whose updates only provided periodical security patches and bug fixes, the Update model in Windows 10 provides continuous security and feature improvements.

3 Next, in the left panel, click **Windows Update**

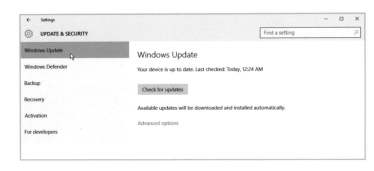

**4** Now, in the right panel, click **Check for updates** – then wait to see if any updates are available

If Automatic Updating has been set, the indication of updates waiting appears immediately when you open Windows Update.

**5** If there are updates waiting, you can click **Install updates** and they will be downloaded and installed

407

**6** When installation completes you may be asked to restart the system, so that appropriate files can be updated

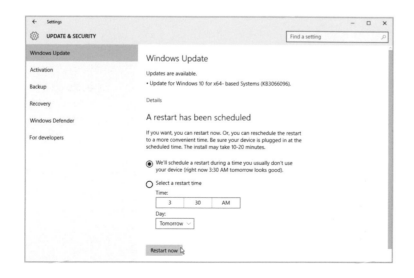

You can selectively apply updates in this manner, but it is much easier to let Windows Update do the job automatically.

# Update settings

**1** Open Settings, **Update & security,** Windows Update, and select the **Advanced options** link

Use Advanced options to turn on Automatic updates and to specify what type of updates take place.

**2** Choose how you want Windows to install updates on your system

**3** Install updates automatically is recommended, or you can choose to receive notifications to schedule restarts

Updates will happen in the background, and you will get an occasional message letting you know about completed updates and actions to be taken, such as restarts.

**4** Simply close this Settings window to apply the changes

# Microsoft Update

**1** Open Settings, **Update & security,** Windows Update, and select the **Advanced options** link

Microsoft Update will provide updates for Office, MSN, Windows Defender, and various Windows Server-related products.

**2** Check the **Give me updates for other Microsoft products when I update Windows** checkbox

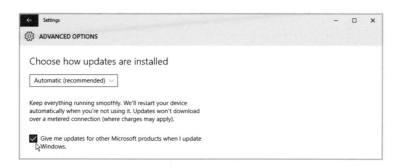

**3** Simply close this Settings window to apply the changes

**4** The next time you open Windows update, you'll see that updates for supported Microsoft products are now being downloaded and installed automatically

# Update sources

**1** Open Settings, **Update & security**, Windows Update, and select the **Advanced options** link

**2** Next, click the **Choose how updates are delivered** link

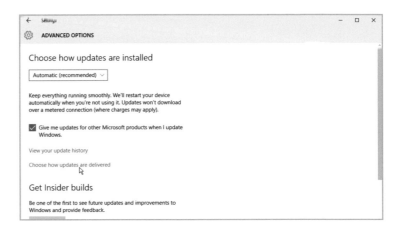

**3** Use the button to turn **On** or **Off** permission to get updates from multiple sources as required

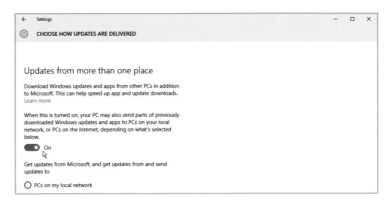

Allow updates from PCs on your local network and from the internet to be received the most quickly.

**4** Simply close this Settings window to apply the changes

# Update history

Updates may be applied automatically, in the background, but you can review the activities:

**1** Open Settings, **Update & security**, Windows Update, and select the **Advanced options** link

**2** Next, click the **View your update history** link

There's an entry for every attempt to apply an update and results are marked as **Successfully installed** or Failed to install.

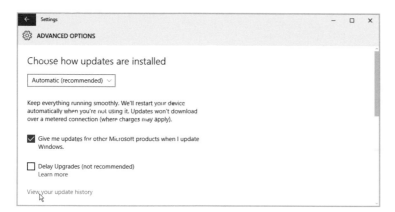

**3** The updates are displayed, latest first

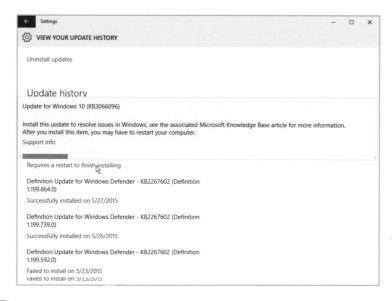

Identify important updates that have failed, and check to ensure that a subsequent update attempt succeeded.

**4** Click the link at the bottom of any update item to see more information about that update

## ...cont'd

You can review the Windows and other updates that have been installed on your computer, and remove any that may be causing problems.

**1** From the "View your update history" screen, select the **Uninstall updates** link

**Hot tip**

There are some updates that cannot be removed this way. If that is the case, there will be no **Uninstall** button shown when you select the update.

**2** Select an update and click **Uninstall** on the toolbar to remove that update

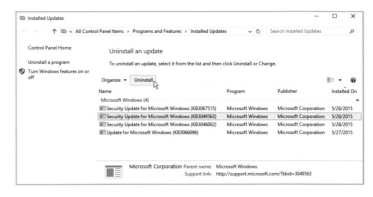

**Hot tip**

You can switch back and forth between the Updates and the Programs list, using the links in the left-hand pane.

**3** You can also change the appearance of the update items using the **More options** button on the toolbar – for example, from the Details view above, to Tiles view below

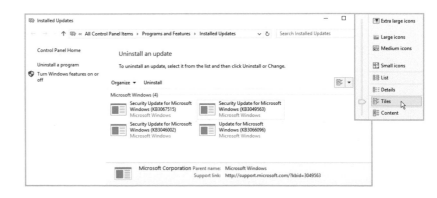

# Installed updates

Installed updates can also be managed via the Control Panel:

**1** Open the Control Panel and **Programs and Features**

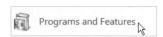
Programs and Features

**2** On the left pane, click **View installed updates**

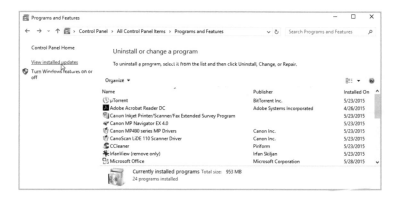

**3** Click the arrow buttons at the right of each category heading to expand or collapse the list of updates for each category, and to view details

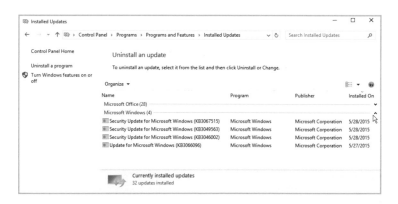

Click the **Uninstall a program** link in the left pane to manage installed programs.

**4** Select an update and click **Uninstall** on the toolbar to remove that update

You can see a comparison of features in each edition of Windows 10 on pages 16-17.

You can install any edition of 64-bit Windows on your computer if it is 64-bit capable and has enough memory to make the transition worthwhile – ideally 4GB of memory.

# Upgrading Windows

Sometimes, adding updates isn't enough – you need to upgrade your edition of Windows to an edition that has the extra functions that you need. Alternatively, you may want to upgrade from 32-bit Windows to 64-bit Windows, so your computer can take advantage of the larger amounts of memory that 64-bit systems can utilize.

### 32 bit to 64-bit
This isn't an upgrade in the usual sense – you cannot install the new operating system and retain existing folders and data files. Instead, you create a completely new system, replacing the existing setup, then install your applications and apply Windows updates. You can backup your data files and folders before you make the change and restore the backup to your revised system. However, you will have to re-install all your apps and may need to install 64-bit versions of drivers for devices unless Windows has them.

### Upgrading editions
Changing editions can be carried out as a true upgrade. You update the operating system files, but leave your data files and folders unaffected. The application programs that you have installed will continue to operate.

### Upgrade paths
With Windows 7 there were a number of upgrade paths possible between the various versions. Windows 10, however, provides only one – if you currently have the entry version, Windows 10 Home, you can upgrade it to Windows 10 Pro. To implement this upgrade you will need to buy the Windows 10 Pro Pack from the Windows Store – open Settings, **Update & security**, Activation, then press the **Go to Store** button:

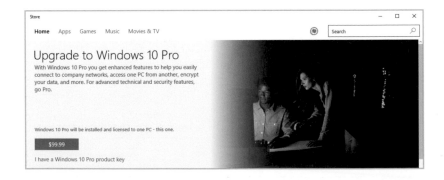

# Resetting your PC

If you want to return your system to its initial state if, for example, you are disposing of a PC, Windows 10 provides an easy way to reset the system. This procedure provides three options of how thoroughly the reset should clean the system:

- **Reset Windows only** – this restores the Windows system files and keeps your personal files and apps intact

- **Reset Windows to new** – this restores the Windows system files and deletes your personal files and apps

- **Reset Windows and clean** – this restores the Windows system files and completely removes your personal files and apps from the hard disk drive

You may just want to reset Windows 10 to its original pristine state if you have, over time, installed many apps or if you feel the system has become sluggish. Again, here, OneDrive proves invaluable as you can simply access your personal files there.

**1** Open Settings, **Update & security**, then select the **Recovery** option on the left pane

**2** Under "Reset this PC", click the **Get started** button

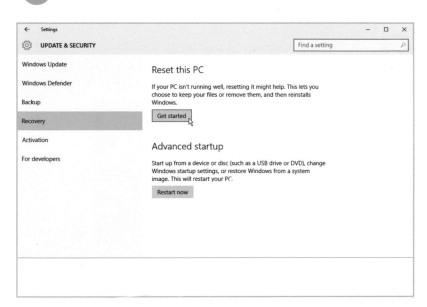

Resetting Windows 10 is like re-installing the operating system, so it does take some time.

Notice that you also have an option here to revert to the previously-installed version of Windows if you recently upgraded the PC to Windows 10.

...cont'd

**3** Choose whether you would like to remove or keep your personal files and apps – e.g., click **Remove everything**

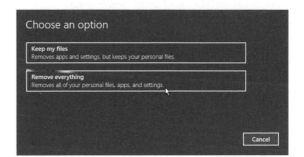

If you are selling the PC you should choose the **Remove files and clean the drive** option.

**4** Now, choose whether you would also like to clean the drives – e.g., click **Remove files and clean the drive**

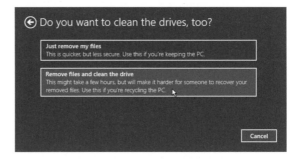

**5** Carefully review the actions to be performed by the reset and, if you are happy with these, click the **Reset** button

The reset process will require you to enter certain information, such as your location and your Wi-Fi key – just like installing Windows 10 for the very first time.

After Windows 10 is re-installed you can sign in with your Microsoft account to sync your files from OneDrive.

# Disk Cleanup

For everyday tasks you can use the tools found in drive properties.

**1** Press **WinKey + X**, select **File Explorer**, **This PC**, then right-click on a drive and click **Properties**

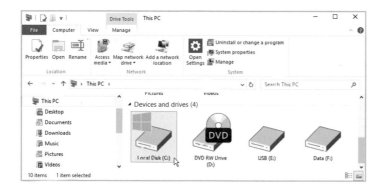

You could also select Disk Cleanup, from the list of **Administrative Tools** via Control Panel.

**2** In the **Properties** dialog box, select the **General** tab and click the **Disk Cleanup** button

**3** Disk Cleanup calculates the space to be released

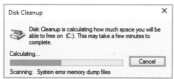

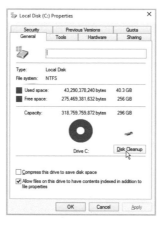

**4** Select or clear file categories and click the **View files** button to see what will be deleted for each category

**5** When you are happy with your selection, click **OK** to proceed with Disk Cleanup

Some categories of file are suggested, but you can select others, e.g. **Recycle Bin** or **Temporary Files**, to increase the amount of space that will be made available.

...cont'd

**6** Click **Delete Files** to confirm that you want to permanently delete the selected files

**7** Disk Cleanup proceeds to free the space used by those files

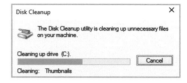

Note that you may be prompted for administrator permission to remove certain types of file. If so, you'll see a box that lets you extend the permission to all the files of that type. Make sure this box is checked and then click **Continue**.

### Clean up system files

If you need more free space, there will almost certainly be some system files that are not really necessary and can be removed safely. Old system restore files are a typical example (these can occupy gigabytes of disk space).

**1** Select **Disk Cleanup** then click **Clean up system files**

**2** Temporary files can also use a lot of disk space. System error memory dump files are also good candidates for deletion

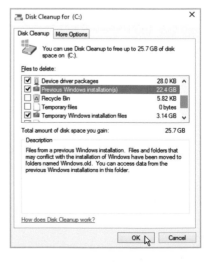

# Defragmentation

**1** From the Properties, Tools tab for any drive, click the **Optimize** button

**2** All drives that can be defragmented are listed, with the latest information about their fragmentation status

The larger the drive, the longer the optimization process takes.

**3** Select a drive and click the **Analyze** button to see the current state of the drive

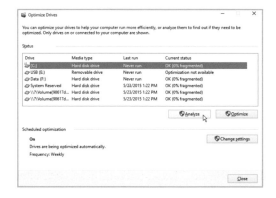

**4** Select the drive and click the **Optimize** button to analyze then defragment the drive

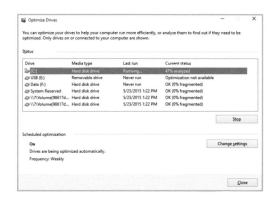

With the schedule turned on, you can still run an immediate defragment. Click **Change settings** to change the frequency or to turn off scheduled optimization entirely.

### ...cont'd

Windows automates the defragmentation process so that it happens in the background on a regular basis. However, you may wish to change the default settings:

**1** If it is not already done, click the **Turn on** button

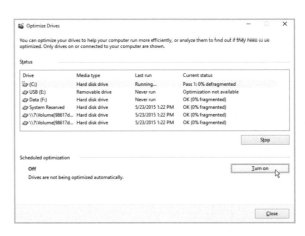

**2** Check **Run on a schedule**. Then set the desired schedule from the drop-down boxes

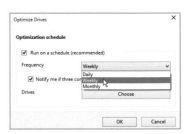

**3** Click the **Choose** button and select the drives to be optimized

**4** Click **OK**. Your drives will now be defragmented according to the settings specified. Click the **Close** button

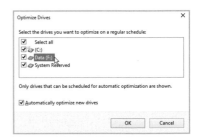

# 25 Windows performance

*Windows provides tools that measure the performance of your PC, and identifies issues affecting its performance. You can use monitoring tools and review detailed information about the PC. Windows will even help you speed up the system by using USB flash drives to act as a cache for system files.*

**Hot tip**

In the Control Panel you'll also display System Properties if you click either **View amount of RAM and processor speed**, or **See the name of this computer**.

# System properties

System Properties is an important location for reviewing and adjusting the performance of your computer, so Windows provides a number of ways for displaying this panel so that it is accessible from various areas within the system.

To display System Properties, use any of the following options:

**1** Open the Power users menu by pressing **WinKey + X** and selecting **System**

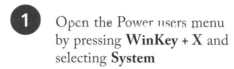

**2** Press **WinKey + X** and select **File Explorer, This PC**. On the ribbon toolbar, click **System properties**

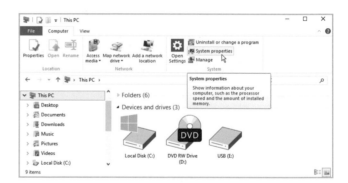

**3** Go to the Control Panel, **System and Security**, and click on the **System** icon link

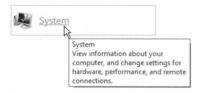

**4** Press **WinKey + Pause/Break**

**5** Whichever method you use, **System Properties** and **System** display basic information about your computer

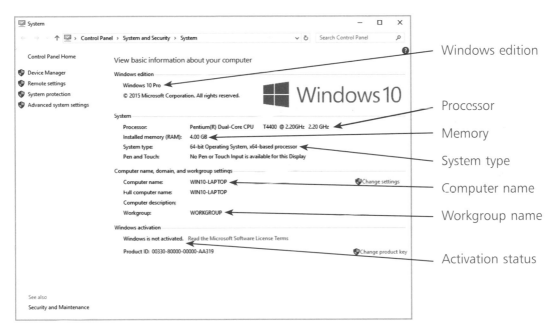

Windows edition

Processor

Memory

System type

Computer name

Workgroup name

Activation status

The pane on the left provides various links, including:

- Device Manager

- Remote settings

- System protection

- Advanced system settings

In the middle, you'll find details of the operating system. This tells you the edition of Windows installed on the PC.

Next are some basic details about the hardware in the PC. Here, you'll see the processor manufacturer, the model number and the speed of the device. Also listed is the amount of memory.

Hot tip

**Device Manager** provides details of the system components. **Advanced system settings** provides the full System Properties.

# Device Manager

As we saw on page 423, System Properties provides a link to the Device Manager at the top-left of the window. You can also access Device Manager directly in the Control Panel.

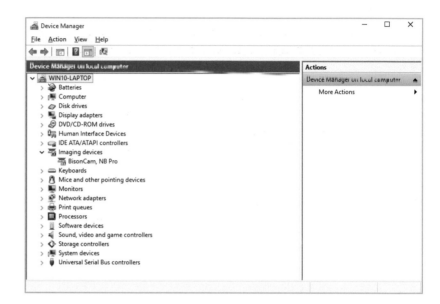

The Device Manager displays a list of your hardware, sorted by category. You can expand these categories to view which hardware you have installed in your computer.

**424**

So what is it, and what does it do? Essentially, the Device Manager is an extension of the Microsoft Management Console that provides a central and organized view of all the hardware installed in the computer.

Its purpose is to provide a means of managing this hardware. For example, hard drives, keyboards, sound cards, USB devices, etc.

Some of the things you can do with the Device Manager include:

- Change hardware configuration
- Manage hardware drivers
- Enable and disable hardware
- Identify and resolve conflicts between hardware devices
- View a device's status
- View a device's technical properties

Click the arrow to the left of the device categories to see what devices are in the category.

We'll take a look at how you can troubleshoot malfunctioning devices with the Device Manager on the next page.

## Troubleshooting with Device Manager

When a device in your computer has a problem, it is flagged as such in the Device Manager. Different symbols indicate specific types of problem. For example:

● A black exclamation point (!) on a yellow field indicates the device has a problem – although it may still be functioning.

In the screenshot on page 424 we see that the camera is flagged as having a problem. To see what the issue is, right-click on the device icon and select **Properties**. On the **General** tab under Device Status we see a message that says "The drivers for this device are not installed". Note that this can also indicate that the driver is present but has been corrupted. To resolve the issue, click the **Update Driver** button, or right-click the device icon and choose **Update Driver Software**. Windows will now try to locate the correct driver for the device and download and install it.

**Don't forget**

When you open the Device Manager, take note of any symbols you see. These indicate issues that will need to be resolved.

Other symbols indicate other issues that may require attention. For example:

● A down-arrow indicates a disabled device. Note that while the device may be disabled it is still consuming system resources and is thus reducing the performance of the system.

Right-click on the device icon and select **Properties**. On the **General** tab under Device Status we see a message that says "The device is disabled". To resolve the issue click the **Enable Device** button, or right-click the device icon and choose **Enable**. Windows will now enable the device ready for use.

**Hot tip**

The Driver tab in a device's Properties offers options to roll back to a previous driver, i.e. one that works properly, to disable the device and to uninstall the device.

# Improving performance

**1** Go to the Control Panel, **System and Security**, System. Click **Advanced system settings**, and then **Settings** under "Performance"

**2** The default **Let Windows choose what's best for my computer** will have most of the effects selected

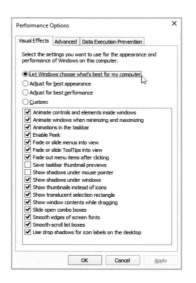

**3** Choosing **Adjust for best appearance** means <u>all</u> the effects will be selected

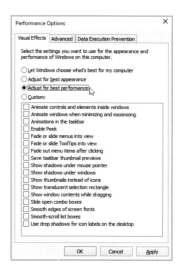

**4** You get <u>no</u> effects if you choose **Adjust for best performance**

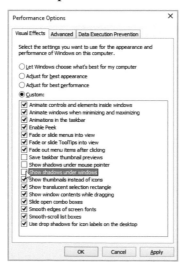

**5** The best balance is to select **Let Windows choose what's best for my computer**, click **Apply**, then deselect effects you can manage without

**6** Click **Apply**, and your choices of effects become the Custom setting

## Processor scheduling

**1** Click the **Advanced** tab, and you can choose to prioritize **Programs** or **Background services**

The usual choice is Programs, but you might choose Background for a computer that acts as a print server or provides backups.

### Virtual memory

Windows creates a Page file to supplement system memory. To review or change the settings:

**1** From the Advanced tab, click the Virtual memory **Change** button

By default, Windows will automatically manage the paging file for your drive or drives. To choose the values yourself:

**1** Uncheck **Automatically manage paging file size for all drives**

**2** Choose an initial size, and a maximum size, then click the **Set** button to apply

Setting the initial size the same as the maximum will avoid the need for Windows to adjust the size of the paging file, though this may not necessarily improve performance.

With multiple drives, choose the one with most space available.

You should only consider changing the processor scheduling on computers that are mainly used for background tasks.

Make sure you always have at least one drive with a paging file, even on a large-memory PC, since some programs rely on the paging file.

427

# Data Execution Prevention

The third tab in the Performance Options is for Data Execution Prevention or DEP. This is a security feature intended to prevent damage to your computer from viruses and other security threats, by monitoring programs to make sure they use system memory safely. If a program tries executing code from memory in an incorrect way, DEP closes the program.

**1** By default, Windows will turn on DEP for essential programs and services only

**2** You can choose to **Turn on DEP for all programs**

**3** Click **Add** to select programs for which you want to turn DEP off

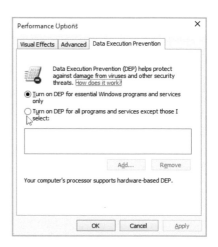

**Don't forget**

If you add a program to the exception list, but decide that you do want it to be monitored by DEP, you can clear the box next to the program.

If DEP keeps closing a particular program that you trust, and your antivirus software does not detect a threat, the program might not run correctly when DEP is turned on. You should check for a DEP-compatible version of the program, or an update from the software publisher, before you choose to turn off DEP for that program.

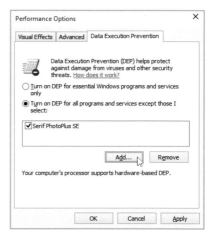

**Beware**

If DEP closes a program that is part of Windows, the cause could be a program you have recently installed that operates inside Windows. Check for a DEP-compatible version.

**428**

### Hardware-based DEP

Some processors use hardware technology to prevent programs from running code in protected memory locations. In this case, you will be told that your processor supports hardware-based DEP. If your processor does not support hardware-based DEP, your computer will still be protected because Windows will use software-based DEP.

# Advanced system settings

Windows provides another way to display the Performance Options:

**1** Open System Properties, **Advanced system settings**

**2** In the Performance section click the **Settings** button

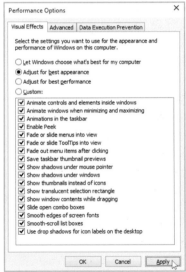

**3** Performance Options is displayed, with **Visual Effects** selected

**4** Select a tab and adjust settings to your liking

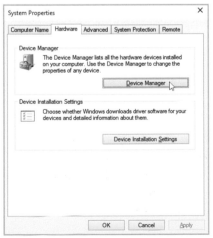

System Properties also gives access to Device Manager.

**5** Click the **Hardware** tab, then click the **Device Manager** button (or click the **Device Manager** link in the System panel)

The Device Manager lists all the hardware devices installed on your computer, and allows you to change their properties.

# Task Manager

Windows Task Manager is a very useful utility that is still available in Windows 10.

To access the Task Manager, right-click on the Taskbar and select **Task Manager**. Another way is to press **Ctrl + Alt + Delete** on the keyboard. Click **More details** at the bottom for an extended view.

The Task Manager allows you to do a number of things. These include viewing each of the tasks currently running on the computer, each of the **Processes**, your **App history**, **Services** and **Startup** programs. It also allows you to monitor the performance of the PC's hardware.

Click the **Performance** tab and on the left you will see entries for the major hardware in the system – CPU, Memory, Disk (hard drive), Ethernet, and Wi-Fi. These let you see how these devices are functioning and see any problems as they arise.

For example, click **Memory** and on the right you'll see two graphs. The first shows memory usage on a scale of 0 to the total amount of memory over a 60-second time frame. The second, **Memory Composition**, shows the memory used by processes, drivers, or the operating system.

Below that are listed various details, such as the amount of memory in use, the amount that is available, its speed, and more.

The CPU, Disk and Ethernet sections provide similar information and will allow you to keep a close eye on how your hardware is performing.

# Event Viewer

Another useful tool provided by Windows with which to monitor your system in regard to performance and troubleshooting is the Event Viewer.

**1** Go to Control Panel, **System and Security**, then click the **Administrative Tools** icon link

**2** Now, click **Event Viewer** then select **Windows Logs**

Hot tip

Advanced users might find the information helpful when troubleshooting problems with Windows or other programs. For most users, the Event Viewer will only be used when directed by technical support staff.

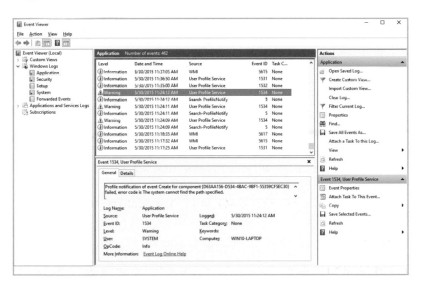

Windows identifies significant events on your computer. For example: when a program encounters an error or a user logs on. The details are recorded in event logs that you can read using the Event Viewer. Windows keeps the following useful logs:

**System Log** – this log records events logged by Windows' system components. For example, the failure of a driver or other system component to load during startup is recorded in the System log.

**Application Log** – the Application log records events logged by programs. For example, a database program might record a file error in the Application log.

**Security Log** – the Security log records security events, such as valid and invalid logon attempts, and events related to resource use, such as creating, opening, or deleting files or other objects. The Security Log helps track and identify possible breaches to security.

# Windows monitors

Open Performance Monitor by going to Control Panel, **System and Security**, **Administrative Tools**, **Performance Monitor**.

The program starts with an overview and a system summary. There's also a link to open the **Resource Monitor** program.

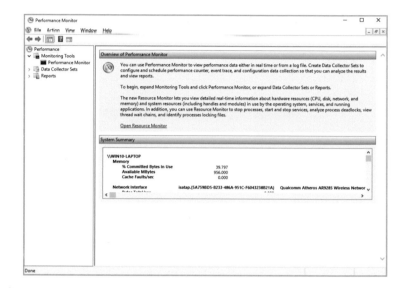

**1** Expand **Data Collector Sets** or **Reports** to see log details

**2** Expand **Monitoring Tools** and click **Performance Monitor** to display the graph of processor activity

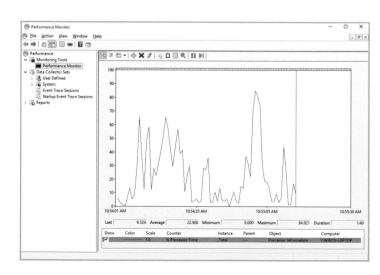

**...cont'd**

**3** Back in **Administrative Tools**, open **Resource Monitor**

With this you can view systems resource usage in real-time, and manage the active applications and services.

**4** Click **Overview** for a summary of computer activity

**5** Click **CPU** for processor details

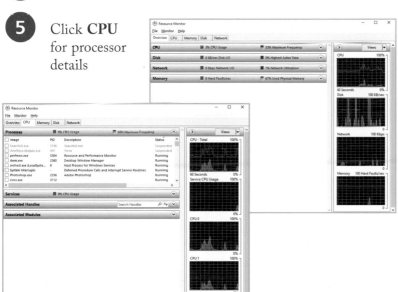

You can open the Resource Monitor utility from Advanced Tools, Performance Monitor or Task Manager.

**6** Click **Memory** for the allocation of physical memory

**7** Click **Disk** for disk activity by process

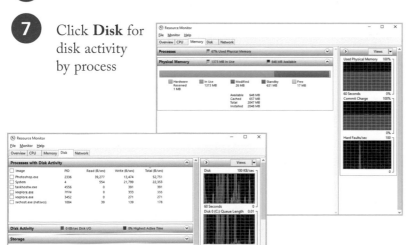

Resource Monitor also includes graphs for network data transfer activity.

# Information on the system

**1** Open Task Manager

This allows you to get information about the programs and processes that are currently running on the computer.

**2** Click **Processes** for a list of all open applications, and background processes for the current user

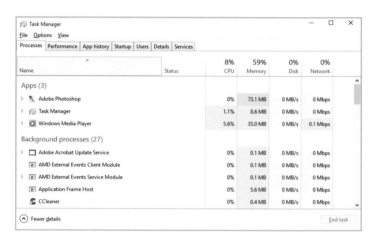

**3** Click **Performance** for graphs of CPU, memory, disk and network usage

**4** Click **App history** to see how each of your apps has used the CPU and the network

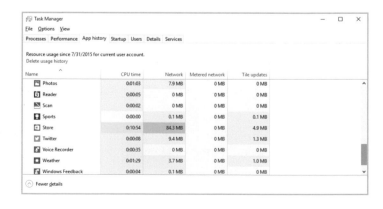

**5** Press **WinKey + R** then type "msinfo32" in the Run box to launch the System Information window

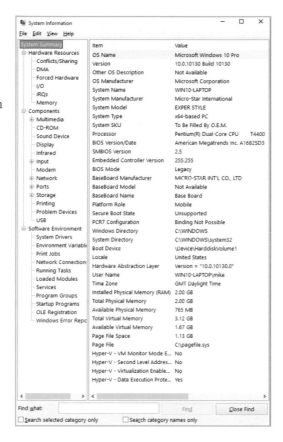

You could also enter "msinfo32" in the Taskbar Search box to open System Information.

435

System Information opens listing details of computer hardware configuration, components, software and drivers in four categories:

- **System Summary** – operating system, computer name, type of BIOS, boot device, username, amount of memory, etc.

- **Hardware Resources** – technical details of the computer's hardware, intended for IT professionals.

- **Components** – details of disk drives, sound devices, modems and other devices.

- **Software Environment** – shows information about drivers, network connections, and other program-related details.

To find a specific detail, type keywords in the **Find what** box, choose **Search selected category only** (if appropriate), then click the **Find** button.

# Reliability Monitor

**1** Go to Control Panel, **Security and Maintenance**, then click the down-arrow to expand the **Maintenance** section

**Security and Maintenance** provides links to several useful Windows tools.

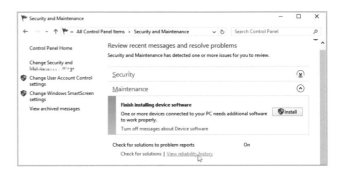

**2** Next, click the **View reliability history** link to launch the Reliability Monitor that records system problems

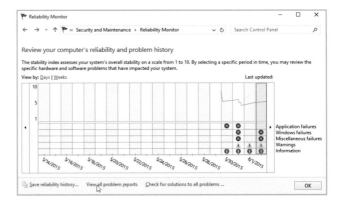

Click the **Check for solutions to all problems** link for help with any problem.

**3** Now, click the **View all problem reports** link to see details of each problem encountered

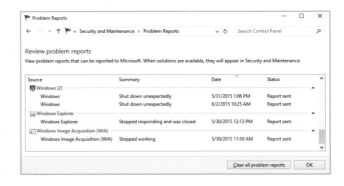

# Boosting performance

There's another way to boost the performance of your computer, without having to make major upgrades to the hardware. You can add USB components such as an external drive or a flash drive.

**1** Connect a second hard drive, for example the external hard disk drive (HDD) shown here:

**2** The first time you do this, Windows installs the device driver software automatically

**3** Windows assigns a drive letter to the drive

The HDD drive is listed under **This PC** in the **Devices and drives** category.

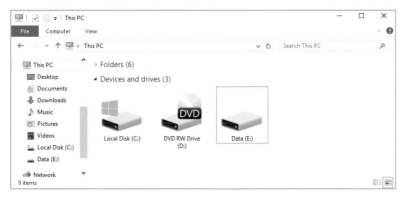

**4** Open **Virtual Memory** (see page 427) to assign the HDD drive a page file

**5** Restart the system to apply

**...cont'd**

If you add a USB flash drive to your computer, you may be able to use ReadyBoost to improve the overall performance.

**1** Connect the USB drive then right-click its icon in File Explorer and select **Properties** from the context menu

**Don't forget**

ReadyBoost is disk caching that uses flash memory to boost your system performance. It can use any form of flash memory such as a USB flash drive, SD card, or CompactFlash.

**2** Next, in the Properties dialog, choose the **ReadyBoost** tab

**3** Now, select **Dedicate this device to ReadyBoost**

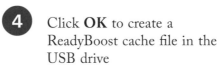

**4** Click **OK** to create a ReadyBoost cache file in the USB drive

**Beware**

ReadyBoost will not work with just any flash drive – it must be a good-quality model.

Sometimes you may be told that a particular drive is not suitable for ReadyBoost. Typically, this is because of insufficient space, or that the device is too slow to support the use of ReadyBoost. Users with a small amount of system memory (RAM) will benefit most from using ReadyBoost.

# 32-bit versus 64-bit

Windows 10 editions are available as either 32-bit or 64-bit. This refers to the addressing structure used by the processor. Desktop computers generally have a 64-bit processor that can run either version of Windows. Some laptop and netbook computers have 32-bit processors, and so can only run the 32-bit Windows. To check the processor level and the current operating system, open System Information (**WinKey + R** and type "msinfo32").

**Don't forget**

You should note the amount of memory as well as 64-bit capability. You need at least 2GB memory to benefit from the 64-bit version of Windows 10.

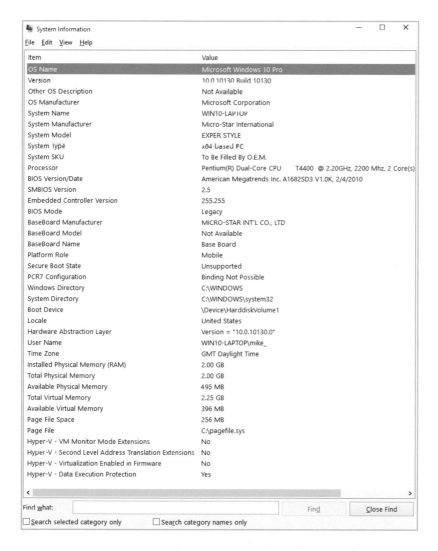

| Item | Value |
|---|---|
| OS Name | Microsoft Windows 10 Pro |
| Version | 10.0.10130 Build 10130 |
| Other OS Description | Not Available |
| OS Manufacturer | Microsoft Corporation |
| System Name | WIN10-LAPTOP |
| System Manufacturer | Micro-Star International |
| System Model | EXPER STYLE |
| System Type | x64-based PC |
| System SKU | To Be Filled By O.E.M. |
| Processor | Pentium(R) Dual-Core CPU     T4400  @ 2.20GHz, 2200 Mhz, 2 Core(s) |
| BIOS Version/Date | American Megatrends Inc. A1682SD3 V1.0K, 2/4/2010 |
| SMBIOS Version | 2.5 |
| Embedded Controller Version | 255.255 |
| BIOS Mode | Legacy |
| BaseBoard Manufacturer | MICRO-STAR INT'L CO., LTD |
| BaseBoard Model | Not Available |
| BaseBoard Name | Base Board |
| Platform Role | Mobile |
| Secure Boot State | Unsupported |
| PCR7 Configuration | Binding Not Possible |
| Windows Directory | C:\WINDOWS |
| System Directory | C:\WINDOWS\system32 |
| Boot Device | \Device\HarddiskVolume1 |
| Locale | United States |
| Hardware Abstraction Layer | Version = "10.0.10130.0" |
| User Name | WIN10-LAPTOP\mike_ |
| Time Zone | GMT Daylight Time |
| Installed Physical Memory (RAM) | 2.00 GB |
| Total Physical Memory | 2.00 GB |
| Available Physical Memory | 495 MB |
| Total Virtual Memory | 2.25 GB |
| Available Virtual Memory | 396 MB |
| Page File Space | 256 MB |
| Page File | C:\pagefile.sys |
| Hyper-V - VM Monitor Mode Extensions | No |
| Hyper-V - Second Level Address Translation Extensions | No |
| Hyper-V - Virtualization Enabled in Firmware | No |
| Hyper-V - Data Execution Protection | Yes |

**Beware**

If the System Type is an x84-based PC it is a 32-bit system that cannot run 64-bit Windows 10.

Here, the System Type is a x64-based PC, which means it has a 64-bit processor and can run both 32-bit and 64-bit editions of Windows, and has Total Physical Memory of 2.00GB.

## ...cont'd

It may improve the performance of your 64-bit-capable computer if you install the 64-bit operating system, but only if there is sufficient memory to make this worthwhile. You'll need at least 2GB – and more if possible.

There's no information report to tell you how much memory you can add to your computer, but you can find free memory scanner tools online to check your system.

**1** Go to **memory-up.com** and click **Memory Scanner (Begin Auto Check)**, then click **Download Scanner**

**2** When prompted choose to **Run the scanner** and it will check your system

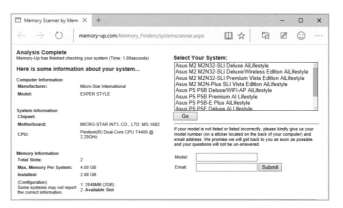

Here the current installed memory is 2GB, and maximum possible memory is 4GB. Switching to 64-bit Windows is possible, but will be of marginal benefit only. 32-bit Windows can use a maximum of 4GB memory, whereas 64-bit Windows can use up to 192GB memory.

You can't upgrade from 32-bit to 64-bit – you must install a fresh system, completely replacing the existing system. So make sure you backup your data first. You also need 64-bit versions of drivers for all of your devices.

With 64-bit Windows installed you will find two Program File folders – one for 32-bit (often called x86) and one for 64-bit applications.

Program Files

Program Files (x86)

# 26 Windows Registry

The heart of the Windows system is the Windows Registry. Windows provides a Registry Editor for working with the Registry, and this may let you carry out tasks that are not otherwise supported. However, do be aware that errors in making such changes could leave your system unusable.

# The Windows Registry

Arguably the most important component in the Windows system, since it records everything about your hardware and software, the Windows Registry is something that in normal circumstances you never need to deal with directly.

The Registry is a structured database that stores the configuration settings and options for applications, device drivers, user interface, services, and all kinds of operating system components. It also stores all the counters that are used to provide the performance reports and charts.

Installation programs, applications and device software all deal directly with the Registry, so all the updates happen in the background. However, the Registry stores user-based settings in a user-specific location, thus allowing multiple users to share the same machine, yet have their own personal details and preferences. The Registry also makes it possible to establish levels of privilege, to control what actions a particular user is permitted to carry out.

### Changes to the Registry Editor
When you make changes to the setup for your user account, Windows writes the necessary updates to the Registry for you. Similarly, when you install new programs or hardware devices, many Registry modifications will be applied. Normally, you won't need to know the details.

### Registry Editor
However, there will be times when the developers have failed to provide a necessary change, and the only way (or the quickest way) to make the adjustment is by working directly with the Registry. Windows includes a Registry Editor that you can use, with caution since the Registry is a crucial part of your system, to browse and edit the Registry.

The Registry is made of a number of separate files, but you never need to be concerned with the physical structure, since the Registry Editor gives you access to the full Registry, displaying the logical structure and taking care of the specifics of updates.

Before you browse or edit the Registry, you should have an understanding of the structure and how changes get applied, and especially how the original values can be saved – just in case changes get applied that have unwelcome effects.

The Windows Registry was introduced in the early versions of Windows as a way of organizing and centralizing information that was originally stored in separate INI (initialization) files.

From time to time, you will encounter Windows tips that are designed to make your system better, faster or easier to use, and such tips often rely on making changes to the Registry.

Change the Registry with care. Only use trusted sources when you do make changes. And make sure you have a Registry Backup before you make any changes.

## The structure of the Registry

The data in the Windows Registry is organized in a hierarchical, or tree, format. The nodes in the tree are called keys. Each key can contain subkeys and entries. An entry consists of a name, a data type and a value, and it is referenced by the sequence of subkeys that lead to that particular entry.

There are five top level keys:

**Beware**

Some products available on the internet suggest the Registry needs regular maintenance or cleaning. Although problems can arise, in general the Registry is self-sufficient and such products are not necessary.

- HKEY_CLASSES_ROOT          HKCR
  Information about file types, shortcuts and interface items
  (alias for parts of HKLM and HKCU).

- HKEY_CURRENT_USER          HKCU
  Contains the user profile for the currently logged on user,
  with desktop, network, printers, and program preferences
  (alias for part of HKU).

- HKEY_LOCAL_MACHINE          HKLM
  Information about the computer system, including hardware
  and operating system data such as bus type, system memory,
  device drivers, and startup control data.

**Hot tip**

Applications read the Registry to check that a specific key exists, or to open a key and select entry values that are included.

- HKEY_USERS          HKU
  Contains information about actively loaded user profiles and
  the default profile.

- HKEY_CURRENT_CONFIG          HKCC
  The hardware profile used at startup, for example to configure
  device drivers and display resolution
  (alias for part of HKLM).

Sections of the Registry are stored in the System32 and User folders, each subtree having a single file plus a log file, for example Sam and Sam.log, or System and System.log. Subtrees associated with files are known as Registry hives. They include:

| | |
|---|---|
| HKEY_LOCAL_MACHINE\SAM | Sam |
| HKEY_LOCAL_MACHINE\SECURITY | Security |
| HKEY_LOCAL_MACHINE\SOFTWARE | Software |
| HKEY_LOCAL_MACHINE\SYSTEM | System |
| HKEY_CURRENT_CONFIG | System |
| HKEY_CURRENT_USER | System |
| HKEY_USERS\.DEFAULT | Default |

**Don't forget**

The tree, subtree, alias, hive, and file structure can be very complex, but the view taken via the Registry Editor is fortunately more straightforward.

443

# Registry backup

Before using the Registry Editor, you should create a restore point using System Restore. The restore point will contain information about the Registry, and you can use it to undo changes to your system.

To create a manual restore point:

**1** Go to Control Panel, System, and click the **System protection** link

You can also back up individual parts of the Registry, just before you make changes to them (see page 449).

**2** Select the **System Protection** tab and click **Create** to create a restore point immediately

**3** Type a description, to remind you of the reason for the restore point

**4** When the restore point completes, click **Close**

**5** On the **System Protection** tab, click the **System Restore** button, then select **Choose a different restore point** and click **Next** – to see your new restore point

This shows that System Restore had made its daily restore point, so this could be used instead of a manual restore point, unless you've already made some changes during the current session.

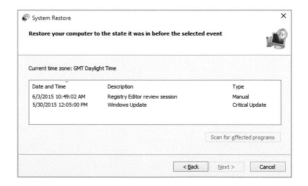

# Open Registry Editor

Registry Editor is not accessible via the Control Panel, Administrative Tools or through any shortcuts. You must run the program **regedit.exe** by name.

**1** Press **WinKey + R** to open the Run box. Enter "regedit" and click **OK**

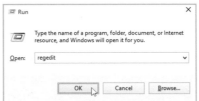

**2** Assuming you have an administrator account, click **Yes**, to allow the Registry Editor to start with full administrator privileges

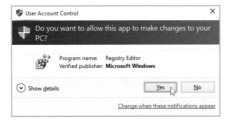

**3** Registry Editor starts, and the first time it runs, you'll see the five main subtrees, with all their branches collapsed

**4** Select a key, e.g. **HKEY_LOCAL_MACHINE** (HKLM), and double-click to expand to the next level

**Don't forget**

This is an advanced program, which will usually be run via an administrator account, though it can be run using a standard account.

**Don't forget**

Registry Editor will save the last key referenced in the session, and open at that point the next time you run the program.

**Hot tip**

The right-hand pane displays the entries and data values for the selected key. You can also click the arrow buttons to open or collapse the branches of the subtrees.

# Example Registry change

Before exploring the Registry further, it will be useful to look at a typical Registry update, used to make changes for which Windows has no formal method included.

One such requirement is to change the registered organization and registered owner for the computer. These names will have been set up when Windows was installed. The names chosen may no longer be appropriate, perhaps because you've changed companies, or because the computer was passed on or purchased from another user.

To see the registration details:

**1** Press **WinKey + R** and type "winver"

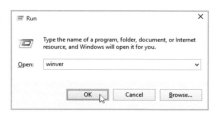

**2** The details of the installed version of Windows are shown, along with the registered owner and organization

**3** Assume that these details need to be revised to "Joanne" and "In Easy Steps"

You'll find many such suggested changes on the internet, usually in lists of Windows hints and tips, and often referred to as Registry "hacks".

Do make sure that the sites you use as sources for Registry changes are reliable, and check the details carefully to ensure the change does exactly what it claims.

**446**

You will find that this particular change is included in a number of Windows hints and tips lists. You'll even find a solution at the Microsoft website **microsoft.com**
All the suggestions follow a similar pattern. They advise you to run **regedit.exe** and find the Registry key named HKEY_ LOCAL_MACHINE\SOFTWARE\Microsoft\Windows NT\ CurrentVersion, where you can change the owner and organization. Some of the websites also discuss the need for administrator authority, and they usually warn about taking backups before making changes.

**1** Locate the subkey **SOFTWARE** and double-click

To locate the key, you can step through the path, subkey by subkey, double-clicking each one in turn.

**2** Scroll down to subkey **Microsoft** and double-click

You can double-click a subkey, or select it and press Enter, to expand it to the next level.

**3** Scroll down to subkey **Windows NT** and double-click

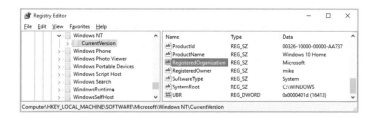

Although the subkeys are shown in capitals or mixed case, as displayed in the Registry, they are, in fact, not case sensitive.

**4** Select subkey **CurrentVersion** and scroll through the list of entries to select **RegisteredOrganization**

# Finding a key

**Don't forget**

Rather than stepping through the path, you could use the **Find** command in Regedit.

**Hot tip**

Pressing **F3** carries out the **Find Next** operation, to locate the next match.

**Beware**

You'll soon discover that subkey names are not unique, and also the same text could appear in the data content of Registry entries.

**Don't forget**

Find is more effective if you restrict the search, for example putting a **Value** entry name, and clearing the Key and Data boxes. You could also search for known text in the data content.

**1** Select the highest level key, **Computer**, and then click **Edit**, **Find** (or press **Ctrl + F**)

**2** Type the required subkey "CurrentVersion" and click **Find Next**

**3** The subkey is in the wrong branch, so keep pressing **F3**

**4** This is the wrong section, and matches data content

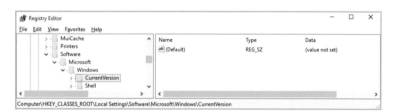

**5** Search instead for the **Value** entry name "RegisteredOrganization"

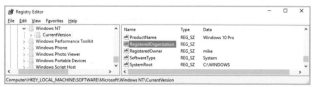

# Back up before changes

**1** Select the subkey, or a value entry within the subkey, and then click **File**, **Export**

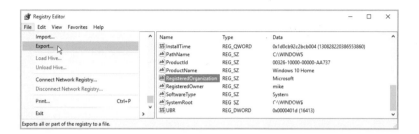

**2** By default, your Documents folder will be selected, but you can choose a different folder if desired

**3** Provide a file name for the Registration File (**.reg**) that is being created and choose **Selected branch**

**4** The Registration file is written to the selected folder

You should make a backup of the branch at the subkey within which changes are required.

You can create a backup of the whole registry, but it is sufficient to back up just the branches being changed.

The **.reg** file will have all the subkeys, value entries and data contents for everything within the subkey selected for Export.

# Change a Value entry

**1** Select the **Value** entry to be changed and double-click

This entry has text data. The value data for other entries could be binary or numbers. You must replace existing contents with the same type of data values.

**2** The Value entry is opened with Value data displayed ready for Edit

**3** Replace the existing contents with the required information

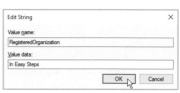

**4** Click **OK** to apply and save the change. It is immediately in effect

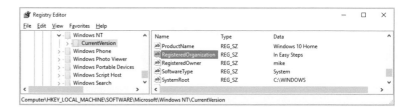

If you change your mind part way through, you cannot just close Registry Editor – you must restore the original values using the branch backup, or else reverse the changes individually.

**5** Repeat for any other values to be changed

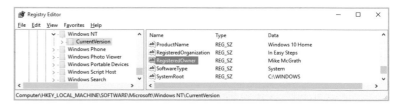

**6** Close Registry Editor when you have finished – no Save is required, since changes are dynamically applied

# Using a standard account

Log off and switch to a Standard user account, making sure no other accounts are active.

**1** Press **WinKey + R** to open the Run box. Enter "regedit" and click **OK**

**2** There's no UAC interception; Registry Editor starts up at **Computer** (or at the last key referenced by this account)

**3** Locate the Value entry **RegisteredOrganization** in the **Windows NT** subkey, and double-click the name

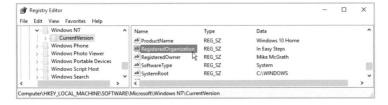

**4** The current value is shown

**5** Change the value to the required text and click **OK**

**6** Registry Editor displays an error message to say it is unable to edit the entry

**Error Editing Value**

❌ Cannot edit RegisteredOrganization: Error writing the value's new contents.

OK

Don't forget

When you run Regedit from a Standard user account, it operates at a lower privilege level.

451

Beware

The standard account can edit and create Registry keys under HKEY_CURRENT_USER, but not entries under HKEY_LOCAL_MACHINE. Some registry entries are even blocked for reading.

## ...cont'd

If you are signed in with a standard user account but you need full Registry Editor access, you must run Regedit as an administrator.

**1** Type "regedit" in the Taskbar Search box and hit **Enter**

**2** Right-click the Regedit search result and select **Run as administrator**

**3** Provide the password for the administrator account displayed and click **Yes**, to allow the Registry Editor to start with full administrator privileges

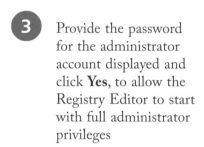

As an alternative, you can open the Command Prompt as an administrator, and start **regedit.exe** from there.

**1** Press **WinKey + X** and click **Command Prompt (Admin)**

**2** Respond to the UAC prompt, then type "regedit.exe" and hit **Enter**. The full Registry Editor will start

# Scripted updates

You'll find that some websites offer scripted versions of Registry updates that you can download and run. These are similar to the Registration files that you create when you back up a branch of the Registry. To illustrate this method, you can create your own script to update the RegisteredOwner details.

**1** Open **Notepad** and type the Registry Editor header, the subkey path and the Value entries required

**2** Select **File**, **Save** and choose a folder if required, or accept the default, normally Documents

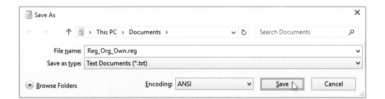

**3** Type the file name and file type, e.g. "Reg_Org_Own.reg"

The quote marks ensure that the file type **.reg** will be used, rather than Notebook's default file type of **.txt**.

**4** Click **Save**, and the Registration file will be added to the specified folder

Using scripts that are provided can make it easier to apply updates, as long as you trust the source websites.

This **.reg** file automates the process followed to find the subkey and amend the Value entries for Organization and Owner.

# Applying an update

**Don't forget**

You use this same process to apply the backup Registration file, if you decide to reverse the changes you have made.

**Hot tip**

The update is applied without any requirement to run Regedit or open the Registry.

**Beware**

It is well worth repeating that you must change the Registry with care. Only use trusted sources when you do make changes. And make sure you have a Registry Backup before you make any change.

**1** To apply an update, double-click the Registration file

Reg_Org_Own.reg

**2** There will be a UAC prompt, and then you will be warned of the potential dangers of updates

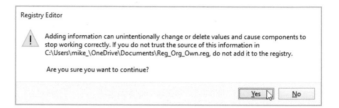

Registry Editor

⚠ Adding information can unintentionally change or delete values and cause components to stop working correctly. If you do not trust the source of this information in C:\Users\mike_\OneDrive\Documents\Reg_Org_Own.reg, do not add it to the registry.

Are you sure you want to continue?

[ Yes ]    [ No ]

**3** If you are happy with the update, click **Yes**

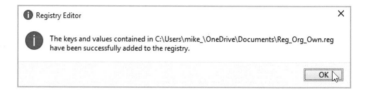

Registry Editor                                          ✕

ℹ The keys and values contained in C:\Users\mike_\OneDrive\Documents\Reg_Org_Own.reg have been successfully added to the registry.

[ OK ]

**4** The keys and values included are added to the Registry

**5** Confirm the update by running **Winver**

About Windows                                          ✕

**Windows 10**

Microsoft Windows
Version 10.0 (Build 10240)
© 2015 Microsoft Corporation. All rights reserved.
The Windows 10 Home operating system and its user interface are protected by trademark and other pending or existing intellectual property rights in the United States and other countries/regions.

This product is licensed under the Microsoft Software License Terms to:

Joanne
In Easy Steps

[ OK ]

**6** You can also open the Registry and check the subkey and its Value entries

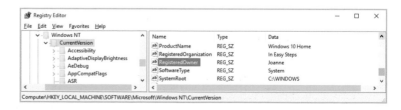

Registry Editor                                    —  □  ✕
File  Edit  View  Favorites  Help

| Name | Type | Data |
|---|---|---|
| ab ProductName | REG_SZ | Windows 10 Home |
| ab RegisteredOrganization | REG_SZ | In Easy Steps |
| ab RegisteredOwner | REG_SZ | Joanne |
| ab SoftwareType | REG_SZ | System |
| ab SystemRoot | REG_SZ | C:\WINDOWS |

Windows NT
  CurrentVersion
    Accessibility
    AdaptiveDisplayBrightness
    AeDebug
    AppCompatFlags
    ASR

Computer\HKEY_LOCAL_MACHINE\SOFTWARE\Microsoft\Windows NT\CurrentVersion

# Resize Taskbar thumbnails

When you move the mouse cursor over a
Windows 10 Taskbar button, you'll see a small
version of the application window.

To make this larger in size:

**1** Open Regedit.exe, and locate the subkey
**HKEY_CURRENT_USER\Software\Microsoft\
Windows\CurrentVersion\Explorer\Taskband**

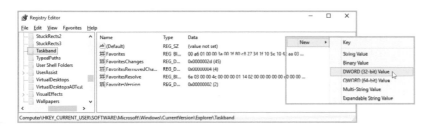

**2** Right-click the right-hand pane and select **New,
DWORD Value,** and name the value "MinThumbSizePx"

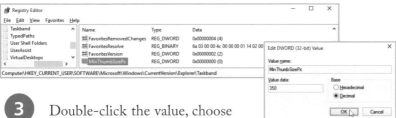

**3** Double-click the value, choose
**Decimal**, make the value "350"

**4** Log off and log on again to put the
change into effect

**5** View a Taskbar thumbnail to see the
enlarged thumbnail results

**Don't forget**

Registry updates require
you to change binary or
number values, or ask
you to create keys or
value entries – like those
in this example.

**Hot tip**

Adjust the value again
to fine-tune the results,
or delete the value entry
to return to the default
thumbnail.

# Remove shortcut suffix

When you create a shortcut on the Desktop, Windows insists on adding the word "Shortcut" to the name.

For example:

**1** Locate the Notepad.exe program file, which is usually found in **C:\windows\system32**

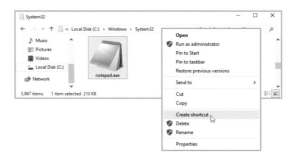

**2** Right-click the program icon and select **Create shortcut**

**3** The shortcut cannot be added to the program folder, so click **Yes** to place it on the Desktop

**4** The shortcut is created and given the program name followed by **Shortcut**

If you find yourself editing the name to remove this addition, you might like to edit the Registry to avoid the suffix for all future shortcuts you create (this change won't affect existing shortcuts).

**1** Run **regedit.exe**, then locate the subkey **HKEY_ CURRENT_USER\Software\Microsoft\Windows\ CurrentVersion\Explorer**

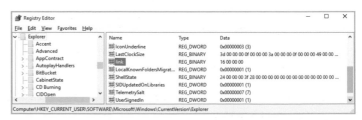

**2** Right-click the "link" entry, then select **Modify** from the context menu

**3** Change the first part of the number (16) to 00 to give a value of **00 00 00 00**

**4** Click **OK** to update the value, then close **regedit.exe**

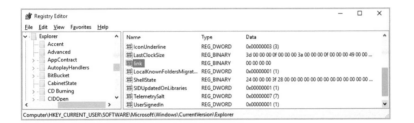

| Registry Editor | | | |
|---|---|---|---|
| Name | Type | Data | |
| IconUnderline | REG_DWORD | 0x00000003 (3) | |
| LastClockSize | REG_BINARY | 3d 00 00 00 0f 00 00 00 3a 00 00 00 0f 00 00 00 49 00 00 ... | |
| link | REG_BINARY | 00 00 00 00 | |
| LocalKnownFoldersMigrat... | REG_DWORD | 0x00000001 (1) | |
| ShellState | REG_BINARY | 24 00 00 00 3f 28 00 00 00 00 00 00 00 00 00 00 00 00 00 ... | |
| SIDUpdatedOnLibraries | REG_DWORD | 0x00000001 (1) | |
| TelemetrySalt | REG_DWORD | 0x00000007 (7) | |
| UserSignedIn | REG_DWORD | 0x00000001 (1) | |

Computer\HKEY_CURRENT_USER\SOFTWARE\Microsoft\Windows\CurrentVersion\Explorer

You must log off and log on again for the change to take effect. Now, when you create a shortcut, it will just receive the program name with no suffix.

### Remove shortcut arrows

You can also use Registry updates to change the shortcut icons, avoiding the shortcut arrow overlay, or using a different, perhaps smaller, arrow to overlay the shortcut icons.

There are a number of different methods suggested for this. They involve adding a reference to an alternative icon file in a value entry in subkey [HKEY_LOCAL_MACHINE\SOFTWARE\ Microsoft\Windows\CurrentVersion\Explorer\Shell Icons].

You can search the internet for articles using a search term such as "Windows remove shortcut arrow" and choose your preferred website. Note that the instructions provided may differ for Windows 32-bit versus Windows 64-bit systems.

As with all Registry updates, make sure that you back up first, before making any changes.

**Hot tip**

Sometimes changes such as these have unexpected side effects, so a backup or restore point will be particularly important.

# Adjust Aero Peek

You can change the time delay before Aero Peek reduces the screen to the Desktop.

**1** Run **regedit.exe** and find the subkey **HKEY_CURRENT_USER\Software\Microsoft\Windows\CurrentVersion\Explorer\Advanced**

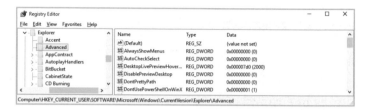

**Don't forget**

When the mouse moves over the Peek button at the bottom-right of the screen, all open windows are replaced by empty frames. This can be distracting when you are just moving the mouse to a corner to help locate the pointer.

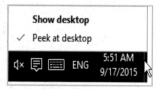

**2** Right-click the right-hand pane and select **New, DWORD Value** (see page 455) and name the value "DesktopLivePreviewHoverTime"

**3** Double-click to edit, select **Decimal** and enter a value in milliseconds, for example "2000" (two seconds), then click **OK**

**Hot tip**

The default is 500 (half a second), 1000 is one second, and 0 is instant. To return to the default, set the value to 500 or delete the Value entry.

Log off, and then log on again to put the Registry update into effect.

# 27 Extending Windows

*Windows 10 provides great extensibility for remote connection, portability, virtual system hosting, and connection to other devices.*

# Remote Desktop connection

Remote Desktop is used to access one computer from another remotely, e.g. connecting to your work computer from home. You will have access to all of your programs, files, and network resources, as if you were sitting in front of your computer at work.

## On the Remote Computer

Before Remote Desktop can be used, the computer to be remotely accessed needs to be configured.

The difference between Remote Desktop and Remote Assistance is that with the latter, both users can control the mouse. With the former, the remote PC is not physically accessible.

**1** Go to the Control Panel and click the **System** icon – to open the **System Properties** dialog box

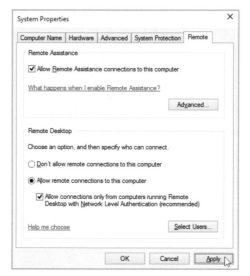

**2** In the System Properties dialog, select the **Remote** tab

**3** Check **Allow remote connections to this computer**

**4** Go back to **System** and make a note of the computer's name – "WIN10-LAPTOP" in the example below

For a secure connection, make sure **Allow connections only from computers running Remote Desktop with Network Level Authentication (recommended)** is checked.

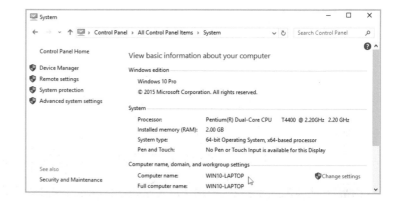

**...cont'd**

## On the Access Computer

You now have to open the Remote Desktop Connection. How you implement this depends on which version of Windows the access PC is using.

**1** If it is Windows 7, click the Start button, go to **All Programs, Accessories** and click **Remote Desktop Connection**

**2** If it is Windows 8, 8.1 or 10, use the Search box for "Remote Desktop Connection". Then press **Enter**

Click **Show Options** to reveal a range of settings with which to enhance the remote connection.

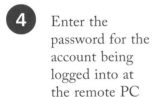

**3** Enter the name of the remote computer – using our example type "WIN10-LAPTOP"

461

**4** Enter the password for the account being logged into at the remote PC

Once the connection is made and authenticated, everything on the remote PC is open to, and can be controlled by, the access computer.

# Windows To Go

Windows To Go is a feature found in Windows 10 Enterprise that enables a fully-functional copy of Windows 10 to be created on a USB drive. The procedure makes the drive bootable in the same way that Windows installation disks are.

Not just any USB drive can be used with Windows To Go. Microsoft has specified certain requirements that manufacturers must meet in order for their USB drives to qualify as a supported Windows To Go device. One such is the Kingston DataTraveler shown below:

Windows To Go is only available on Windows 10 Enterprise and Windows 10 Education editions.

External USB drives can be used, as well as flash drives.

The minimum storage space required by Windows To Go is 32GB. This is enough for Windows 10 itself, but if you also need to transport applications such as Microsoft Office, plus files, a larger USB drive will be required. Currently, flash drives up to 512GB are readily available.

A Windows To Go drive can be plugged into a USB socket on any computer and, because it is bootable, a Windows 10 session can be loaded on that computer. Once booted, it functions, and is controlled by standard enterprise management tools such as System Center Configuration Manager (SCCM) and Active Directory group policies.

Windows To Go provides an ideal solution for anyone who needs mobile computer access. For example, business representatives out in the field will be able to work from any computer. Also, it's more cost-effective for IT departments to replace a faulty USB drive than it is to deal with the downtime and expense of returning a laptop to the office, repairing it, and returning it to the field.

Windows To Go is also ideal for trying out Windows 10 (or other software) on a machine without affecting that machine.

Windows To Go will only work on USB drives built specifically for it.

# Virtual machine

A virtual computer is one that is created by, and run within, a computer virtualization program. It is a fully-functional replica of a physical computer and can run programs, access the internet, etc.

Popular programs of this type include VMware and VirtualBox – the latter being a free download from **www.virtualbox.org** However, with some versions of Windows 10 there is no need for third-party virtualization software – one, called Hyper-V, is supplied with Windows 10 Pro edition. It does need to be installed first, though, as explained below:

Client Hyper-V has very stringent hardware requirements. Not every PC will be able to run it.

**1** Type "Turn Windows features on or off" into the Taskbar Search box, then click the result to open the Windows Features dialog box

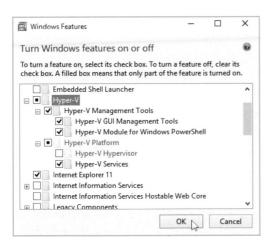

**2** Check the boxes next to **Hyper-V**, then click **OK**

**3** Restart the computer when prompted to launch Hyper-V

**4** Now, in the Taskbar Search box, type "hyper" and press **Enter**. The Hyper-V Manager opens, as shown below

# Install guest system

To demonstrate Hyper-V, we are going to create a Windows 7 virtual PC.

We show how to create a Windows 7 guest system. However, you can create guest systems for other operating systems.

**1** At the top-left of the Hyper-V Manager, select the computer name, then click **Action**, **New**, **Virtual Machine** – to open the New Virtual Machine Wizard

**2** Click the **Next** button, then name the new virtual machine "Windows 7" and click **Next** again

**3** Choose **Generation 1**, click **Next** and assign a valid startup memory allocation, then click **Finish**

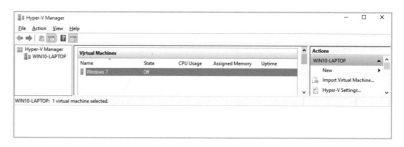

Hyper-V's Hardware options provide a range of settings for all the hardware components found in a computer.

**4** On the right under "Windows 7", click **Settings** to open the "Hardware and Management options" screen, then select **Legacy Network Adapter** and click **Add**

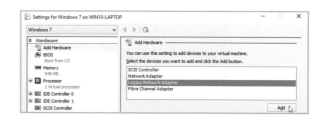

**5** Click **Hard Drive** under "IDE Controller 0". By default, size is set at 127GB but can be enlarged by clicking Edit, Choose Action, Expand, Next and **Configure Disk** – then enter a higher-size figure, such as "500GB"

**6** Select **DVD drive** under "IDE Controller 1". Here, you can specify an image file (ISO) or optical drive for installation of the operating system. To use an installation disk select **Physical CD/DVD drive**, then click **Apply**

**7** Insert the Windows 7 installation disk in the drive, go back to the Actions pane in the Hyper-V Manager, scroll down to the "Windows 7" virtual machine section and click the **Connect** command

Potential uses for virtual PCs include sandboxed software evaluation, other operating systems, and safe web browsing.

**8** Click **Start** to begin building the virtual PC within Hyper-V

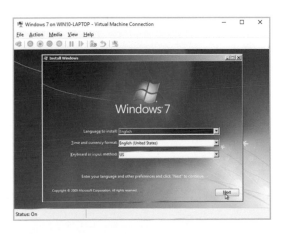

Hyper-V has a feature called Snapshots. These let you save the state of a virtual PC, so you can revert back in much the same way as a system backup lets you roll back to the point when the backup was made.

# Windows devices

Windows 10 is a unified operating system that will run on desktop PCs, laptops, tablets, and smartphones. The same great features are available across all these devices, with only minor modifications tailored to better suit screen sizes below 8".

Windows 10 supports direct access to a connected Windows Phone via File Explorer. This lets you drag-and-drop content to and from your phone – just as you can with any USB hard disk drive or flash drive.

**Hot tip**

First, connect the cable to your phone, then connect to a USB socket on your computer.

**1** Connect a Windows Phone to your Windows 10 computer via a USB cable connection

**2** Next, launch File Explorer on your computer and expand the **This PC** item in the Navigation pane to see your phone icon appear under "Devices and Drives" category

**Hot tip**

The phone here is named WIN10-PHONE but your connected phone will bear its own name.

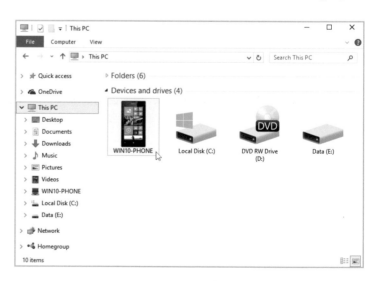

**3** Now, use File Explorer on your computer to select any file on your computer that you want to copy to your phone

**4** Right-click on a selected file icon and choose **Send To**, then click your phone's item on the context menu

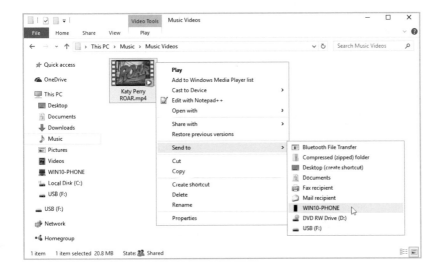

The selected file here is a video within a sub-folder of Music, but will be intelligently copied to the phone's Videos folder.

**5** The selected file now gets copied to your phone

**6** Use the File Explorer app on your phone to see that the file has been copied to an appropriate folder

Always use the **Safely Remove Hardware** feature to disconnect your phone from your computer – just as you should with any other USB device connection.

# Phone Companion app

The Phone Companion app that is included with Windows 10 lets you easily copy music, photos, videos, and documents between your computer and ANY smartphone or tablet device.

**1** Connect a smartphone to your Windows 10 computer via a USB cable connection

The Phone Companion is new in Windows 10 and this Universal Windows App works with Windows, Android, iPhone and iPad devices.

**2** A notification invites you to choose what happens with this device – click on the notification

**3** From the pop-up menu that appears, choose the **Phone Companion** option to "Get your stuff on your PC, tablet and phone"

You can also launch the Phone Companion app at any time from the Start menu.

**4** The Phone Companion app will now open. Click the **Show** link at the bottom-center of the screen to see information about the connected device

**5** Click the **Import photos and videos** link to copy media files from your phone into the Pictures folder on your PC

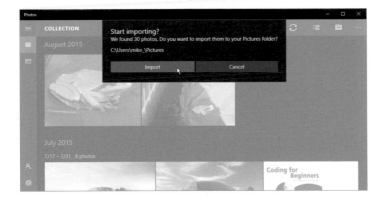

**Hot tip**

Click the Hide link to collapse the information and explore the demonstrations on this screen of what you can do with many apps.

**6** Click the **Transfer other files** link to copy any files between your phone and your PC with File Explorer

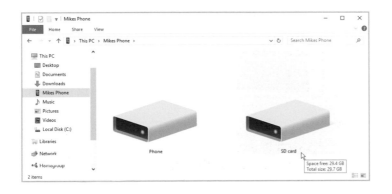

**Don't forget**

The links in the Phone Companion app let you quickly launch the Photos app Import feature or File Explorer already in your device's drive.

# Windows news

Microsoft intends to introduce new features into Windows 10 as it evolves. You can follow the development of the latest features by regularly visiting the official Windows blog online at **blogs.windows.com**

**Hot tip**

Users of Windows 10 Mobile may also be interested in the "Windows Central" at windowscentral.com

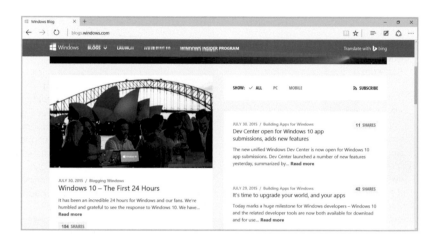

Sometimes you can learn of new features for Windows 10 before their official announcement on websites that claim to have inside knowledge. There are several of these, such as the "SuperSite for Windows" at **winsupersite.com**

Windows 10 revolves around its convergence for all devices, from phones to PCs, in Microsoft's battle against Android, iPhone and iPad. Only time will tell if this will be enough.

# Index

472

## T

## U

# V

# W

23.99

WITHDRAWN